THE COALITION AND THE CONSTITUTION

'England', Benjamin Disraeli famously said, 'does not love coalitions.' But 2010 saw the first peacetime coalition in Britain since the 1930s. The coalition, moreover, may well not be an aberration. There are signs that, with the rise in strength of third parties, hung parliaments are more likely to recur than in the past. Perhaps, therefore, the era of single-party majority government, to which we have become accustomed since 1945, is coming to an end. But is the British constitution equipped to deal with coalition? Are alterations to the procedures of parliament or government needed to cope with it?

The inter-party agreement between the coalition partners proposes a wide-ranging series of constitutional reforms, the most important of which are fixed-term parliaments and a referendum on the alternative vote electoral system, to be held in May 2011. The coalition is also proposing measures to reduce the size of the House of Commons, to directly elect the House of Lords and to strengthen localism. These reforms, if implemented, could permanently alter the way we are governed.

This book analyses the significance of coalition government for Britain and of the momentous constitutional reforms which the coalition is proposing. In doing so it seeks to penetrate the cloud of polemic and partisanship to provide an objective analysis for the informed citizen.

The Coalition and the Constitution

Vernon Bogdanor

·HART·
PUBLISHING

OXFORD AND PORTLAND, OREGON
2011

Published in the United Kingdom by Hart Publishing Ltd
16C Worcester Place, Oxford, OX1 2JW
Telephone: +44 (0)1865 517530
Fax: +44 (0)1865 510710
E-mail: mail@hartpub.co.uk
Website: http://www.hartpub.co.uk

Published in North America (US and Canada) by
Hart Publishing
c/o International Specialized Book Services
920 NE 58th Avenue, Suite 300
Portland, OR 97213-3786
USA
Tel: +1 503 287 3093 or toll-free: (1) 800 944 6190
Fax: +1 503 280 8832
E-mail: orders@isbs.com
Website: http://www.isbs.com

British Library Cataloguing in Publication Data
Data Available

ISBN: 978-1-84946-158-0

Typeset by Hope Services, Abingdon
Printed and bound in Great Britain by
TJ International Ltd, Padstow, Cornwall

'Society in this country is perplexed, almost paralysed; in time it will move, and it will devise. How are the elements of the nation to be again blended together? In what spirit is that reorganization to take place?'

'To know that', replied Coningsby, 'would be to know everything.'

Disraeli, *Coningsby*

Acknowledgements

I would like to thank for their critical comments on earlier drafts of this book- Chris Ballinger, Andrew Blick, Lord Butler of Brockwell, Diane Coyle, Guy Lodge, Kenneth Morgan, Peter Riddell, Andrew Stockley and Anthony Teasdale. But they are not to be implicated either in my arguments or in my conclusions. I would also like to thank Roger Mortimore and Ben Page of Ipsos-MORI for supplying me with survey data.

I owe a great debt of gratitude to Lord Owen, former leader of the SDP, for taking the time to explain to me how SDP thinking influenced the Liberal Democrat 'Orange Book', and helped to speed up changes in Liberal Democrat attitudes. I owe a debt also to those civil servants who have been kind enough to spare the time from their busy schedules to discuss constitutional issues with me. Their comments have greatly helped my understanding of the constitution.

I am grateful to John Curtice, doyen of British psephologists, for providing me with material relating to the 2010 election, and for many stimulating discussions on electoral matters; and to Oonagh Gay, Head of the Parliament and Constitution Centre of the House of Commons Library, for providing me with valuable material. Arne Bjoernstadt of the Royal Norwegian Embassy in London was kind enough to discuss with me the workings of fixed-term parliaments in Norway. Philip Joseph, Professor of Law at the University of Canterbury, New Zealand, and author of the authoritative text *Constitutional and Administrative Law in New Zealand*, the third edition of which was published in 2007, generously sent me material on hung parliaments and on the working of proportional representation in New Zealand. I have in addition benefited from many stimulating conversations with Professor Joseph. I am grateful also to Hans van Leeuwen for providing me with much helpful information concerning electoral systems in Australia.

I would like to thank the incomparable London Library for the cheerfulness and efficiency with which they have kept me supplied with relevant books.

But my greatest debt is to my wife, Sonia, for her encouragement and support at all stages in the writing of this book.

Vernon Bogdanor
London, November 2010

Contents

Introduction

We are currently living under the first peacetime coalition government in Britain since the 1930s. The coalition arose out of Britain's first hung parliament since 1974. It was an unexpected outcome. Previously coalitions have arisen not from hung parliaments, but from national emergencies – war in 1915, 1916 and 1940, financial emergency in 1931. In the past, hung parliaments have led to short-lived minority governments, not coalitions. The process by which the 2010 coalition came into being raises fundamental questions about the British constitution, about the process of government formation in a hung parliament, and about the role of the incumbent Prime Minister in a hung parliament. Some argued that Gordon Brown should have resigned as soon as it was clear that he had not won the election. Others argued the opposite – that he resigned too soon, before it was clear whether a coalition could be formed. The coalition also raises the question of the role of the electorate. To what extent is it in accordance with the norms of democracy for the nature of the government to be determined after the votes have been counted? The voters were given no chance to endorse or repudiate the Conservative/Liberal Democrat coalition, and it may be that many who voted Conservative or Liberal Democrat would in fact have repudiated it. Nor were the voters given a chance to endorse or reject the coalition's Programme for Government, drawn up by the two coalition partners shortly after the election and held by them to supersede any promises made in their election manifestoes. That claim too has excited controversy, particularly on the issue of tuition fees in higher education, a policy rejected by the Liberal Democrats in their election manifesto but accepted by them in government. This raises anew the question of the role of the mandate in British politics, its relevance and limits.

These issues are not only of importance in relation to the coalition formed in 2010. If, as there is good reason to believe, the hung parliament of 2010 was not an aberration, but a culmination of long-term trends in social change and electoral behaviour, then the 2010 coalition could prove the first of many. In the mid-nineteenth century Disraeli famously said that England does not love coalitions, but perhaps England, and indeed Britain as a whole, will have to get used to them. Scotland and Wales have certainly done so since devolution came into effect in 1999: most of the governments in Scotland and Wales since then have been coalitions.

Not only is the formation of a peacetime coalition following a hung parliament a constitutional innovation, but the coalition promises a whole raft of constitutional reforms, the most important of which are fixed-term parliaments, a directly elected second chamber and a referendum on the alternative vote method of election, to be held in May 2011. The Deputy Prime Minister, Nick Clegg, in a speech shortly after the formation of the coalition, on 19 May 2010, declared that these reforms amounted to 'the most significant programme of empowerment by a British government since the great enfranchisement of the nineteenth century . . . the biggest shake-up of our democracy since 1832, when the Great Reform Act redrew the boundaries of British democracy, for the first time extending the franchise beyond the landed classes'. This may be dismissed as the natural hyperbole of a politician catapulted, no doubt to his surprise, into a leading position in government. But both those who favour these reforms and those who are opposed to them claim that they are radical and will permanently alter the way we are governed. Whether that is so or not, it is already apparent that the era of constitutional reform, which began with the Blair government in 1997, and which was charted in my earlier book, *The New British Constitution*, published in 2009, is by no means over. Far from the British constitution having reached a stable resting-place, it remains in flux. Reform of the constitution is most definitely a process not an event.

The working and evolution of a constitution cannot be independent of political circumstances. The British constitution, after all, worked very differently between the wars, when Britain was governed for all but six of the 21 years from 1918 to 1939 by coalition or minority governments, than in the years since 1945, when single-party majority government has been the norm. If we are once again entering a world of multi-party politics, hung parliaments and coalition governments, the constitution will have to change to accommodate this changed political landscape. *The Coalition and the Constitution* seeks to analyse this changed landscape, to consider how coalitions might work in Britain, and to evaluate the constitutional consequences of regular coalition government. *The Coalition and the Constitution* is therefore in a sense both a pendant and a sequel to *The New British Constitution*. The earlier book sought to analyse the constitutional reforms of the Blair government from 1997, radical reforms indeed, but reforms which did not seriously alter the working of the central institutions of British government – Parliament, the Cabinet, and the electoral system for elections to the House of Commons. The reforms of the coalition government, by contrast, do seek to reform the working of these central institutions. The Fixed-Term Parliaments Act proposes to alter the relationship between government and parliament by making dissolution more difficult, while the alternative vote proposes to make the electoral system more fair. The Cabinet system could also come to be altered, not through legislation, but by the very working of a coalition government which superimposes upon the normal search for collective government an additional layer of inter-party negotiation. Indeed, in John Morley's biography of Walpole – a *locus classicus* on Cabinet government, a *locus classicus* supervised by Gladstone – it was suggested that Cabinet government actually presupposed single-party government.[1] How, then, is its working likely to be altered by coalition?

---

[1] John Morley, *Walpole* (Macmillan, 1889) 156.

The Coalition and the Constitution seeks to chart the future of a constitution whose fabled adaptability and flexibility are likely to be severely tested in the years ahead. It is an attempt to write the history of the future.

1

The General Election of 2010 and the Formation of the Coalition

I. OUTCOME OF THE ELECTION

THE GENERAL ELECTION of 2010 occurred at the end of a Parliament that had seen two major crises. First, there was the economic crisis: the credit crunch, and the downturn and collapse of the financial markets, including a run on Northern Rock in September 2007 – the first run on a British bank since the nineteenth century. These economic events seemed to shape public attitudes, causing resentment, if not anger, directed not only towards bankers and financiers, who were held to have acted recklessly and ceased to deserve – if indeed they had ever deserved – their huge salaries and bonuses, but also towards the government of Gordon Brown, which, so it was alleged, had failed to prevent the collapse.

Second, there was the expenses crisis – the abuse by a large number of MPs of their expenses claims. These abuses included some fraudulent claims and many unreasonable or unwise ones – a pattern of behaviour summed up by *The Daily Telegraph*, the newspaper that exposed the abuse, as 'a systematic and deliberate misappropriation of public funds on an extravagant scale'.[1] The expenses crisis increased public resentment and anger towards MPs, and led to the first resignation since 1695 of a Speaker of the House of Commons: Michael Martin, many believed, had been lax in failing to investigate abuses. The expenses crisis also fuelled the demand for constitutional reform, which, for the first time since the struggles over the House of Lords and Irish Home Rule before the First World War, became a genuinely popular issue, exciting, albeit for only a short period of time, considerable interest in constitutional questions. The three party leaders responded to this sentiment by competing with each other during 2009 and 2010 to produce lists of constitutional reforms, some of which were of very dubious relevance to the expenses crisis. There was, nevertheless, a general feeling that Parliament had become too insulated from the voters and that Westminster had become remote from popular concerns. The pressure for constitutional reform was eventually to find its outlet in some of the proposals set out in the Programme for Government produced by the coalition that took office after the election.

---

[1] Quoted in Dennis Kavanagh and Philip Cowley, *The British General Election of 2010* (Palgrave Macmillan, 2010) 26.

Many believed that the popular disenchantment resulting from these two crises would lead to populist or radical reactions. Some predicted that the public would vent their feelings by not voting at all, since they would think that all MPs were rascals, and therefore not worth bothering to vote for. The previous two general elections, in 2001 and 2005, had seen the lowest levels of turnout since the introduction of universal male suffrage in 1918 – 58% and 62% respectively. There were fears that turnout would be even lower in 2010.

Others feared, and some hoped, that there would be a rise in support for hitherto unrepresented parties, such as the Greens or the United Kingdom Independence Party, or for extremist parties, such as the British National Party. Some predicted a surge in support for the Liberal Democrats, since they seemed less tainted by the expenses scandal and were less strongly identified with the Westminster club than the Conservatives and Labour.

In the event, all of these predictions proved false. The outcome of the general election was as follows:

	% share of vote	Change from 2005	Seats	Change from 2005[2]	Votes
Conservative	36.1	+3.7	307	+97	10,726,614
Labour	29.0	−6.2	258	−91	8,609,527
Liberal Democrats	23.0	+1	57	−5	6,836,824
UKIP	3.2	+0.9	0	0	919,546
BNP	1.9	+1.2	0	0	564,331
Greens	1.0	−0.1	1	+1	285,616
SNP	19.9 in Scotland	+2.3	6	0	491,386
Plaid Cymru	11.3 in Wales	−1.3	3	+1	165,394
Others	1.5	−0.2	1	−3	469,591
Northern Ireland parties	3.2 in Northern Ireland	0	17	0	622,551

There was no evidence of a general reaction against sitting MPs. Indeed, in all parties, incumbents fared better than new candidates, although in some cases incumbents tainted by expenses performed badly.[3] Part of the reason indeed why the Conservatives failed to win an overall majority was that some sitting Labour MPs were able to hold on to a personal vote and to resist the national swing against their party. The largest swings to the Conservatives were in seats they already held, rather than in the marginals where Lord Ashcroft, the party's fundraiser, had concentrated his efforts. However, a record number of incumbents stood down because of the expenses scandal, and it is possible that their replace-

---

[2] Because of boundary changes after 2005, the change in seats must be calculated on the basis of 'notional' results. The calculation here is taken from David Denver, 'The Results; How Britain Voted' in Andrew Geddes and Jonathan Tonge (eds), Britain Votes 2010 (Oxford University Press, 2010) 11. 'Others' include the Speaker, whose seat was not contested by the Conservatives, Labour or the Liberal Democrats.

[3] See the table in Denver, ibid, 16, and also the comments by John Curtice, Stephen Fisher and Robert Ford in 'Appendix 2: An Analysis of the Results' in Kavanagh and Cowley (n 1) 393 and 298.

ments were punished for the supposed misdeeds of their departed colleagues by facing larger swings against them.

Turnout was at 65%, slightly higher than the low levels of 2001 and 2005. New and extremist parties made little impact, although the Greens did succeed in winning their first parliamentary seat in Brighton Pavilion, while the United Kingdom Independence Party gained 3.2% of the vote – 'the largest share of the vote ever won by a minor party' – over 900,000 votes – though failed to win a seat.[4] The British National Party, which put up 338 candidates, as compared with 119 in 2005, doubled its vote to 1.9% – the largest share of the vote ever won by a far-right party – and slightly increased its percentage of the vote per candidate – although it too failed to win a seat. The Liberal Democrats, despite gaining 1% of the vote, lost five seats, reducing the party's parliamentary strength from 62 to 57. The Liberal Democrat share of the vote, at 23%, although 2% lower than the best third-party vote since the war – that of the Liberal/SDP Alliance in 1983, which gained 25% of the vote – was nevertheless the second best electoral performance by any third party since 1929.

Before the election, Mervyn King, the Governor of the Bank of England, was reported as saying that the 2010 general election was one that any rational party would wish to lose. The scale of cuts in public expenditure needed to eliminate a budget deficit of nearly £170bn would, King believed, be so severe that any government implementing them would then find itself in opposition for a very long time. Although, no doubt, all the major parties fought hard to win the election, perhaps King's remark had some subconscious impact. For each of the three major parties had good reason to be disappointed with the outcome. There is a sense in which all three lost the election.

The Labour Party was the most obvious loser. Its share of the vote, at 29%, was its second lowest since it became a mass party in 1918, the lowest being that of 1983, when the party fought a disastrous campaign under the leadership of Michael Foot. In 2010, Labour lost over 6% – one-sixth – of its 2005 vote. In large parts of southern England it had been all but wiped out. In the south, outside London, the party now holds just 10 out of 197 seats. Labour now has no MPs at all in Cornwall, Somerset, Wiltshire, Dorset, Sussex, Kent, Essex, Norfolk, Cambridgeshire, Northamptonshire, Rutland, Warwickshire, Buckinghamshire, Hertfordshire, Gloucestershire, Worcestershire or Herefordshire. The BBC's electoral analyst, David Cowling, was right, therefore, to describe the outcome in 2010 as 'the dismembering of New Labour's 1997 electoral triumph'.[5] For Tony Blair had striven hard to make Labour sympathetic to aspirational voters in the south of England, as well as to its traditional voters in the conurbations of the Midlands and the North, and Scotland and Wales. That indeed was the central theme of New Labour – the attempt to reconnect with skilled C2 aspirational voters who had found a home with Margaret Thatcher and John Major, and without

---

[4] Kavanagh and Cowley (n 1) 404.
[5] Quoted in Patrick Diamond and Giles Radice, *Southern Discomfort Again* (Policy Network, 2010) 11.

whom Labour could not hope to win power. But the Blair project now seemed to be at an end, with the party having been forced back into its traditional heartlands. New Labour seemed, for the time being at any rate, dead.

The Liberal Democrats had high hopes of making an electoral breakthrough in 2010, since the banking crisis and the expenses crisis seemed to make their calls for a radical overhaul of the political system more relevant and more popular than ever before. They had a further important advantage, in that the introduction of televised debates between the party leaders gave them equal billing with the leaders of the two larger parties and therefore helped to make their leader, Nick Clegg, appear, with Gordon Brown and David Cameron, a genuine contender for the premiership.

In the past, the Liberal Democrats had often benefited from the extra publicity they were able to gain during the immediate pre-election campaign period, and which drew them to the attention of voters who might otherwise have ignored them. A no doubt unscientific survey at the Cheltenham races, taken before the first debate, found that while 98% could name the favourite for the Gold Cup, just 26% knew who Nick Clegg was! Clegg, however, took advantage of the opportunity that the television debates gave the party, for he was widely thought to have performed better than the other two contenders in the first debate. Indeed, during this debate, Gordon Brown said on more than one occasion, 'I agree with Nick', and this encouraged Liberal Democrat supporters to wear T-shirts embellished with the slogan, 'I agree with Nick'. But the Liberal Democrats, although gaining a small percentage of the vote as compared with 2005, failed to achieve the gains they had hoped for or to make a breakthrough, and in fact won five seats fewer than in the previous general election of 2005. The party's position became pivotal not because of its electoral success, but because the Conservatives failed to win an overall majority. Its pivotal position depended upon the pattern of votes for the other two parties, not upon its own electoral performance.

The Conservatives had perhaps the greatest reason to be disappointed with the outcome. Until the summer of 2009, the party had appeared well on course for an overall majority. Survey evidence seemed to indicate that they enjoyed the support of around 40% of the voters, as compared to Labour's 30%, a lead sufficient for an overall majority. But the Conservatives failed to achieve that overall majority, despite facing an unpopular government and a Prime Minister whom it accused of having presided over, and indeed having caused, a very severe recession.

The 307 Conservative MPs were elected on just over 36% of the vote. That was the lowest Conservative share of the vote since the Second World War, except for the general elections of October 1974, 1997, 2001, and 2005. But in all those elections the Conservatives had been comprehensively defeated. In 1945, when the Conservatives were so thoroughly beaten by Attlee's Labour Party, they gained 39.8% of the vote, nearly 4% more than in 2010. The Conservative vote in 2010 was lower than at the time of the last hung parliament in February 1974, when Edward Heath had secured 37.1% of the vote. But the outcome of that election had been a Labour minority government. When David Cameron entered Downing Street, it was with the lowest percentage of the vote of any Conservative Prime Minister in modern times.

Had the election led to a Conservative minority government, which seemed at one point a likely outcome, it would have been the second successive British government to have been based on just over one-third of the vote. Labour, although it enjoyed a comfortable overall majority of 67 seats after the 2005 general election, had won that majority on just 35.2% of the vote, a smaller share than the Conservatives achieved in 2010. The vagaries of the electoral system allowed Labour, therefore, to secure an overall majority on 35.2% of the vote in 2005, while denying the Conservatives an overall majority on 36.1% of the vote in 2010. All the same, nearly two-thirds of those voting had voted against the Conservatives, just as nearly two-thirds of those voting had voted against the majority Labour government of 2005. These two election results cast perhaps an ironic light on the notion of democracy as majority rule, and on the proposition that the first past the post electoral system generally yields a government supported by the majority of the voters. The Conservative/Liberal Democrat coalition, formed after the election, does, however, enjoy an overall majority of 78 in the House of Commons, while over 59% of those voting supported either the Conservatives or the Liberal Democrats. In this sense, the coalition can claim to be the first government to enjoy majority support since Stanley Baldwin's National Government in 1935. But it can make this claim only on the highly dubious assumption that all those who voted for the Conservatives and Liberal Democrats would have endorsed the coalition. It is doubtful, to put it no higher, whether the Liberal Democrats would have won 57 seats had voters been told before the election that the party would form a coalition with the Conservatives.

The Liberal Democrats, though winning 23% of the vote – nearly a quarter of the vote – won just 57 out of 650 seats – fewer than one-10th of the seats – in the House of Commons. They were, as has been the case ever since the 1920s when they became a third party, harshly treated by the electoral system. It took 33,468 votes to elect a Labour MP, and 35,028 votes to elect a Conservative MP, but 119,780 votes to elect a Liberal Democrat MP.

The Liberal Democrats, however, were not the only party to be disadvantaged by the electoral system. The fourth party in terms of votes in the election was the United Kingdom Independence Party, which won over 900,000 votes, 400,000 votes more than in 2005. In a proportional system, their 3.2% share of the vote would have given them around 20 seats. But, under first past the post, they won no seats at all.

Nevertheless, UKIP may not have been without influence in the election. In 21 constituencies, the total of the UKIP and Conservative vote was higher than that of the winning Labour or Liberal Democrat.[6] If one makes the assumption that, in

---

[6]   Sean Carey and Andrew Geddes, 'Less is More: Immigration and European Integration at the 2010 General Election' in Geddes and Tonge (n 2) 277.

the absence of a UKIP candidate, UKIP voters would have supported the Conservatives, then the intervention of UKIP cost the Conservatives their overall majority. If that is so, then, ironically, the intervention of the most anti-European of the parties fighting the election handed the balance of power to the most pro-European of the parties fighting the election, namely the Liberal Democrats.

There was also a fifth party that was strikingly under-represented – the British National Party. Many were delighted that Nick Griffin, the leader of the party, was defeated in Barking. Few noticed that the BNP increased its vote by 50%, to secure nearly 2% of the vote, the highest percentage vote ever secured by a far-right party in Britain at a general election. Indeed, there were twice as many votes for the BNP as there were for the Greens. Under an entirely proportional system, the BNP would have won around 13 seats. Admittedly, the number of BNP candidates had increased threefold since the last election, and the party's vote per candidate increased only slightly. Nevertheless, the fact remains that in 2010, nearly two in every hundred British voters were prepared to support a far-right party. The BNP performed far better than Oswald Mosley's British Union of Fascists, which, in 1935, the only general election to occur before the party was proscribed by law in May 1940 as a danger to national security, put up no candidates and advised its supporters not to vote – a striking confession of weakness.

Seven parties with lower votes than UKIP and the BNP succeeded in securing representation in the House of Commons – the Democratic Unionist Party of Northern Ireland, the Scottish Nationalists, Sinn Fein, Plaid Cymru, the Social Democratic and Labour Party of Northern Ireland, the Greens, and the Alliance Party of Northern Ireland. But of these parties the Greens were the only national, rather than regional, party, and thus were the only one of those parties to fight the election on a nationwide basis. The others fought seats in only one of the territories comprising the United Kingdom.

The total vote secured by the two major parties – Conservatives and Labour – was, at 65.1%, the lowest since 1918, beating the previous low of 2005, when the two major parties between them secured just 67.6% of the vote. There were 84 MPs who, together with the Speaker, owed no allegiance to either the Labour or Conservative Parties – the second highest figure since the war (the highest, 92, occurring in 2005). The three-party vote was, at 88.1%, by far the lowest since the war. In Northern Ireland, not one MP was returned from the three major parties, and Sir Reg Empey, leader of the Ulster Unionist Party, which was allied to the Conservatives, was defeated in the constituency of Down South.

These outcomes contrast sharply with the results of general elections immediately after the war. In 1951, for example, no fewer than 96.8% of those voting supported Labour or the Conservatives. The Liberal Party, the predecessor of the Liberal Democrats, put up just 109 candidates and secured 2.5% of the vote, winning only six seats. In Scotland and Wales, all the seats were won by candidates from the three major parties – with none of the nationalist candidates securing representation. In Northern Ireland, all but three of the 12 seats were won by the Ulster Unionists, who took the Conservative whip in the House of Commons.

It is difficult to do more than speculate on the reasons for these changes, but one cause, surely, must be the gradual unfreezing of the class structure – the breaking up of the large socio-economic blocs based on occupation and social class that characterised the first half of the twentieth century. Partly for this reason, no doubt, party membership is far lower today than it was in the 1950s. Whereas in the 1950s around one in 11 of us belonged to a political party, today just one in 88 of us do. Party identification is also lower. Tribal politics has been undermined. There are not many voters who say today, 'I've always been Labour', or 'My family have never voted anything other than Conservative'. Just as the great nationalised monopolies have broken up in response to consumer demand for wider choice, so the monolithic party allegiances of yesteryear have, at a glacially slow pace admittedly, been dissolving, and voters have begun increasingly to shop around to seek the deal that best meets their individual preferences, rather than the preferences of their class or occupational grouping. This greater social fluidity is perhaps the most important of all the many changes to have taken place in British society during the post-war period, and it has had radical consequences for electoral behaviour.

Britain is also a far more geographically and socially fragmented society than it was 60 years ago. In 1951, outside Northern Ireland, there was a fairly standard Conservative/Labour battle in every constituency, with the Liberals reduced to the role of impotent onlookers, while the nationalists seemed to many to be irrelevant, cranky even, and, as Attlee suggested in the late 1950s, 'out of date'.[7] In 2010, by contrast, there were different electoral battles in the different parts of the United Kingdom. In Northern Ireland the battle was between parties representing the mainstream Unionist and Nationalist communities. Only one party – the Alliance Party – sought to straddle the two communities, and it succeeded in gaining its first parliamentary seat. The Alliance Party is a sister party to the Liberal Democrats, although it does not support the Conservative/Liberal Democrat coalition. None of the other parties which won seats in Northern Ireland has any connection with the parties on the other side of the Irish Sea.

In Scotland, the electoral battle was primarily between Labour and the SNP. The Conservatives could do no more than hold on to their single seat in Scotland, and were serious contenders in only a very few of the constituencies north of the Tweed. This meant that the dominant party at Westminster remained the fourth party in Scotland. In the South West of England, by contrast, the electoral battle was between the Liberal Democrats, the majority party in the region, who, before the election, held 12 out of the 25 seats, and the Conservatives, with nine seats, while Labour, with just four seats in the region, was very much the third party. Before the election, the Conservatives targeted 24 seats which they hoped to win from the Liberal Democrats. Of these, no fewer than 11 were in the South West.

The geographical fragmentation of Britain was not only between the nations and regions comprising the United Kingdom, but also between the cities and the countryside. By contrast with 1951, when the Conservatives were strongly repre-

---

[7] Brian Harrison, *Seeking a Role: The United Kingdom 1951–1970* (Clarendon Press, 2009) 425.

sented in the cities, they entered the general election of 2010 without a single seat in the large industrial conurbations of the Midlands, the North or Scotland. They were totally unrepresented in Birmingham, Bradford, Edinburgh, Glasgow, Leeds, Leicester, Liverpool, Manchester, Newcastle, Nottingham and Sheffield. Although the Conservatives won 97 seats in the election, these cities stubbornly refused to return a single Conservative.

The outcome of the general election, as we have seen, was as follows:

Conservative	36.1%
Labour	29.0%
Liberal Democrats	23.0%

In the previous general election, that of 2005, the percentages were as follows:

Labour	35.2%
Conservative	32.4%
Liberal Democrats	22.0%

The gap between the two major parties was far smaller in 2005 than in 2010, yet the election of 2005 yielded not a hung parliament, but a comfortable Labour majority of 66 seats. Had the result in 2010 been the other way around: Labour 36%, Conservatives 29%, Liberal Democrats 23%, Labour would again have won a comfortable majority, perhaps near to 100. In 2010, the Conservatives, although failing to win an overall majority, secured 6.9% of the vote more than Labour. That was a larger Conservative lead over Labour than the party had secured in any general election since the war, except for those of 1979, 1983, 1987 and 1992. It was a larger lead than that secured by Anthony Eden in 1955, when the Conservatives secured an overall majority of 58, by Harold Macmillan in 1959, when the Conservatives secured an overall majority of 100, and by Edward Heath in 1970, when the Conservatives gained an overall majority of 30. It was nearly as large as the 7% lead that Margaret Thatcher secured in the first of her election victories in 1979, when the Conservatives won an overall majority of 43.

	Conservative lead	Conservative majority
1955	3.3%	58
1959	5.6%	100
1970	3.4%	30
1979	7.0%	43
2010	6.9%	No overall majority

It is clear, then, that the electoral system is biased against the Conservatives vis-a-vis Labour. If Labour and the Conservatives had won exactly the same share of the vote in 2010, Labour would have won 54 more seats than the Conservatives. The Conservatives would indeed need to have won around 11% of the vote more than Labour to have secured an overall majority. Labour, by contrast, could have won an overall majority had it been just 3% ahead of the Conservatives; while in 2005,

Labour could have secured an overall majority even if it had secured 1% less of the vote than the Conservatives![8] For a working majority of 20, Labour needs a lead of 4% over the Conservatives, but the Conservatives need a lead of over 12%.[9] It is, in these circumstances, ironic that the Conservatives are the only major party to support retention of the first past the post voting system.

II. A HUNG PARLIAMENT

The 2010 general election yielded a hung parliament, the first since February 1974. But the options in 2010 seemed clearer and less complex than had been the case in 1974, when the result was as follows:

	Seats	% votes
Conservative	297	37.9
Labour	301	37.1
Liberals	14	19.3
SNP	7	2.0
Plaid Cymru	2	0.6
United Ulster Unionist Council	11	1.8
SDLP	1	0.9
Others	2	0.4
Total	635	100

The Conservatives, under Edward Heath, had lost their overall majority, and Labour was now the largest party, although the Conservatives had won more votes than Labour. Labour, however, was 17 seats short of an overall majority. The difficulty was that no single minor party held the balance of power. The only combination of two parties capable of securing an overall majority was a grand coalition of Labour and the Conservatives, and that was highly unlikely. An alliance between a major party and a single minor party – even the largest minor party, the Liberals – would have been insufficient to secure an overall majority. The support of at least two of the minor parties would have been necessary. In the event, the election led to a Labour minority government, which lasted for seven months before a second general election in October yielded a small overall majority of three seats for Labour.

In 2010, by contrast, there was the possibility of a government with a comfortable overall majority of 78 if a Conservative/Liberal Democrat coalition could be formed. In practice, the overall majority would be slightly larger than that, since the five Sinn Fein MPs from Northern Ireland, who do not recognise British rule over Northern Ireland, do not take their seats at Westminster. Therefore

---

[8] John Curtice, 'So What Went Wrong with the Electoral System? The 2010 Election Result and the Debate about Electoral Reform' in Geddes and Tonge (n 2) 54.

[9] 'An Analysis of the Results' in Kavanagh and Cowley (n 1) 416–17.

323 seats rather than 326 would be sufficient for an overall majority, and a Conservative/Liberal Democrat coalition would in practice have an overall majority of 83. The second possibility was a coalition of the Left – a so-called 'rainbow' coalition. This would comprise Labour and the Liberal Democrats, together with the three Social Democratic and Labour MPs, the Alliance Party MP from Northern Ireland, and the Green MP. Such a coalition would have commanded 321 seats in the House of Commons, not quite sufficient for an overall majority. However, the nationalists indicated that they wished at all costs to avoid a Conservative government, and that they would not therefore support any motion that would have the effect of bringing down a government of the Left; they would instead abstain on crucial votes. The third possibility was a Conservative minority government, perhaps sustained by an agreement with the Liberal Democrats along the lines of the Lib-Lab pact between March 1977 and October 1978 – a so-called 'confidence and supply' agreement – by which the party outside the government would agree not to vote against it in confidence or supply motions, in exchange for policy concessions and a promise of consultation on legislation. A confidence and supply agreement provides for a parliamentary but not a governmental coalition.

Every previous hung parliament in the twentieth century – in 1910, 1923, 1929 and 1974 – had led to a minority government rather than a majority coalition. A minority government can survive in the House of Commons provided that the other parties do not successfully combine against it. That was how the Labour minority government survived in the seven-month minority parliament of 1974, and again during the years from 1976 to 1979, since by 1976 it had lost, through defections and by-election defeats, the small overall majority which it had won in the October 1974 general election. For around half of the period 1976–79, the minority Labour government survived through the Lib-Lab pact, but for the rest of the time it survived because the other parties were unable or unwilling to combine against it, until, in March 1979, following the failure of devolution referendums in Scotland and Wales, the government was defeated in the House of Commons on a confidence motion by one vote, and was forced to go to the country. Britain also had experience of minority government during the inter-war years, under the first two Labour governments – the first lasting for 10 months in 1924, and the second lasting for just over two years between 1929 and 1931.

A Conservative minority government seemed, for a time, to be the most likely outcome following the election. But perhaps David Cameron had noticed that the experience of minority government in Britain has not been an altogether happy one. The minority government of 1924 lasted less than a year and achieved little; the minority government of 1929 lasted just over two years with the help of an agreement with the Liberals, but collapsed in the financial crisis of 1931, and in the election that followed Labour was reduced to just 52 seats, though ironically it won 33% of the vote, 4% more of the vote than Labour gained in the 2010 election. In 1974, the Wilson minority government felt unable to take strong measures to control inflation, which would soon reach 26%, since it knew that it would shortly have to face the voters in another general election. The Callaghan minority government of 1976 lasted longer because of the pact with the Liberals, but after the pact ended it collapsed in 1979 following the public sector strikes that marked the 'winter of discontent', and Labour went into opposition for 18 years.

It perhaps comes as no surprise that in the Coalition Agreement David Cameron and Nick Clegg declared: 'After the election . . . there was the option of minority government – but we were uninspired by it.' A minority government would almost certainly have meant a second general election within a few months. But, even if the Conservatives had been able to win that second election, their troubles would not had been over, unless they had won with a large majority. For, not only have minority governments been short-lived, but governments with small majorities have not lasted long either. The 1950 Labour government, returned with a majority of five, lasted 18 months; the Labour government of 1964, which had a majority of four, also lasted 18 months. John Major in 1992 found that even an overall majority of 21 was barely sufficient to secure passage of the Maastricht Treaty through Parliament. David Cameron had been a Special Adviser during the period of the Major government, first to Norman Lamont, the Chancellor, and then to Michael Howard, the Home Secretary. It was perhaps the unhappy experience of that government, wracked by conflict between Europhiles and Eurosceptics, that helped to persuade Cameron that, even if he could win a small overall majority in a second general election, a coalition with a comfortable majority would provide a better solution to the problems facing the country. But, whatever the motives of the participants, the hung parliament of 2010 was the first to result in a coalition, rather than a minority government. In the past, coalitions resulted not from general elections, but from crises occurring between general elections – war led to the formation of the Asquith coalition in 1915, the Lloyd George coalition in 1916 and the Churchill coalition in 1940, and a financial emergency in 1931 led to the formation of the National Government.

There is, however, one striking difference between the coalitions of 1916 and 1931 and that of 2010. Unlike the coalition of 2010, those of 1916 and 1931 were endorsed by the voters **after** they had been formed – in the general election of 1918 (the so-called 'coupon' election[10]), and in the general election of 1931. The coalition of 2010 has received no such electoral endorsement. It was formed after a general election, not before it.

III. A HUNG PARLIAMENT AND THE CONSTITUTION

With a number of alternative possible governments in a hung parliament situation, agreed procedures needed to be in place to regulate the government formation process, so that whatever government was eventually to be formed would enjoy a

---

[10] See Chapter 4, p 72.

secure measure of legitimacy. In the past these procedures were unwritten, forming part of the 'tacit understandings' that sustained so much of the British constitution. In a modern democratic society, however, such tacit understandings are no longer sufficient. Most of the officials involved in the process of government formation believed that they ought now to be codified. Many politicians agreed. In early February 2010, aware of the strong possibility of a hung parliament, Gordon Brown asked Sir Gus O'Donnell, the Cabinet Secretary, to produce a Cabinet Manual bringing together the laws and conventions relating to Cabinet government. By the end of February, the Cabinet Office had produced a chapter laying out the procedures to be followed in the event of a hung parliament. This was sent to the Justice Select Committee of the House of Commons, which, after examining various witnesses, including Sir Gus himself, issued a short report in March endorsing these procedures.[11] The procedures were generally accepted as appropriate, and it was striking that they gave rise to hardly any controversy during the period of government formation. This part of the Manual was therefore, in Sir Gus O'Donnell's words, 'tested under fire'.[12]

The guidelines were not intended to lay down any new constitutional principles – indeed the Cabinet Office would not have had the authority to carry out such a task; rather their purpose was to codify and, where necessary, clarify existing principles. But, in evidence to the House of Commons Justice Select Committee on 24 February 2010, Sir Gus drew its attention to two matters. The first was a clarification of the role of the civil service after an election resulting in a hung parliament. The civil service, of course, must continue to advise the incumbent government until it resigns, but the guidelines declared that, in a hung parliament situation, it was 'open to the Prime Minister to ask the Cabinet Secretary to support the Government's discussion with opposition or minority parties on the formation of government'. That was a suggestion that Brown was to follow after the election, when he authorised officials to support the talks between the Conservatives and Liberal Democrats.

Secondly, and perhaps even more importantly, Sir Gus noted that the Manual also clarified the fact that the incumbent government in a hung parliament – before it had won, in effect, a vote of confidence on the Queen's Speech – was under an obligation 'to observe discretion in taking significant decisions', although '[t]he normal and essential business of government at all levels . . . will need to be carried out'. The New Zealand Cabinet Manual has gone further than the chapter in the British Cabinet Manual and codified the conventions governing a so-called caretaker government in much greater detail. For, in New Zealand, since the introduction of proportional representation in 1996, every parliament has been a hung parliament. The New Zealand Cabinet Manual lays down the

[11] The complete Manual can now be found on the Cabinet Office website, www.cabinetoffice.gov. uk. The author was one of a small group of academics called upon to advise on the procedures, and was questioned on it by the Select Committee on 24 February 2010.

[12] Oral evidence to House of Commons Political and Constitutional Reform Committee, 4 November 2010.

principle that where it is not clear who is to form the next government, the incumbent government should defer making controversial decisions whenever possible. When that is not possible, such decisions should be 'handled by way of temporary or holding arrangements that do not commit the government in the longer term (that is, by extending a board appointment or rolling over a contract for a short period); or if neither deferral nor temporary arrangements are possible, be made only after consultation with other political parties to establish whether the proposed action has the support of a majority of the House'.[13]

But the main emphasis of the chapter in the Cabinet Office Manual was on the fundamental constitutional principle regulating the formation of a government. This fundamental principle is that a government must be able to command the confidence of the House of Commons, although this does not, as we have seen, mean that it need enjoy an overall majority, so long as the opposition parties are not prepared to combine together to defeat it. The test that any new government, whether a coalition or minority government, has to meet after a general election yielding a hung parliament is the vote, as soon as Parliament meets, on the Queen's Speech, which is in effect a vote of confidence. Of course, when, as has been the case at every general election since the war, with the exception of those of February 1974 and 2010, there is a clear result, it is obvious which party will be able to command the confidence of the Commons. If an opposition party has won an overall majority, the Prime Minister will resign as soon as the election results are known. He may, if he wishes, wait to meet Parliament, and indeed until 1868 it was the custom for incumbent Prime Ministers to test opinion by meeting Parliament, but Disraeli, after the general election of that year, which returned an overall majority for his Liberal opponents, resigned immediately so as to avoid wasting time. Disraeli's precedent has since been followed by every Prime Minister when a general election has resulted in an overall majority for an opposition party.

From a strictly constitutional point of view, however, it is the composition of the House of Commons that determines who is able to form the government. The role of the voters is restricted to that of electing a House of Commons. Of course, under normal circumstances, when a single party has won an overall majority, the House of Commons acts as an electoral college, mandated to support the government that has won the election. With a hung parliament, however, the situation becomes more complex, although the fundamental principle that a government needs to secure the confidence of Parliament remains.

Since it is Parliament and not the people that decides upon a government, an incumbent Prime Minister, faced with an inconclusive general election result, is entitled, in the words of paragraph 16 of the Cabinet Office Manual, 'to await the meeting of the new Parliament to see if it can command the confidence of the House of Commons'. That was the course taken by Stanley Baldwin, the Conservative Prime Minister, after he lost his overall majority in the inconclusive general election of December 1923. The outcome of the election was as follows:

---

[13]   Cabinet Office, Wellington, 2008, para 6.20.

	Seats
Conservative	258
Labour	191
Liberals	159
Others	7
Total	615

Baldwin decided to wait until Parliament met in January 1924. He was then immediately defeated in the vote on the King's Speech by a combination of Labour and the Liberals. He at once resigned, to be succeeded by Ramsay MacDonald at the head of a minority Labour administration.

Baldwin had a tactical motive for deciding to meet Parliament. He wanted to show the voters that the Liberals were allowing a government of the Left, a government dedicated to socialism, to take office. He hoped that, as indeed turned out to be the case, the Conservatives could win over much of the Liberal but anti-socialist vote at the next general election. But Baldwin could also argue that he had a good constitutional reason to meet Parliament since, although he had lost his overall majority, the Conservatives were still the largest party. To find an instance of the Prime Minister of a party which was **not** the largest party in the House of Commons meeting Parliament, we have to go back to January 1886. The general election of November 1885 left the Conservative government of Lord Salisbury 86 seats behind the Liberals. There were, in addition, 86 Irish nationalists, who held the balance of power. Salisbury decided to meet Parliament, but was defeated, shortly after the Queen's Speech, on an amendment to a bill relating to agrarian legislation, which he took as a vote of no confidence in his government. Salisbury promptly resigned and Gladstone formed a Liberal administration committed to Irish Home Rule. Salisbury, however, had as good a tactical motive for meeting Parliament in 1886 as Baldwin did in 1923. For just as Baldwin wanted to display the dependence of Labour on the Liberals, so Salisbury wanted to display the dependence of Gladstone's Liberals on the Irish Home Rule Party, a party which, in the view of the Conservatives, was proposing a policy that would lead to the disintegration of the United Kingdom. Whether, therefore, an incumbent Prime Minister in a hung parliament situation decides to meet Parliament depends in part upon tactical considerations.

Before meeting Parliament, a Prime Minister in a hung parliament situation may seek to strengthen his position by means of a coalition or an agreement with another party. That was what Edward Heath tried to do when the February 1974 election produced a hung parliament. Heath's Conservatives were the second largest party in terms of seats, but the Conservatives had won more votes than Labour. Instead of resigning immediately, Heath sought a coalition with the Liberals, offering them places in a reconstituted Cabinet. He also offered the whip to some though not all of the Ulster Unionists, who had resigned the Conservative whip in 1973 in protest at the Sunningdale Agreement, which provided for power-sharing between the Unionists and the Nationalists in a new Northern Ireland

Assembly. The Liberals declined Heath's offer of coalition, but said that they would be prepared to support his government from the outside on a 'confidence and supply' basis – the same basis on which they later supported Labour during the Lib-Lab pact in 1977–78. Heath, however, declined this offer and resigned following a weekend of negotiation, on the Monday after the general election.

Brown followed Heath's example and, fortified perhaps by the Cabinet Manual, remained in office after the election, hoping to negotiate a coalition or agreement with the Liberal Democrats. Although, as we have seen, Brown was constitutionally entitled to remain, he had perhaps rather less justification than Heath in 1974. Heath had lost the election very narrowly, and the Conservatives had in fact won more votes than Labour. Brown, by contrast, had been comprehensively defeated. In the view of Lord Adonis, Transport Secretary in the Brown government, the Manual 'performed its crucial role of overcoming the knee-jerk expectation that there must be a new Prime Minister in post by Friday afternoon, which of course has been the general practice in British Government over recent decades'.[14] Had it not been for the publication of the Cabinet Manual and the dissemination of its doctrines, there might have been more public criticism of Gordon Brown than in fact there was.

It is interesting to speculate whether the Conservatives would have been able to construct a coalition had Brown resigned immediately on the Friday after the election, rather than after five days of fruitless negotiation with the Liberal Democrats. Had Brown resigned immediately, David Cameron would have been called to the Palace the day after the election, and would have had to form a Cabinet rapidly. He might have offered Cabinet places to the Liberal Democrats, but perhaps successful negotiations with the Liberal Democrats would have required more time than was available on the Friday and Saturday after the election, and he would have had to be content with a 'confidence and supply' agreement. But that, of course, is speculation.

In a hung parliament situation, instead of waiting to meet Parliament or seeking an arrangement with another party, there is, of course, a third alternative: the incumbent Prime Minister may resign immediately. That was the course taken by Stanley Baldwin after the 1929 general election, when the result was as follows:

	Seats
Labour	288
Conservative	260
Liberals	59
Others	8
Total	615

In 1929, by contrast with 1923, Labour and not the Conservatives were the largest party, although, as in February 1974, the Conservatives had won more votes than Labour. Some Conservatives, including Winston Churchill, Chancellor of the

[14] Oral evidence to House of Commons Political and Constitutional Reform Committee, 14 October 2010, HC 528-i, Q 39.

Exchequer in Baldwin's government, and Sir Austen Chamberlain, who had been Foreign Secretary, thought that Baldwin ought to follow the 1923 precedent and meet Parliament, but Baldwin told the King's Private Secretary, Lord Stamfordham, that '[h]e had appealed to the people to trust him, as in 1924, and they had refused. He was beaten and he accepts it and thinks this sporting attitude will count in his favour next time. If he hangs on they will say, "Here is this man clinging to office, he won't take his defeat, he is trying to prevent the Labour Party from enjoying their victory".'[15] That was perhaps a better judgment of the public mood than Heath showed in 1974 or Gordon Brown in 2010. But, just as in 1923, Baldwin had a tactical motive. He did not want to form a Conservative government which would be dependent on Lloyd George, the Liberal leader, and a politician whom he thoroughly distrusted. The Deputy Cabinet Secretary, Tom Jones, who discussed the matter with Baldwin and colleagues at Chequers after the election, wrote in his diary, 'What we all feared was that Lloyd George might keep S.B. [Baldwin] in office for a week or a month, and humiliate him and his party in every conceivable way. S.B's instinct was to go out at once . . . If this were not done, there would be a scream from Labour that S.B. was denying them the fruits of victory.'[16]

When a Prime Minister resigns, he will normally be asked by the sovereign for a recommendation as to his successor. The sovereign is not obliged to seek such a recommendation, but on only three occasions since the resignation of Gladstone in 1894 is it known that a Prime Minister has not been asked for one. The first was in 1894, when Queen Victoria chose Lord Rosebery as Gladstone's successor, someone Gladstone would certainly not have recommended. The second was in 1908, when Edward VII, who was in Biarritz, appointed Asquith, without asking the resigning Prime Minister, Campbell-Bannerman, for a recommendation. But Campbell-Bannerman was a dying man, and the choice of Asquith, unlike Rosebery in 1894, was obvious and acceptable to all. The third occasion was in 1923 following the resignation of Bonar Law. But Bonar Law too was a dying man and had indicated that he did not wish to be asked.

When a resigning Prime Minister is asked for his recommendation, his answer is of course in no way binding, or it would be open to a Prime Minister who had lost the support of Parliament or the electorate to make a mischievous recommendation. Gordon Brown, for example, could have recommended David Davis, a Conservative opponent of Cameron's, for the succession. In 1957, upon his resignation, Sir Anthony Eden recommended RA Butler as his successor, but the consensus of the Conservative Party was clearly for Harold Macmillan, whom the Queen duly sent for.[17]

When, in a hung parliament situation, the incumbent Prime Minister has decided to resign, or has been defeated on the Queen's Speech, normal practice is to call for the leader of the largest party in the Commons and ask him if he can

---

[15] Keith Middlemas and John Barnes, *Baldwin* (Weidenfeld and Nicolson, 1969) 527.

[16] Tom Jones, *Whitehall Diary, Vol 2, 1926–1930* (Oxford University Press, 1969) 192.

[17] Vernon Bogdanor, *The Monarchy and the Constitution* (Oxford University Press, 1995) 94.

form a government. He is not, however, asked whether he can form a government which can command a *majority* in the House of Commons. It is open to the leader of the largest party either to form a minority government, as Ramsay MacDonald did in 1924 and 1929, and Wilson did in 1974, or to form a coalition, as David Cameron did in 2010. Indeed, when Cameron was appointed Prime Minister, it was not absolutely certain that he would be leading a coalition rather than a minority Conservative government, since the Coalition Agreement had not, at that stage, been accepted by both parties; and Cameron apparently told the Queen that he was uncertain. In a later television documentary, *Five Days that Changed Britain*, he declared: 'I said I *hoped* to [form a coalition] but I might have to come back in the morning and tell [the Queen] it was something rather different.'[18] In such a situation, the Queen will normally ask only whether the candidate called to the Palace can form a government. She will not stipulate the form that this government might take, which is a matter for the new Prime Minister.

It is of course possible that the person called to the Palace following an inconclusive general election will be uncertain whether he can form a government. In such circumstances he may accept a conditional commission. Instead of kissing hands upon appointment as Prime Minister, he will reply to the Queen's question of whether he can form a government by replying that he will try. That was the course taken by Lord Home when asked to form a government after the resignation of Harold Macmillan as Prime Minister in 1963. Home could not be sure whether he could form a government, not because there was a hung parliament – the Conservatives enjoyed a comfortable majority in the Commons – but because there seemed to be significant Cabinet opposition to his appointment, and it was by no means clear whether major figures in the Cabinet, and in particular RA Butler, himself a candidate for the premiership, would agree to serve, in which case Home would have had to report failure. After Home was called to the Palace in October 1963, the Court Circular declared simply that 'The Queen has received the Earl of Home in audience and invited him to form an administration'. The press magnate, Lord Beaverbrook, predicted that Home would succeed. 'He has got the loaves and fishes. There is no stopping him now.' That prediction proved correct. Butler and his supporters agreed to serve, and Home was able to report success when he saw the Queen the next day. The Palace then issued a Court Circular declaring, 'The Queen this morning received in audience the Earl of Home who kissed hands upon his appointment as Prime Minister and First Lord of the Treasury'.[19]

One important motive behind publishing the rules governing the appointment of a Prime Minister in a hung parliament was to ensure that the Queen was not drawn into the process. Were the Queen to be involved in discussions between the parties, her political neutrality could be compromised. The role of the Queen is not one of participating in the government formation process, but of endorsing

---

[18] Rob Wilson, *5 Days to Power: The Journey to Coalition Britain* (Biteback, 2010) 274.
[19] DR Thorpe, *Alec Douglas-Home* (Sinclair Stevenson, 1996) 313–15.

decisions made by the political leaders. In the words of the Justice Committee of the House of Commons, in paragraph 19 of its report, *Constitutional Processes Following a General Election*,[20] written in bold: 'Our witnesses were unanimous that, in the circumstances of a House with no overall majority, it was for the politicians to conduct negotiations to clarify who was most likely to be able to command the House's confidence and the Sovereign would not, and should not be expected to, take a role in that process.' It is for the political parties, not the Queen, to determine who should be the next Prime Minister. The Queen then endorses that choice. The non-involvement of the Queen was symbolised by her remaining at Windsor, rather than returning to Buckingham Palace, during the five days of negotiations between the parties that followed the 2010 general election.

That was a striking contrast to the stance adopted by George V when the last peacetime coalition government was formed, following the economic crisis of 1931. Responding to the crisis, Ramsay MacDonald, the Prime Minister of a minority Labour government, had sought to make cuts in public expenditure, but his Cabinet found itself unable to agree on a reduction in the standard rate of unemployment benefit. MacDonald accordingly went to the Palace in order to resign. But the King 'impressed on the Prime Minister that he was the only man to lead the country through the crisis and hoped he would reconsider the situation'. The King had previously asked MacDonald whether he might consult with the leaders of the two opposition parties, the Conservatives and Liberals, and MacDonald had agreed. The King's consultations had convinced him that the opposition parties 'would support him [MacDonald] in restoring the confidence of foreigners in the financial stability of the country'. MacDonald then asked the King if he would call a conference of the three party leaders at Buckingham Palace the next day. The King again agreed.[21]

When the party leaders met at the Palace, the King virtually instructed them to form a National Government, under MacDonald's leadership. The memorandum of events recorded by the King's Private Secretary, Sir Clive Wigram, states: 'The Prime Minister said that he had the resignation of his Cabinet in his pocket, but the King replied that he trusted there was no question of the Prime Minister's resignation: the leaders of the three Parties must get together, and come to some arrangement. His Majesty hoped that the Prime Minister, with the colleagues who remained faithful to him, would help in the formation of a National Government, which the King was sure would be supported by the Conservatives and the Liberals. The King assured the Prime Minister that, remaining at his post, his position and reputation would be much more enhanced than if he surrendered the government of the country at such a crisis.'[22] When the National Government went to the country in October 1931, George V said to the Cabinet Secretary, Sir Maurice Hankey, 'Of course you are going to vote'. Hankey replied that, since

---

[20] HC 296, March 2010.
[21] Harold Nicolson, *King George V: His Life and Reign* (Constable, 1952) 449, 464.
[22] Sir Clive Wigram's memorandum is reprinted in Nicolson, ibid, 465–66.

assuming his post, he had 'rather made a point of not voting'. 'But this time', the King retorted, 'it is different. I want the National Government to get every vote possible.' Hankey inquired whether this was in the nature of 'a command', and, on being told that it was, he declared, 'Very well, Sire. Your Majesty can claim to have canvassed one vote for the National Government.'[23]

In 1931 George V played an active role as a facilitator, if not indeed also as the instigator, of the National Government.[24] In 2010, by contrast, the Queen and her advisers were insistent not only that she would in no way be involved in the government formation process, but that she should be *seen* not to be involved. Part of the reason for the difference between the two situations is that economic conditions were not as serious in 2010 as they had been in 1931, when politicians feared an immediate collapse of the currency if finances were not stabilised. It is true that there were considerable anxieties also in 2010; indeed, on the first weekend after the election, it seemed as if the currency crisis in Greece might force that country to leave the eurozone, with serious consequences even for countries such as Britain which were not members. Nevertheless, the atmosphere in 2010 cannot be compared to the near panic that gripped political leaders in 1931.

But there is a further important reason underscoring the difference in the role of the monarch between 1931 and 2011. It lies in changing perceptions of the monarchy. In 1931, and indeed until the 1960s, there was widespread deference and an almost religious reverence for the monarchy, whose workings were enveloped in an atmosphere of mystery. Today, however, attitudes towards the monarchy have become more questioning and sceptical. The institution has come to be seen in a more practical light, and its activities have come to be much more open to public scrutiny. This could cause difficulties for the monarchy, for the Queen occupies not only the constitutional position of head of state, but also the role of head of the nation. During the twentieth century, the monarchy came increasingly to be seen as a symbolic institution, indeed the only institution that is capable of representing the whole nation to itself. To fulfil this role successfully, it is vital that the monarchy is not only above party – it must also be clearly seen to be above party. This means that the remaining discretionary powers of the sovereign, to appoint a Prime Minister and to agree to a dissolution of Parliament, must be exercised in such a manner that they cannot give rise to accusations of partiality, even from those who may be ill-disposed towards the monarchy. It is for this reason that the Palace welcomed the adoption by the Conservative Party in 1964 of rules for the election of the party leader, following the fracas attending the choice in 1963 of Lord Home as the successor to Harold Macmillan under the older more opaque system of 'customary processes of consultation'.[25]

---

[23] Stephen Roskill, *Hankey: Man of Secrets, Vol II, 1919–31* (Collins 1972) 569.

[24] The argument that George V was the instigator of the National Government is discussed in Vernon Bogdanor, '1931 Revisited: The Constitutional Aspects' (1991) *Twentieth Century British History* 1–25 and, more briefly, in Bogdanor (n 16) 105–12.

[25] The problems raised by the selection of Lord Home are discussed in Bogdanor (n 16) ch 4, while ch 3 of that book discusses the role of the Queen in the appointment of the Prime Minister.

The adoption of the Cabinet Manual is an important stage in the evolution of constitutional monarchy. In the past, it was held that the precise extent and scope of the sovereign's personal prerogatives, including the choice of a Prime Minister, should deliberately be left undefined. For if these prerogatives were to be precisely defined, so it was argued, they would limit the sovereign's freedom of choice; the sovereign, it was held, could not be bound by precedent, but ought to have the discretion to act as she thought best in circumstances that cannot, in the nature of events, be foreseen. In *The English Constitution*, Bagehot declared that 'There is no authentic explicit information as to what the Queen can do any more than of what she does'.[26] In 1910, Lord Esher, an adviser to Edward VII, went so far as to say that there ought not to be any public discussion of the prerogative at all, since 'the principle is entirely dependent upon the circumstances in which the prerogative is used'.[27] In 1953, one authority declared that the 'precise limits' of the sovereign's power 'have never been defined'.[28] In 1974, the Queen's Private Secretary, Sir Martin Charteris, told Tony Benn that the discretion to refuse a dissolution must be preserved 'because I think there has to be some risk attached in order to provide excitement for the monarchy'.[29]

Such a doctrine can hardly be maintained in the modern world, where every institution has come to be exposed to the pressures of transparency. But there is in any case a tension between the idea of a wide and undefined discretion for the sovereign and that of political neutrality. The greater the discretion, the greater the possibility that the sovereign might use it in a manner that offends one of the principal parties in the state. The sovereign should therefore be protected from having to use her discretion in a controversial way. This is best achieved if the party leaders are able to present her with an agreed solution to the problem of government formation in a hung parliament. In New Zealand, when proportional representation was introduced for the general election of 1996, with the likelihood that most general elections would yield hung parliaments, the Queen's representative, the Governor-General, Sir Michael Hardie Boys, declared that his role was 'to ascertain the will of Parliament . . . and make an appointment accordingly'. Were negotiations between the parties to become difficult, then 'a little encouragement may not be out of place. My role . . . is simply that of a facilitator'.[30] But even that goes too far for a sovereign, who, unlike a Governor-General, does not relinquish office after a period of years, but remains on the throne for the rest of her life. Were the Queen to be seen to be offering 'a little encouragement', she would undoubtedly come to be criticised by those politicians whom she had not encouraged! In modern times, therefore, the sovereign will be expected to use her prerogative powers only in those very rare situations when politicians fail to

[26] Bagehot, 'The English Constitution' in *The Collected Works of Walter Bagehot*, vol 5 (The Economist, 1974) 243.

[27] Quoted in Bogdanor (n 16) 75.

[28] LS Amery, *Thoughts on the Constitution*, 2nd edn (Oxford University Press, 1953) 6.

[29] Tony Benn, *Against The Tide: Diaries 1973–86* (Hutchinson 1989) 94–95.

[30] Quoted in Colin James, *Under New Sail: MMP and Public Servants* (Institute of Policy Studies, Wellington, 1997) 45.

behave with constitutional propriety. If, for example, after failing to win an over-all majority, Gordon Brown had sought an immediate second dissolution before meeting Parliament, the Queen would have been entitled to refuse this request. In these circumstances, the Queen is a kind of constitutional long-stop, an ultimate guardian of the constitutional proprieties. But, on other occasions, the Queen waits for the politicians to come to their decisions, and then endorses them. She is not herself an active facilitator.

*   *   *

After the general elections of February 1974 and 2010, which resulted in hung parliaments, the incumbent Prime Ministers – Edward Heath and Gordon Brown – decided not to resign immediately, but to explore whether they could continue by forming a coalition – with the Liberals in 1974, and with the Liberal Democrats in 2010. Some criticised them for this. Both Heath and Brown, critics argued, had sought a renewed mandate from the voters, but had failed to achieve it. Therefore, they ought to do what Baldwin had done in 1929 and resign immediately. In fact, as we have seen, they were perfectly within their constitutional rights to remain, and indeed, had they wished to do so, to meet Parliament and test the opinion of the House of Commons. It is possible to question their political judgment in remaining, but not the constitutional propriety of their doing so.

Some commentators, however, have criticised Gordon Brown from an oppo-site viewpoint. They have suggested not only that an incumbent Prime Minister in a hung parliament situation has a *right* to remain, but that he is under a *duty* to do so until the formation of an alternative government is assured, so as to protect the Queen. The Cabinet Secretary, Sir Gus O'Donnell, adopted this view when he told the House of Commons Justice Committee before the election that 'it was the "responsibility" of the incumbent Prime Minister not to resign until the position was clear'. Other witnesses told the Committee that it was 'the "national duty" of the Prime Minister "above and before party political considerations as primary adviser to the Crown . . ." to remain'.[31] Lord Armstrong, a former Cabinet Secretary, concurred with the view expressed by Sir Gus O'Donnell in a letter sent to *The Times* on 15 May 2010.[32] He argued that, if no party has won an overall majority, it is the incumbent's 'duty to remain in office until, following political negotiations, he is in a position either to form a government himself or to tender his resignation and make a recommendation as to whom the Queen should send for to take his place'. In New Zealand, it is in fact the convention that the incum-bent Prime Minister continues in a caretaker capacity until it is clear that a new government can be formed. On this view, Gordon Brown was at fault, not for failing to resign immediately, but for the opposite reason: he resigned too soon,

---

[31] HC 296, para 19.
[32] I am grateful to Lord Armstrong for sending me the full copy of his letter to *The Times*, and also for many stimulating discussions on these matters. But he is not, of course, to be implicated in my arguments or conclusions.

before it was clear whether Cameron could form a coalition. Indeed, it appears that Nick Clegg sought to persuade Brown to delay his resignation until the talks between the Liberal Democrats and the Conservatives had been brought to fruition, though it was of course clear well before Brown resigned that Cameron would be able to form a government, even if there was doubt as to whether it would be a minority government or a coalition.

The purpose of the Armstrong doctrine is not merely to protect the Queen, but to ensure that she is not left without advisers, to ensure that there is always a Prime Minister in place. In 1922, however, Britain found herself without a government for four days. A meeting of Conservative MPs, the majority element in the Lloyd George coalition government, decided, against the advice of the party leader, Austen Chamberlain, that it did not wish to continue with the coalition. Lloyd George resigned immediately on hearing of this decision, without waiting for Parliament to meet or for the Conservatives to elect a new leader. It would have been pointless for the King to have summoned Chamberlain, since he had been repudiated by his party. He therefore called for the leader of the anti-coalition Conservatives, Bonar Law, a former party leader. But Bonar Law, although pressed by the King's Private Secretary, declared that he would not accept appointment until he had been formally elected as Conservative Party leader. This was to take four days. The Court Circular, therefore, simply declared that the King had granted Bonar Law an audience, and he did not kiss hands as Prime Minister for another four days.[33]

It might be argued that in the more dangerous world of today, when terrorism is an ever-present threat, Britain cannot afford to take the risk of being left without a Prime Minister for four days. Even so, the Armstrong doctrine may go too far. The question of when a Prime Minister ought to resign is a matter for his political judgment. He should not be required to incur odium by having to hang on when it is clear that he no longer enjoys political support. It is not the incumbent's responsibility alone to protect the Queen, but that of all the political actors involved. Brown, therefore, acted perfectly constitutionally in resigning once it became clear that he could not form a government, there being no possibility of agreement on a coalition between Labour and the Liberal Democrats.

It would, however, have been perfectly open to Heath in 1974 or Brown in 2010 to decide, as Baldwin did in 1929, that, while the verdict of the voters might be unclear, what was clear was that they had been rejected. In all of these situations, the successor as Prime Minister was obvious and uncontroversial – MacDonald in 1929, Wilson in 1974 and Cameron in 2010. Even if there is no obvious successor, however, the incumbent Prime Minister is entitled to make a decision as to when he should go on political grounds. No doubt advisers might suggest to the Prime Minister that he ought to stay until there is a successor, in order to protect the

---

[33] The collapse of the Lloyd George government and formation of the Bonar Law government are discussed in Robert Rhodes James, *Memoirs of a Conservative: JCC Davidson's Memoirs and Papers, 1910–37* (Weidenfeld and Nicolson, 1969) 128; and also in Robert Blake, *The Unknown Prime Minister: The Life and Times of Andrew Bonar Law, 1858–1923* (Eyre and Spottiswoode, 1955).

Queen, but he is in no way required to accept such a suggestion. It will then be for the other party leaders to ensure that the Queen is not brought into the negotiations or caused political embarrassment.

The rules regulating the government formation process, codified in the Cabinet Manual, emphasise that, while a hung parliament may lead to a political crisis, there is no reason why it should lead to a constitutional crisis. A hung parliament, after all, merely makes transparent the fundamental principle of parliamentary government – a principle that, since 1868 at least, has normally been covert: the principle that a government depends upon the confidence of Parliament. Even if, therefore, hung parliaments become a regular feature of British politics, as they almost certainly would were proportional representation to be introduced, existing institutions and procedures would be perfectly capable of dealing with them without the need for constitutional innovation. The experience of New Zealand, a country with a Westminster model of government, and, like Britain, without a codified constitution, which introduced proportional representation in 1996, confirms this view. For proportional representation in New Zealand has proved perfectly compatible with that country's traditional political institutions. The working of government alters, and the political relationships between government and parliament may be different, but from the point of view of constitutional principle 'little had changed', the leading authority on the New Zealand constitution declared in 2008. 'Politics continue to be organized around the linchpin of the Westminster system – the need for governments to secure and retain the confidence of the popularly elected House.' What is notable, as a former New Zealand Prime Minister has noted, is 'not how much [the Cabinet system] has changed but how little'. The only change was the introduction of 'agreements to differ'.[34] Proportional representation has radically changed politics in New Zealand but not the constitution.

Nevertheless, the publication of Chapter 6 of the Cabinet Manual was a constitutional innovation of some importance, since the very act of writing down rules which hitherto were unwritten has served to clarify them and to emphasise the apolitical role of the monarchy. It has proved a further stage in constitutionalising the monarchy.

Chapter 6 of the Cabinet Manual, which deals with the procedures to be adopted in case of a hung parliament, was published in March 2010. The draft Cabinet Manual as a whole was published, following Cabinet approval, in December 2010. But the precise constitutional status of the Manual is not wholly clear. In reply to questioning by the House of Commons Political and Constitutional Reform Committee, the Cabinet Secretary accepted that while the Manual might be the nearest we have come to a written constitution, and indeed might serve as a first step towards such a constitution, it is nevertheless 'a long, long way from a written constitution'. Whether Britain does or does not develop

---

[34] Philip Joseph, 'MMP and the Constitution' (2009) *New Zealand Journal of Public and International Law* 113. This article is based on a lecture given in 2008. The former New Zealand Prime Minister was Sir Geoffrey Palmer. For 'agreements to differ', see p 51 below.

a written – or more properly a codified – constitution is of course a matter for politicians, not for officials.[35]

The Cabinet Manual brings together existing laws and conventions. Sir Gus O'Donnell has suggested that in Britain, as in New Zealand, the Manual would be 'owned by the Cabinet'.[36] But it is not clear what happens if a newly elected government declares that it does not accept one of the conventions. In New Zealand, it is open to a newly elected government to decide whether or not to abide by the Manual, although the changes so far made to it have in fact been effected by civil servants and not by ministers. But, neither in New Zealand nor in Britain is any legal sanction available should a new government decide not to abide by the rules set out in the Manual.

Insofar as the Manual has a constitutional status, it seems pertinent to ask what legitimacy or authority it can have when drawn up in private by non-elected officials with the assistance of a small number of selected academics. Neither Parliament nor the people played any role in drawing it up, and, while it will no doubt be scrutinised in due course by Select Committees of Parliament, there is no intention to submit it to the public for popular endorsement. Nevertheless, in an unplanned and unforeseen way, typical perhaps of much of British constitutional development, the Manual, drawn up to meet a particular exigency, might well prove, not only a stage in constitutionalising the monarchy, but a further stage in the long process of transforming a constitution based on 'tacit understandings' into one based on a written document. Perhaps the other constitutional reforms proposed by the coalition, and in particular the proposal for a wholly or mainly elected House of Lords, will accelerate that process. For, as we shall see in Chapter 7, a wholly or mainly elected House of Lords will almost certainly require codification of the powers of the Lords vis-a-vis the Commons. Gradually, therefore, and almost imperceptibly, the building blocks of a codified constitution are coming into view. Publication of the Cabinet Manual is an important step in that direction.

---

[35] Some of the problems of drawing up a codified constitution are discussed in Vernon Bogdanor, *The New British Constitution* (Hart Publishing, 2009) ch 9.

[36] Oral evidence to the Political and Constitutional Reform Committee, 4 November 2010.

2

Formation of the Coalition

I. THE POLITICS OF COALITION FORMATION

ONCE APPRISED OF the election result, Gordon Brown decided to remain in office to seek a coalition of what he regarded as the two 'progressive' parties, Labour and the Liberal Democrats. On Monday 10 May, four days after the election, he made a statement claiming that the outcome had shown the existence of 'a progressive majority' in Britain, and declared his belief that 'it could be in the interests of the whole country to form a progressive coalition government'. The answer to the question whether such a progressive coalition could be formed lay with the Liberal Democrats. They were in a dilemma best summed up by their former leader, Paddy Ashdown, who declared that the voters seemed to have 'invented a deliciously painful torture mechanism for the Liberal Democrats because our instincts go one way [Labour] but the mathematics go the other [the Conservatives]'.[1]

Many Liberal Democrats, although instinctively drawn towards co-operation with Labour, felt that Brown was a tribal politician unable to embrace the power-sharing which a coalition would require. In their view, Labour had missed the chance to create a progressive coalition under the Blair and Brown governments, and it was too late, now that Labour had lost the election, to make amends. David Cameron, on the other hand, had sought to modernise his party since becoming Conservative leader in 2005 and this took him in a liberal direction, while Nick Clegg was less sympathetic to the progressive alliance than his predecessors in the Liberal Democrat leadership. The party leadership changes since 2005, therefore, made a progressive alliance less likely and a Conservative/Liberal Democrat coalition more likely. As David Laws, one of the Liberal Democrat negotiators, suggests, 'It is difficult to imagine a Lib Dem-Conservative coalition government being formed if the Conservative Party had been led by Michael Howard, and the Liberal Democrats by either Charles Kennedy or Menzies Campbell'.[2]

Brown, however, could claim that a coalition of the Left was more logical than a Conservative/Liberal Democrat coalition, since most Liberal Democrat voters regarded themselves as being on the Left, and would have preferred to join with

---

[1] Andrew Geddes and Jonathan Tonge (eds), *Britain Votes 2010* (Oxford University Press, 2010) 27.
[2] David Laws, *22 Days in May: The Birth of the Liberal Democrat-Conservative Coalition* (Biteback, 2010) 268.

Labour in a hung parliament. In a YouGov survey published the day before the general election, 34% of those questioned put the Liberal Democrats on the Left of the political spectrum, while only 11% put them on the Right. Amongst Liberal Democrat voters, 39% described the party as being centre-Left or Left, 33% as centrist, and just 5% as being centre-Right or Right. Further, 43% of Liberal Democrat voters placed *themselves* on the Left, while 29% described themselves as centrist, and only 9% on the Right.[3] An Ipsos-MORI telephone poll, also published the day before the election, showed that, with a hung parliament, just 22% of Liberal Democrats would prefer to work with the Conservatives, while 40% would prefer to work with Labour, and 35% would like to see all three parties working together.[4] Psephological studies confirmed this view by showing that, while the social profile of Liberal Democrat voters was somewhat similar to the Conservatives, ideologically they were closer to Labour.[5]

On the central issue of the election – how rapidly the structural budget deficit should be eliminated – the Liberal Democrats had sided with Labour in their belief that reducing the deficit should be achieved gradually when economic recovery was assured, rather than, as the Conservatives proposed, within a single parliament. Speaking to the Liberal Democrat spring conference in Birmingham in March, Nick Clegg declared that, if the Conservatives were the largest party, he would try to stop them from carrying out their pledge to begin cutting the deficit immediately.[6] Of the Conservative programme for rapid cuts he declared: 'If we want to go the direction of Greece, where you get real social and industrial unrest, that's the guaranteed way of doing it.'[7] Indeed, the Liberal Democrat manifesto went even further, declaring: 'To boost the economy and create jobs for those who need them, we will begin our term of office with a one-year economic stimulus and job creation package.' Moreover, just one week before the election, on 30 April 2010, Nick Clegg told *Guardian* readers that there was 'a gulf in values between myself and David Cameron', and that the Conservatives had 'no progressive reform agenda at all'.[8] Addressing the Liberal Democrat spring conference in Liverpool in March 2008, Nick Clegg had said: 'The day before I was elected leader, Mr Cameron suggested we join them. He talked about a "progressive alliance". . . . So I want to make something very clear today. Will I ever join a Conservative government? No.' But he also said, 'Will I ever join a Labour government? No.'

Gordon Brown had seemed, as Prime Minister, by no means unsympathetic to the Liberal Democrats. On forming his government in 2007, he had suggested the possibility of a coalition to Sir Menzies Campbell, the then leader of the Liberal Democrats, and had offered a Cabinet post to Paddy Ashdown, the former Liberal

   [3] Geddes and Tonge (n 1) 37.

   [4] 3% were 'other' or 'don't know'.

   [5] Andrew Russell and Edward Fieldhouse, *Neither Left Nor Right? The Liberal Democrats and the Electorate* (Manchester University Press, 2005).

   [6] 'I'll Try to Prevent Tory Cuts, Says Clegg', *Daily Telegraph*, 15 March 2010.

   [7] Guy Lodge and Anthony Seldon, *Brown at 10* (Biteback, 2010) 457.

   [8] Admittedly Clegg had also told *Sun* readers on 23 November 2009, 'I would back Tories in hung poll', and had told *The Daily Mail* on 11 March 2010 of his 'admiration for Thatcher'.

Democrat leader. Although Ashdown declined this offer, three Liberal Democrat peers – Lord Lester, Lady Neuberger and Lady Williams (the former Labour Cabinet minister, Shirley Williams) – accepted advisory posts, but were allowed to retain their independence by remaining outside the government and continuing to accept the Liberal Democrat whip.[9] Labour's 2010 election manifesto made a gesture in the direction of the Liberal Democrats by proposing fixed-term parliaments, which had long been a Liberal Democrat aim, and a referendum on the alternative vote method of election, which, although not meeting the Liberal Democrat wish for proportional representation, did at least offer hope of electoral reform. The Conservatives, by contrast, had been adamantly against electoral reform even though, as we have seen, the first past the post system disadvantages them so considerably. In addition, Labour and the Liberal Democrats had been able to work together well in coalition governments in the devolved governments in Scotland and Wales. All of this seemed to provide evidence of some ideological similarity, and that ideological similarity appeared to have a long history.

From the time of Jo Grimond's leadership of the Liberals in the 1950s, the party had stressed its ideological kinship with the moderate wing of the Labour Party and had sought to bring about a progressive realignment of British politics such as had enjoyed hegemony before 1914 under the Liberal governments of Campbell-Bannerman and Asquith. Grimond insisted, unlike his predecessor, Clement Davies, that the Liberals were a party of the Left, but that they belonged to a different sort of Left from the statist Left represented by the Labour Party, which, so Grimond believed, was shackled by its fundamentalist socialist element. As early as 1958, Grimond had called for 'a new Lib-Lab alignment . . . leading to a party of the Left'. After Labour's third election defeat in 1959, he wrote: 'I have always said we should have a new progressive party, and it would have to attract many people who at present lean towards the Labour Party . . . We should try and have a new alternative to the Conservatives.' His long-term aim was 'to build up an effective radical non-socialist alternative to the Tories'.[10] In 1962, he declared that 'the divisions in politics fall in the wrong place. The natural breakdown should be into a conservative Party – a small group of convinced Socialists in the full sense – and a broadly based progressive Party. It is the foundations of the last named that the Liberal Party seeks to provide.'[11]

Grimond's search for realignment proved abortive, but hopes of an agreement between the two parties were resurrected during the period of the Lib-Lab pact of 1977–78. Then, after Labour's election defeat in 1979, Roy Jenkins, the former Labour Cabinet minister, in his Dimbleby lecture, 'Home thoughts from Abroad', called for 'a strengthening of the radical centre'.[12] In 1981, the Social Democratic Party, led by four ex-Labour Cabinet ministers – Jenkins, Shirley Williams, David

---

[9]   Menzies Campbell, *My Autobiography* (Hodder and Stoughton, 2008) 278, 284.
[10]   Peter Barberis, *Liberal Lion: Jo Grimond: A Political Life* (IB Tauris, 2005) 85–86, 127.
[11]   Matt Cole, 'An Out-of-date-World: Grimond and the Left' (2010) *Journal of Liberal Democrat History* (Summer) 54.
[12]   Roy Jenkins, 'Home Thoughts from Abroad', *The Listener*, 29 November 1979, 738.

Owen and Bill Rodgers – was formed as a breakaway from Labour, in alliance with the Liberals, and the two parties merged to form the Liberal Democrats in 1988. Jo Grimond, by now retired as Liberal leader, mischievously predicted that the Alliance would be a great success, since Roy Jenkins, leader of the Social Democrats, was such a good liberal, while David Steel, the Liberal leader, was such a good social democrat![13]

The first leader of the merged Liberal Democrats was Paddy Ashdown. As the 1992 election approached, Ashdown made it clear that his party would not prop up John Major if the Conservative leader failed to retain his overall majority; instead it would be more sympathetic to Labour. This, however, enabled Major to claim that a vote for the Liberal Democrats was equivalent to a vote for Labour, and it seems that some Conservative-inclined Liberal Democrats swung to the Conservatives late in the campaign. Nevertheless, the Liberal Democrats continued to seek an accommodation with Labour; indeed, the impetus towards realignment seemed to accelerate after Labour's fourth election defeat in 1992, when it appeared to some that Labour might never again be able to win a general election on its own. In 1993, even before Tony Blair was to become leader of the Labour Party, he and Ashdown 'agreed we would need good relationships between the parties if there were ever a hung parliament. . . . When Smith died [in 1994] the relationship took off and we worked very closely together, co-coordinating our campaigns, including attacks on Major at Prime Minister's Questions, to a much greater extent than anyone has ever realized.'[14] In a speech at Chard in 1992, Ashdown called, as Grimond had done, for a 'new forum' for those wishing to see 'a viable alternative to Conservatism'. This speech fitted in with the developing sentiment amongst Liberal Democrat voters. Until 1992, the British Election Survey showed that they had seen themselves since 1974 as closer to the Conservatives, except for the time of the 1979 election, held in the aftermath of the Lib-Lab pact. But, from 1992, Liberal Democrat voters came to be more evenly split, and then closer to New Labour – 'The change was dramatic'. In May 1995, Ashdown declared: 'It should surprise no one when we say that if the Conservatives lose their majority in Parliament, and seek our support to continue in office, they will not receive it. People must know that if they kick the Tories out through the front door, we Liberal Democrats will not allow them to sneak in through the back.' By 1997, two-thirds of Liberal Democrats preferred Labour to the Conservatives, and in the election, 43 of the 46 Liberal Democrat MPs defeated Conservative challengers, with Labour in third place.[15] The Liberal Democrats had clearly become an anti-Conservative, not an anti-Labour, party. On the day of the election, Blair concurred. 'I am absolutely determined to mend the schism that occurred in the progressive forces in British politics at the start of the century.'[16]

---

[13] Michael McManus, *Jo Grimond: Towards the Sound of Gunfire* (Birlinn, 2001) 350.

[14] Letter from Ashdown to Charles Kennedy, his successor as Liberal Democrat leader, in 1999, reprinted in Campbell (n 9) 131.

[15] Russell and Fieldhouse (n 5) 106, 108.

[16] ibid, 40.

Even Blair's landslide election victory in 1997 did not put paid to what Ashdown called 'the Project' of realignment. Indeed, it appears that Blair went so far as to propose a merger of the two parties.[17] As Prime Minister, Blair established a joint Labour/Liberal Democrat Cabinet committee on constitutional reform, a remarkable constitutional innovation, and an independent commission on electoral reform under Roy Jenkins, promising to hold a referendum on its recommendations. In 1998, the Jenkins Commission reported in favour of proportional representation. But it soon became clear that important sections of the Labour Party were opposed both to proportional representation and to 'the Project', and no referendum was held. In 1999, Ashdown resigned as Liberal Democrat leader and, under his successor, Charles Kennedy, the joint Cabinet committee gradually atrophied, ceasing to exist in 2001.[18] But although Ashdown, like Grimond and Steel, had failed to secure realignment, he could claim some success for 'the Project' in that he had helped to secure coalitions between Labour and the Liberal Democrats in the devolved administrations in Scotland and Wales, as well as proportional representation for the European elections.

It seemed hopeful, therefore, that the long period of ideological convergence between Labour and the Liberal Democrats might herald a coalition of the Left. Indeed, by 2010, even the trade unions, who had hitherto been hostile to realignment, had come to favour it in preference to a Conservative government. Gordon Brown appreciated that, having led Labour to an election defeat, he might himself prove to be an obstacle to realignment. He therefore announced on the Monday, four days after the election, that he would resign as Labour Party leader, and therefore as Prime Minister, at the time of the Labour Party conference in September. Later he was to declare that he would resign immediately if that would assist the negotiation process; and indeed, after resigning the premiership, he did in fact resign as Labour leader with immediate effect without waiting for the party conference. For the Liberal Democrats, Paddy Ashdown spoke on the radio on the Tuesday morning, arguing that Labour and the Liberal Democrats could form a minority government and 'dare' the smaller parties to vote them out. But he later changed his mind and came to support the Conservative/Liberal Democrat coalition.

There are a number of different versions of what transpired in the negotiations between Labour and the Liberal Democrats, and a definitive version will undoubtedly be unavailable for some time, if ever.[19] It seems, however, that Labour went a

---

[17] Campbell (n 9) 143.

[18] The story of the negotiations between Ashdown and Blair is told in great detail in the two volumes of Paddy Ashdown's diaries: vol 1, 1988–97 (Allen Lane Penguin, 2000); vol 2, 1997–99 (Allen Lane Penguin, 2001).

[19] Two books have been published on the negotiations, the first by Rob Wilson, Conservative MP for Reading East (*5 Days to Power: The Journey to Coalition Britain* (Biteback, 2010)); the second by David Laws (*22 Days in May* (n 2)). In addition, two of the participants in the negotiations, Lord Adonis and David Laws, gave oral evidence of what transpired to the House of Commons Political and Constitutional Reform Committee on 12 November 2010, HC 528-i. See also the review by Lord Adonis of David Laws' book in *The New Statesman*, 29 November 2010, and Laws' reply in *The New Statesman*, 6 December 2010. There is also some material in Peter Mandelson's autobiography, *The Third Man: Life at the Heart of New Labour* (Harper, 2010).

long way to meet Liberal Democrat wishes on policy, going beyond the promise of a referendum on the alternative vote by declaring that it would consider a multi-question referendum on the New Zealand model,[20] which would include the option of proportional representation as well as the alternative vote. The difficulty, perhaps, was that some Liberal Democrats were sceptical as to whether Labour would or could deliver on this promise. After all, in 1997 Tony Blair had promised the Liberal Democrats a referendum on electoral reform, but he had given no date for it, and it had not occurred. The 2010 promise of a referendum was made under the auspices of Gordon Brown, but there would soon be a new leader of the Labour Party, and it was not clear who the new leader would be – or whether he would feel bound by a commitment given by his predecessor. Brown, however, insisted that he would make the vote in the Commons on a multi-option referendum a confidence vote to ensure its passage; and he promised that Labour would actively campaign for the alternative vote. This was an advance on the Labour manifesto, which simply committed the party to a referendum. The Conservatives were to offer less – a referendum on the alternative vote which they would campaign against. It seemed, then, that the progressive alliance was tantalisingly close. But the Liberal Democrats then confusingly argued that they wanted the alternative vote to be introduced before a referendum, so that the referendum, when it came, would be held to endorse, as it were, a *fait accompli.*

The Liberal Democrat negotiators were careful to bring their parliamentary party along with them in the discussions. Labour, by contrast, did not consult its parliamentary party; and it soon became obvious that there were many in the party, led by Jack Straw, the Justice Secretary in the Brown government, who were hostile to electoral reform and might well vote against it in Parliament. Even while negotiations with the Liberal Democrats were taking place, senior Labour figures, such as Straw, Andy Burnham (the Health Secretary) and two former Cabinet ministers, David Blunkett and John Reid, were insisting that the party had been defeated in the election and should go immediately into opposition. Blunkett declared that the Liberal Democrats were 'behaving like every harlot in history'.[21] Lord Falconer, Lord Chancellor in the Blair government, gave a radio interview on the Tuesday after the election, declaring that the party was doing itself 'damage now in trying to do a deal. The sense that people will bargain on any basis in order to stay in power is unacceptable.' Labour, he said, should 'call it quits' and go into opposition.[22] Therefore, it was not clear, even if there was the necessary goodwill, whether a new leader could in fact deliver on the promise of a referendum on electoral reform. So the Liberal Democrats could have been forgiven for treating Labour proposals with some scepticism. Indeed, one Liberal Democrat negotiator believed that Labour was less interested in a coalition than in adding one or two Liberal Democrats on to what would remain basically a Labour government.

---

[20]   See p 92.

[21]   Wilson (n 19) 244.

[22]   Quoted in Dennis Kavanagh and Philip Cowley, *The British General Election of 2010* (Palgrave Macmillan, 2010) 218.

Labour, this negotiator insisted, saw it 'as a continuation of the old government, just with a few irritants added in'.[23]

If the Liberal Democrats were suspicious of Labour, the Labour negotiators came to be equally suspicious of the Liberal Democrats. Some thought that the Liberal Democrats never intended to negotiate seriously, but were taking part in discussions with Labour solely in order to improve their bargaining position with the Conservatives. Their worries were confirmed when the Liberal Democrats insisted that any coalition with Labour would have to commit itself to eliminating the structural budget deficit within the course of one parliament. This was a clear departure from the position taken in the Liberal Democrat manifesto and the party's election campaign. The feeling, on the part of the Labour negotiators, that the Liberal Democrats had not been wholly straightforward seemed confirmed when David Cameron persuaded Conservative MPs to support the Liberal Democrat proposal for a referendum on the alternative vote by claiming that Labour had offered the alternative vote without a referendum, something that Labour had not in fact done. Some Labour supporters argued that Clegg had deceived Cameron, others that Cameron had deceived his party. Probably the confusion was the outcome of an honest misunderstanding. It almost certainly made little difference to the outcome.

The fundamental problem with the Labour/Liberal Democrat negotiations always remained: the parliamentary arithmetic simply did not favour a coalition of the Left. On the contrary, it seemed to dictate, not a Labour/Liberal Democrat coalition, but a Conservative/Liberal Democrat one. In addition, both Labour and the Liberal Democrats had lost seats in the election, and the Labour government had been rejected by the voters. Therefore a Labour/Liberal Democrat government would take on the character of a losers' coalition, a sheltering from the storm by two defeated parties, a rejection of the verdict of the voters. It is ironic that, in 1997, Labour had been too strong to realign with the Liberal Democrats; in 2010 it was too weak.

The arithmetic helped to make possible a Conservative/Liberal Democrat coalition in another way. At one time it had seemed that the Conservatives would be unwilling to concede a referendum on the alternative vote, the fundamental condition without which the Liberal Democrats would not have agreed to a coalition. They agreed to do so solely because they were aware that the Liberal Democrats did have the alternative possibility of an agreement with Labour. That increased the leverage of the Liberal Democrats. As David Laws points out, '[a] small difference in the election result could have had major consequences'.[24] Paradoxically, if the Conservatives had done better in the election, and won, say, five more seats from Labour, the outcome might have been a Conservative minority government based on a 'confidence and supply' agreement rather than a coalition. For a Liberal Democrat/Labour agreement then would have been impossible. The Liberal

---

[23] ibid, 216. Chapter 10 of this book, 'Five Days in May: The Formation of the Coalition', benefits from the extensive interviews carried out by the authors.

[24] Laws (n 2) 266.

Democrats therefore would have had less bargaining power, and the Conservatives would have felt under no pressure to agree to a referendum on the alternative vote.

Nick Clegg, the Liberal Democrat leader, had indicated before the election that, by contrast with Ashdown in 1992 and 1997, he had no preferred coalition partner, and that, if there were to be a hung parliament, his first step would be to talk to the party with the 'strongest mandate'.[25] This meant that it was the voters who would determine the Liberal Democrats' most likely coalition partner. They were to find the Conservatives more congenial than they had at first suspected. David Cameron had already shown himself to be more sympathetic to the Liberal Democrats than his predecessors. In March 2007, shortly after Nick Clegg became Liberal Democrat leader, he made an explicit appeal for co-operation in opposition. 'Gordon Brown', he insisted, 'and the philosophy which drives him will only be defeated if the Liberal and Conservative supporters rally behind an alternative government-in-waiting. I believe that we need a new Liberal-Conservative consensus in our country.'[26] In May 2007, the former Director General of the BBC, Greg Dyke, invited the Conservatives and Liberal Democrats jointly to support him as a candidate for Mayor of London. The Liberal Democrats rejected this proposal immediately, but the Conservatives did not. On the day after the election, David Cameron continued with his conciliatory approach by declaring that he would make the Liberal Democrats 'a big, open and comprehensive offer', a clear hint that he would be prepared to discuss coalition. By mid-morning on Tuesday 11 May 2010, five days after the election, it was clear that negotiations between the Liberal Democrats and Labour would not succeed. Gordon Brown therefore resigned in the afternoon, and the Queen appointed David Cameron as Prime Minister. Cameron was able successfully to conclude negotiations with the Liberal Democrats, and duly announced the formation of Britain's first peacetime coalition in nearly 80 years. The Liberal Democrats were given five out of the 23 Cabinet posts and 14 junior ministries. Nineteen – one-third – of the 57 Liberal Democrat MPs were to be in the government, a generous tally.

In their book on the 2010 election, Philip Cowley and Dennis Kavanagh conclude by pointing out 'the final paradox':

> that it was the Liberal Democrats – the weakest of the three parties – who decided who should form the government – and on the basis of a policy of immediate expenditure cuts which was diametrically opposed to the one on which they fought the election. The general election did not determine who would be Prime Minister; the Liberal Democrats did. Moreover, the crucial policy agreement that cemented the Conservative-Liberal Democrat coalition was a referendum on the Alternative Vote, a policy that in the election both the Conservatives and Liberal Democrats had opposed, and which had been supported only by Labour (and to which, after the election, Labour promptly declared themselves opposed).[27]

---

[25] He refused to be drawn on what he would do if the party with the most seats had not won the most votes.

[26] *The Independent*, 24 March 2007.

[27] Kavanagh and Cowley (n 22) 348.

The agreement was endorsed by Conservative MPs, who perhaps had little alternative. The Liberal Democrats, to the surprise of some, succeeded with ease in undoing the 'triple lock' imposed by the party in 1998, a set of preconditions that had to be met before a coalition was formed. The triple lock, a product of Liberal Democrat disillusionment with Paddy Ashdown's lack of success in securing realignment with Tony Blair, provided that any proposal to bring the party into coalition with another party required, first, a majority in the parliamentary party and the Federal Executive: second, if a 75% majority was not achieved in these two bodies, a majority at a Special Conference; third, if a two-thirds majority was not achieved at the Special Conference, a vote of the whole membership, where a simple majority would be sufficient. In the event, MPs voted 50–0 in favour of coalition, the abstainers including Charles Kennedy, the former party leader, while the Federal Executive supported it by 27 to 1. Although the conditions of the triple lock had now been met, it was decided all the same to call a Special Conference so as to give the Coalition Agreement legitimacy amongst Liberal Democrat members. Opposition to the coalition proved much less vociferous than many expected. Liberal Democrat MPs were fearful of a second general election, and the party lacked the funds to fight it. They were fearful also that, if they did not join a coalition, the ensuing period of weak government would damage not only them but also the prospects for electoral reform. For electoral reform would undoubtedly lead to further hung parliaments, and the voters would feel that this would lead to further periods of weak government.

In the country, even though, as we have seen, most Liberal Democrats before the election would have preferred an arrangement with Labour, survey evidence showed that the coalition, after it had been formed, was strongly endorsed by Liberal Democrat voters. An Ipsos-MORI poll on 12–13 May 2010 asked, 'Do you think that Nick Clegg was right or wrong to form a coalition with the Conservatives?' Of those who said that they had voted Liberal Democrat, 74% thought that he was right and only 22% that he was wrong. However, a Populus poll, published in *The Times* on 8 May, revealed that amongst all voters a minority Conservative government was the favoured option, attracting 53% support, while a Liberal Democrat/Labour coalition was preferred to a Liberal Democrat/ Conservative one by 51% to 46%.

The Liberal Democrats perhaps felt a special responsibility to help ensure a stable government. They had always argued that proportional representation, with its concomitant, hung parliaments, would not necessarily lead to instability, but could presage a new form of power-sharing government, in which men and women holding different views would learn to work amicably together. In the 1950s, Jo Grimond had argued that 'if electoral reform led to the results for which Liberals hoped and which statistics foretold, that is the fifty to seventy MPs to which our vote entitled us, then, if government was to be carried on, coalitions of some sort would often be essential'. 'I was right', he insisted, 'in telling the Party that it could not by some miracle of parthogenesis spring from six MPs to a majority in the House of Commons. It would have to go through a period of coalition.'[28] In 1997, the Liberal Democrats' campaign manager, Lord Holme, told the party that '[a]nyone who campaigns for proportional representation but rules out a coalition in any circumstances is suffering from a serious logic deficit'.[29] The Liberals had been given the chance of coalition with Edward Heath, but that would not have yielded a parliamentary majority. Besides, the Liberal gain in votes in that election had been largely at Conservative expense and the Conservatives had been rebuffed by the voters. But the Liberal leader, Jeremy Thorpe, had nevertheless suggested that his party 'might give consideration to offering support from the opposition benches to any minority government on an agreed and limited programme', an offer similar to that later accepted by Labour in 1977 as the basis for the Lib-Lab pact.[30]

In 2010, there seemed a great opportunity for the Liberal Democrats to prove that coalition government and power-sharing could work. If it did, that might strengthen the case for electoral reform. But, if they refused to play any part in government, not only would the case be weakened, but in the second general election likely to follow fairly soon, they would almost certainly be squeezed between the Conservatives and Labour as they had been after past hung parliaments – in 1924, when their parliamentary representation had been reduced from 159 seats to 40, and in October 1974, when they had lost one of their 14 seats and nearly a million of the six million votes they had gained in the previous February election.

A possible alternative for the Liberal Democrats in 2010 would have been a 'confidence and supply agreement' along the lines of the Lib-Lab pact of 1977–78. But many Liberal Democrats felt scarred by the pact, believing that they had come to share in the unpopularity of the Labour government without being able to exert much influence on its policies, and that this was one of the reasons why they had lost over 4% of their October 1974 vote in the general election of 1979. The agreement with Labour had provided that the Labour government would use its best endeavours to secure the main Liberal policy demand – proportional representation for the European elections – but proportional representation was defeated in a free vote in the House of Commons. The Liberals, therefore, seemed to have little of substance to show for supporting an unpopular Labour government from the outside.

The prime factor making the coalition possible, however, was the parliamentary arithmetic. A Labour/Liberal Democrat coalition, with the support of various of the smaller parties, might just have been able to secure an overall majority. But its day-to-day survival would have been at the mercy of snap votes, and it would have been difficult for such a government to provide the strong leadership that many thought was needed to deal with the budget deficit. Such a broad coalition was known in Germany as a 'traffic light' coalition of 'red, yellow, green'. David

---

[28]   Jo Grimond, *Memoirs* (Heinemann, 1979) 211–12, 204. But he adds: 'The prospect of coalition in those days scared Liberals out of their wits.'

[29]   Peter Joyce, *Realignment of the Left? A History of the Relationship between the Liberal Democrat and Labour Parties* (Longman, 1999) 291.

[30]   David Butler (ed), *Coalitions in British Politics* (Macmillan, 1978) 103.

Laws, however, thought it would prove, not a traffic light, but a car crash.[31] Paddy Ashdown, the former Liberal Democrat leader, summed up the problem:

> A 'rainbow coalition' of parties would be the worst sort of advertisement for the politics of coalition and partnerships, which must necessarily come with proportional representation. A weak coalition of this kind would kill stone dead the prospect of winning a referendum on voting reform, which would be crucial if such a coalition is to be formed. Can you imagine weeks of indecisive government, having to buy off the Irish, Welsh and Scottish on every single vote, and then after months of this you go to the people and say, 'Please could you vote for AV or PR or whatever, so we can have much more of this type of government in the future?' It would be utterly dotty and it would kill PR stone dead for a generation. Look. A coalition with Labour is impossible. Doing nothing is impossible. That must point to a deal with the Conservatives.[32]

A Conservative/Liberal Democrat coalition, by contrast with a rainbow coalition, could yield a stable majority. David Cameron seems to have taken the view, as soon as the election result was known, that in the difficult economic circumstances which the country faced, a coalition would provide a more stable administration than a minority Conservative government could do. But, in any case, a minority government, if the precedents of 1924, 1929–31 and 1974 were anything to go by, could not be expected to last long. Therefore, there would be a fairly rapid second election. But in that election, as in 2010, the Conservatives would have to be around 10% ahead of Labour to secure an overall majority, and there was no guarantee that this would occur. In 1924, Ramsay MacDonald had lost office after 10 months of minority government; in 1974, Harold Wilson had indeed secured an overall majority, but it was an overall majority of just three, and soon removed by by-election defeats and defections. Moreover, even if Cameron did secure an overall majority, that would not end his troubles. In 1992 John Major had gained an overall majority of 21, but his administration had been wrecked by Eurosceptics, just 11 of whom could destroy his majority. Cameron, similarly, would have been at the mercy of his right wing had he won a small majority. He no doubt preferred to work with the Liberal Democrats, especially as the personal chemistry between him and Clegg seemed so good.

This element of personal chemistry should not be underestimated, for the Conservative/Liberal Democrat coalition was by no means foreordained by the electoral arithmetic. Had either of Clegg's two predecessors, Charles Kennedy or Sir Menzies Campbell, remained as Liberal Democrat leader, a Conservative/Liberal Democrat coalition would have been highly unlikely. It would also have been unlikely if, as had at one time seemed possible, David Davis rather than David Cameron had been elected Conservative leader in 2005; or perhaps if Tony Blair or David Miliband had been leader of the Labour Party rather than Gordon Brown.

But it was not only that Nick Clegg proved personally congenial to David Cameron. There was also some ideological similarity. Clegg belonged to the 'Orange

---

[31] Laws (n 2) 93.

[32] ibid, 73. But, as Laws admits, Ashdown was later to change his mind! See p 90.

Book' wing of the Liberal Democrats, rather than their 'social' wing. *The Orange Book* was a volume of essays published in 2004, edited by Paul Marshall and David Laws, containing essays by, amongst others, Clegg, Chris Huhne and Vince Cable. In his own essay, 'Reclaiming Liberalism', David Laws quoted with approval Jo Grimond, who, by 1980, seemed to have abandoned his earlier views on realignment to the Left, and declared that 'Much of what Mrs Thatcher and Sir Keith Joseph say and do is in the mainstream of liberal philosophy'. Laws went on to ask how it was that 'over the decades up to the 1980s the Liberal belief in economic liberalism was progressively eroded by forms of soggy socialism and corporatism . . .'. There had been 'a progressive dilution of the traditional liberal beliefs in the benefits of markets, choice, the private sector and capitalism'. We must, Laws insisted, 'reject nanny-state liberalism'.[33] This was the central theme of *The Orange Book*. In a second essay on health care, Laws went so far as to call for the National Health Service to be replaced by a National Health insurance scheme, based on the Continental model.

The 'social' wing of the Liberal Democrats continued to look to the Left and to realignment. The 'Orange Book' Liberal Democrats, by contrast, believed that the party had become too statist in its approach, and that as a liberal party it ought to give more emphasis to the market, which provided for a widening of choice and greater freedom for the individual. The origins of this approach lie with David Owen, one of the 'Gang of Four' who had founded the Social Democratic Party in 1981, but who had refused to merge with the Liberals in 1988 and instead relaunched a continuing SDP which lasted until 1990. Owen saw the Liberal Democrats as a party of the 'soft centre', while the SDP by contrast had been 'destined to be the hard centre'.[34] Owen reacted against what he saw as the excessive internationalism of the Liberal Democrats, being strongly in favour of retention of an independent deterrent, and hostile to British membership of the euro. He shared the view of Margaret Thatcher's Conservatives that Britain had become too corporatist a society, and argued that the SDP had 'been brought into existence by many of the same forces that projected Margaret Thatcher to victory in 1979'.[35] Even before the Conservatives came to support the social market, Owen argued that the SDP should embrace it. He also favoured an internal market in the National Health Service. The Conservatives refused to support this in their 1987 election manifesto, but it did find a place in the SDP/Liberal Alliance 1987 manifesto. During the 1987 election campaign, David Butler and Dennis Kavanagh noticed that '[i]t became plain . . . that Dr Owen would be much more ready to do business with Mrs Thatcher than would Mr Steel'.[36]

When it came to the 1992 election, David Owen took part in discussions – abortive in the event – for an electoral pact with John Major, who had adopted the

---

[33] David Laws, 'Reclaiming Liberalism' in Paul Marshall and David Laws (eds), *The Orange Book: Reclaiming Liberalism* (Profile Books, 2004) 29, 30.
[34] David Owen, *Time to Declare* (Michael Joseph, 1991) 719.
[35] ibid, 766.
[36] David Butler and Dennis Kavanagh, *The British General Election of 1987* (Macmillan, 1988) 115.

SDP idea of an internal market in health, and he endorsed Major in preference to Neil Kinnock, the Labour leader.[37] Significantly, Owen hoped for an agreement with Major and Chris Patten, Chairman of the Conservative Party, on the basis of the alternative vote and fixed-term parliaments. Major, he wrote in 1991, 'opposes proportional representation for the Westminster Parliament but there are other ways of evolving and building bridges across our polarized politics. Chris Patten is wisely talking about fixed-term Parliaments. . . . The alternative vote system . . . is worth contemplating . . . This is a far fairer system than the one we have now, though not as fair as proportional representation.' Nevertheless, Owen presciently declared, 'it might have some attractions to the Conservative Party'.[38] Owen can claim to be one of the intellectual ancestors of *The Orange Book* and of the stream of Liberal Democrat thought which led to the 2010 coalition.

Most of the 'social liberals' amongst the Liberal Democrats felt much more comfortable with Labour than with the Conservatives. But Owen's view of the role of a party of the centre such as the SDP, and that of the 'Orange Book' Liberal Democrats, left open the question of which party the Liberal Democrats would work with in the event of a hung parliament. In an essay published in 2010 for a book celebrating Shirley Williams's 80th birthday, Owen praised Nick Clegg for 'emerging as a Liberal in the continental tradition, at ease with the market economy, perfectly happy with being seen by the electorate as able to negotiate with either Conservative or Labour'.[39] On the Continent, a number of liberal parties, such as the Dutch VVD and the German Free Democrats, are seen as parties of the Right, combining a strong belief in the market economy with an equally strong belief in personal freedom and civil liberties, and work happily with Christian Democrat parties of the Right. Nick Clegg began his political career in the European Parliament, where the Liberal group sits to the Right of the Christian Democrats.

But the Orange Book grouping was very much a minority stream of thought within the Liberal Democrats. '*The Orange Book*', it was alleged in 2007, 'received a cool reception from most of the party when it was published in 2004'.[40] Its most contentious recommendation, to reshape the National Health Service using a social insurance model, was widely criticised. Social liberalism, it was argued, has always been the dominant strand in the Liberal Party's philosophy, and in 2007, in a counterblast to *The Orange Book*, it was claimed that '[t]he limitations of the market . . . are becoming increasingly obvious. Conservative and Labour governments obsessed with market-based solutions have built a more unequal and unfair

---

[37] Owen (n 34) 789.

[38] ibid, 793. Owen reiterated his support for fixed-term parliaments in the revised edition of his memoirs, *Time to Declare: Second Innings* (Politico's, 2009), writing in the context of a possible coalition government (pp 625–26). He is now, however, more sceptical of the merits of the alternative vote. See his essay in Andrew Duff (ed), *Making the Difference: Essays in Honour of Shirley Williams* (Biteback, 2010) 59–60.

[39] Duff, ibid, 55.

[40] Duncan Brack, Richard S Grayson and David Howarth, *Reinventing the State: Social Liberalism for the 21st Century* (Politico's, 2007) ix.

society than Britain has experienced at any time since the First World War.' British Liberals, it went on, 'have argued for well over a century that the market suffers from a number of limitations, and that there is, therefore, an important role for the state'. 'The need', it insisted, 'for a collective response to the problems we face remains overwhelming'. David Cameron was not slow in pointing to the division with the Liberal Democrat camp. 'There is a question mark', he noticed, 'over the future direction of the Liberal Democrats between the Orange Book Liberals and what we might call the Brown Book Liberals – those who look forward to a coalition government with Gordon'.[41] The Orange Book Liberal Democrats were to receive a great boost when, in 2007, Nick Clegg was elected party leader. This was, David Laws believes, 'of particular importance' in paving the way for a coalition with the Conservatives since 'Nick was the first leader for decades who felt genuinely equidistant in his attitude to the other two parties. . . . If we had fought the 2010 general election on the 2005 manifesto, it would have been much tougher to reach policy agreement with the Conservatives, given our previous policies on free personal care for the elderly, immediate abolition of tuition fees, higher taxes, and opposition to most reforms in health and education.'[42]

Part of the difference between the two wings of the Liberal Democrats was generational. Nick Clegg's four predecessors as Liberal or Liberal Democrat leader, David Steel, Paddy Ashdown, Charles Kennedy and Sir Menzies Campbell, had spent much of their parliamentary careers in opposition to Conservative governments, during the long period of Conservative hegemony which lasted from 1979 to 1997. It was natural for them to believe that the only way to destroy this Conservative hegemony was through a realignment, leading to an alliance between the two parties on the progressive side of politics. The parliamentary experience of Nick Clegg, by contrast, not elected to the Commons until 2005, and that of his closest allies, such as David Laws, elected in 2001, and Danny Alexander, elected in 2005, had been in opposition not to a Conservative government, but to the Labour governments of Tony Blair and Gordon Brown, governments which they saw as excessively statist and hostile to civil liberties. Above all, they blamed Labour for the Iraq war, which they saw as illegal and a breach of international law. Admittedly, the Conservatives, too, had supported the war, but they had been in opposition at the time, and it could be argued that they had been misled by the evidence produced by the Blair government relating to weapons of mass destruction in Iraq. Most Liberal Democrats saw the Iraq war as Blair's war and as Labour's war.

During the period of the Iraq war, the Liberal Democrats had appeared more anti-American and less committed to the Atlantic alliance than the Conservatives. But the election of Barack Obama to the United States presidency in 2008 tended to bring the two parties together, since Obama had himself opposed the Iraq war.

[41] Wilson (n 19) 47.
[42] Laws (n 2) 270.

Therefore support for the United States and the Atlantic alliance was less divisive than it had been under President Bush. Europe also proved a less divisive factor between the two parties than might have been predicted, for the Lisbon Treaty, which transfers various competencies to the European Union, had already been ratified by the time of the general election. Had that not been so, Europe would indeed have been a major source of conflict between the Conservatives and the Liberal Democrats: the Conservatives had insisted that there should be a referendum before Lisbon were to be ratified, a proposal opposed by the Liberal Democrats. The Conservatives did admittedly propose in their election manifesto a renegotiation of the Lisbon Treaty in order to repatriate social and employment powers from the European Union. But David Cameron was perhaps not too unhappy at having to drop this proposal in the Coalition Agreement, since, faced with opposition from the other 26 Member States of the European Union, repatriation was almost certainly unrealistic. The Member States had undergone such efforts to agree an *acquis communautaire* with the new, ex-communist Member States entering the Union in 2004 that they were not likely to reopen the package in order to assist a new Eurosceptic Conservative administration in Britain. The most that Cameron could have hoped to achieve was a symbolic renegotiation of the kind carried out by Harold Wilson in 1974–75, which would have generated considerable ill-will on the Continent for little practical benefit. With the ratification of Lisbon, therefore, there was some hope that the toxicity of the European issue might disappear from British politics. The process of treaty amendment and constitutional change in the European Union, which had begun with the Single European Act in 1986, and which had led to five amendments to the Treaty of Rome in addition to the treaties enlarging the European Union, seemed to have come to an end. None of the Member States wanted any further major constitutional amendments of the kind that had caused so much trauma, first over Maastricht in 1992, then over the Constitutional Treaty, rejected by France and the Netherlands, and finally over the Lisbon Treaty.

The most fundamental difference between the Conservatives and the Liberal Democrats lay in their opposing views on the fiscal crisis, with the Conservatives arguing that the structural deficit should be eliminated within one parliament, and the Liberal Democrats agreeing with Labour on a slower approach. But, in an odd way, the severity of the fiscal crisis helped in the formation of the coalition. One reason for this was that the coincidence of the crisis in Greece with the general election gave the Liberal Democrats a reason – some would say an excuse – to alter their policy and adopt the Conservative approach. But the fiscal crisis also made irrelevant the old dispute between the two parties as to whether spending more to improve public services should take precedence over reductions in taxation – the Liberal Democrats taking the former view, the Conservatives the latter. In past general elections the Liberal Democrats had been the only major party to propose an increase in taxation – a penny on income tax to improve education – though by 2008 a Liberal Democrat policy document entitled *Make It Happen* was proposing 'ways to cut Britain's overall tax burden, so ordinary families have more of their money to help themselves'. But, in any case, the conflict between tax cutters and spenders was rendered obsolete by the fiscal crisis, which left no scope either for reducing taxes or for higher public expenditure. So, even though the pre-election policies of the Conservatives and the Liberal Democrats were diametrically opposed, the fiscal crisis helped to bring the two parties together. Without the pressures of the crisis, the coalition might well not have come into existence.

The formation of a centre-Right coalition, therefore, was favoured not only by the arithmetical logic of the election result and the personal chemistry between the two leaders, but also by political contingencies and a certain degree of ideological convergence.

II. THE ELECTORAL GEOGRAPHY OF COALITION FORMATION

A government of the centre-Right would have one further striking advantage over a 'rainbow' coalition of the centre-Left. A Labour/Liberal Democrat government would have commanded just 234 seats in England, as compared with 298 for the Conservatives; therefore a government of the Left would have been able to secure its legislation only through the votes of MPs sitting for non-English constituencies. MPs from outside England would have been deciding legislation for England on such issues as education, health and transport – matters which are devolved in Scotland and Wales. Critics would have claimed that a government of the Left had no mandate to govern England. Such a government might, therefore, have been seen as illegitimate by English voters and might have given rise to a demand that only MPs representing English constituencies should be allowed to vote on matters affecting England – 'English votes for English laws'.

A coalition of the Left, therefore, would have resurrected the West Lothian Question with a vengeance. This Question is named after Tam Dalyell, MP for West Lothian from 1962 to 1983 and then, until 2005, when he retired from the Commons, MP for Linlithgow.[43] The West Lothian Question is a consequence of asymmetrical devolution. There is now devolved government in the non-English parts of the United Kingdom – Scotland, Wales and Northern Ireland – but not in England, by far the largest part of the United Kingdom with 85% of its population. This means that domestic matters affecting England – such as education, health, housing and transport – can be decided by non-English MPs. English MPs, however, have no right to decide these matters for Scotland, Wales or Northern Ireland. They are instead decided by the devolved bodies in these areas.

The West Lothian Question asks whether it is right that Scottish MPs should be able to vote at Westminster on English domestic legislation pertaining to issues such as city academies or higher tuition fees for university students – legislation

---

[43] See, for a fuller exposition of the Question, Vernon Bogdanor, 'The West Lothian Question' (2010) *Parliamentary Affairs* 156–72, and Vernon Bogdanor, *The New British Constitution* (Hart Publishing, 2009) 109–14.

which does not apply in Scotland, where domestic affairs are devolved and have become the responsibility of the Scottish Parliament. Bills on such matters as education and health are, it is argued, mainly English bills; yet Scottish MPs are entitled to vote on them. A government of the Left would have brought this Question to the forefront of the political debate, and may possibly have aroused an English backlash.

There is little danger, by contrast, of the Conservative/Liberal Democrat coalition arousing an English backlash, since it enjoys a majority in England as well as in the United Kingdom as a whole. A Conservative minority government, however, would have been a majority government in England, but not in the United Kingdom as a whole. It could have been defeated by the votes of MPs sitting for non-English constituencies. Were it to have been defeated by the votes of such MPs on matters which are devolved in Scotland, matters such as education or health, that too might have given rise to an English backlash. The Conservative/ Liberal Democrat coalition, therefore, is the best form of government from the point of view of assuaging English worries over the extent of devolution to the non-English parts of the United Kingdom.

From another point of view, however, the Conservative/Liberal Democrat coalition could threaten the unity of the United Kingdom as much as a coalition of the Left, but for a different reason. The coalition is very far from enjoying a majority in either Scotland or Wales. So, although it may appear to enjoy a clear mandate in England, critics in Scotland and Wales will argue that it has no mandate to govern the non-English parts of the United Kingdom. In Scotland the Conservatives hold just one seat, and the Liberal Democrats 11 of the 59 seats. In Wales the Conservatives hold eight and the Liberal Democrats three out of the Principality's 40 seats. This could give rise to serious problems, especially when cuts in public expenditure come to be implemented. For these cuts are likely to be felt with particular severity in Scotland and Wales, which are more dependent upon public sector jobs than the south of England. Labour might dispute the mandate of the coalition in Scotland and Wales, but the nationalists will claim that these territories could avoid the cuts altogether by becoming independent. In the late 1980s, introduction of the poll tax to Scotland by a Conservative government representing only a minority in Scotland served to strengthen both Labour and the nationalists and to fuel the argument for devolution. It may be that the expenditure cuts of the Conservative/Liberal Democrat coalition will similarly strengthen both the radical devolutionists and the nationalists.

But the geographical fragmentation of the country could give rise to another problem for the coalition government, since neither the Conservatives nor the Liberal Democrats are strongly represented in the major conurbations of the Midlands and the North, the very areas in England in which the public expenditure cuts are likely to be felt most deeply. The Conservatives, as we have seen, hold no seats at all in Birmingham, Bradford, Edinburgh, Glasgow, Leeds, Leicester, Liverpool, Manchester, Newcastle, Nottingham or Sheffield. The Liberal Democrats hold only six, and most of these are not in the inner-city areas likely to feel the cuts most severely. This could also lead to problems of legitimacy for the government. Indeed, shortly before the election, Nick Clegg declared that if a Conservative government imposed cuts on the inner cities, the result could be 'serious social strife'.[44] The problems could be almost as great for the Conservative/Liberal Democrat coalition.

Of course, the lack of Conservative representation in the large cities and in Scotland or Wales does not mean that there are no Conservative voters in these areas. In Scotland, for example, 16.7% – around one-sixth of the voters – supported the Conservatives, but they were able to elect just one Scottish MP, while Labour, with just over two-fifths of the Scottish vote – 42% – secured over two-thirds – 41 out of 59 – of the Scottish seats. There is also a substantial Conservative vote in the major cities, but it is a minority vote and therefore not represented. It is a commonplace that the electoral system discriminates against third parties such as the Liberal Democrats. It is less often noticed that it discriminates also against second parties in areas where that party is weak. The consequence is to make Britain appear a more divided country than in fact it is.

Under the first past the post system, the imbalance of representation between England and the non-English parts of the United Kingdom makes it appear as though a government of the Left has no mandate to govern England, and as though a Conservative government or a Conservative/Liberal coalition has no mandate to govern Scotland or Wales; for there are, outside England, just nine Conservative MPs but 108 non-Conservative MPs. The Conservatives proposed in their election manifesto to provide for English votes for English laws – that only English MPs should vote for English laws. After the formation of the coalition, this proposal was kicked into the long grass by being sent to a commission for review. The proposal for English votes for English laws to answer the West Lothian Question gives rise to two further constitutional conundrums. The first is that, when there are different majorities in England and the United Kingdom, government would become bifurcated. There would be one government, presumably a government of the Right, for England, and an opposing government, presumably a government of the Left, for the United Kingdom as a whole. There would, therefore, be one government for English domestic affairs such as education and health, and another government for UK-wide matters, such as economic policy, social security, foreign affairs and defence. Ministers would therefore have to move rapidly to the opposition benches when the matter for legislation or debate switched from being about economic policy to being about education or health; which would be absurd. A government has to be collectively responsible for all the issues that come before it, not merely a particular selection of them.

The second difficulty to which the notion of English votes for English laws gives rise relates to the fact that the revenue which the Scottish Parliament receives depends upon expenditure levels in England, the Scottish Parliament having min-

---

[44] 'Tight Election Win could Plunge UK into Social Chaos – Nick Clegg', *The Observer*, 11 April 2010.

imal taxation powers.[45] The amount of money Scotland receives from the block fund depends, through the Barnett formula, on English spending. If the government at Westminster decides, for example, to cut public expenditure in England on education and health, there is a knock-on effect in Scotland, and Scotland receives less revenue. So the fundamental argument for the Scots to continue to be represented at Westminster and to be able to vote on all matters is that otherwise they would become subject to taxation without representation. This means that the proposal for English votes for English laws only makes sense in relation to matters that do not involve public expenditure, such as hunting. It would otherwise be unreasonable for the Scots to be expected to abstain on any matter involving public expenditure since the size of the block fund provided by London depends upon expenditure in England.

The answer to the West Lothian Question and the imbalance between England and the other nations making up the United Kingdom lies, therefore, not in altering parliamentary procedure, but in altering the electoral system. We have already seen that the first past the post electoral system grossly distorts the relationship between votes and seats. It may, in addition, now have become a cause of territorial instability, artificially polarising England against Scotland and Wales, and the conurbations against the suburbs and the countryside. A government of the Right threatens to reawaken the forces of Scottish separatism, while a government of the Left, which can secure its measures only through the aid of the votes of non-English MPs, threatens to arouse an English backlash against the Celtic nations. If this analysis is correct, then continuation of the first past the post electoral system could come to threaten the continued unity of the United Kingdom. The formation of the Conservative/Liberal Democrat coalition may serve temporarily to obscure this problem. It will not, in the long run, resolve it.

---

[45] The coalition government is proposing to give the Scottish Parliament wider revenue-raising powers. Even so, the point of principle discussed in this paragraph will remain so long as the level of public expenditure in Scotland is determined primarily by its level in England.

3

Governing with a Coalition

I. THE STRUCTURE OF THE COALITION

THE CONSERVATIVE/LIBERAL DEMOCRAT coalition was agreed late on Tuesday 11 May 2010, five days after the general election. The two parties immediately issued a Coalition Agreement. It began by declaring:

> The parties agree that deficit reduction and continuing to ensure economic recovery is the most urgent issue facing Britain. We have therefore agreed that there will need to be a significantly accelerated reduction in the structural deficit over the course of Parliament, with the main burden of deficit reduction borne by reduced spending rather than increased taxes.

On this issue, the Liberal Democrats had accepted the Conservative position in contradiction to the stance they had taken in their election manifesto. The document also set out agreed policies on taxation, banking reform, immigration, pensions and welfare, education, relations with the European Union, civil liberties, the environment, and political reform. On political reform, considerable concessions were made to the Liberal Democrats. The parties agreed to five-year, fixed-term parliaments, and stated that the next general election would therefore be held on the first Thursday of May in 2015. Somewhat confusingly, the document also declared that legislation would be brought forward to provide for an earlier dissolution if 55% or more MPs voted in favour of it. The parties also promised to 'bring forward a Referendum bill on electoral reform, which includes provision for the introduction of the Alternative Vote'. The parties would 'whip their Parliamentary Parties in both Houses to support a simple majority referendum on the Alternative Vote', but would be free to advocate either a 'Yes' or a 'No' vote in the referendum. The parties furthermore agreed to provide for legislation for 'the creation of fewer and more equal sized constituencies', and to introduce a power of recall to force a by-election where an MP 'was found to have engaged in serious wrongdoing'. They would also bring forward proposals 'for a wholly or mainly elected upper chamber on the basis of proportional representation'.

The Coalition Agreement was followed by a more detailed Programme for Government on 30 May, signed by David Cameron as Prime Minister, and Nick Clegg as Deputy Prime Minister, covering the full range of policy issues over 31 policy areas, including areas such as foreign and defence policy which had not been covered in the initial document. The foreword to the Programme declared that it was 'an historic document in British politics: the first time in over half a century two parties have come together to put forward a programme for partnership government'. 'Three weeks ago', Cameron and Clegg declared, 'we could never have predicted the publication of this document. After the election, of course, there was the option of minority government – but we were uninspired by it. Instead, there was the option of a coalition in the national interest – and we seized it.' The Programme declared that a coalition was actually a better option than single-party government.

> We have found that a combination of our parties' best ideas and attitudes has produced a programme for government that is more radical and comprehensive than our individual manifestos'; and it reaffirmed that 'the most urgent task facing this coalition is to tackle our record debts, because without sound finances, none of our ambitions will be deliverable.

The Programme for Government was, as it were, the coalition manifesto. The Cabinet Secretary, Sir Gus O'Donnell, referred to it as 'the overarching framework', and as 'the document we, as the Civil Service, work towards'.[1] The Programme would supersede the manifestoes of the two parties. There were indeed a number of items in the manifestoes which did not feature in the Programme for Government. There were also some cases where the Programme directly contradicted items in one if not both of the party manifestoes. But it was to be the Programme, not the party manifestoes, that was to be the guiding document for the new government. This, however, raised a problem. Not only had no one voted for the coalition, but no voter had been able to endorse the Programme. Whereas a single-party government could claim, however implausibly, a mandate for its policies, the coalition, it seemed, could claim no such mandate.

This could have some importance when government legislation comes to be considered by the House of Lords. For the Lords, since 1945, when it faced, for the first time since the 1911 Parliament Act, a majority government of the Left, had decided voluntarily to bind itself by the so-called Salisbury convention.[2] This doctrine held that the Lords should not defeat on second reading nor wreck any item in a government's programme which had been foreshadowed in the governing party's manifesto, on the ground that the government had a mandate for such legislation. The Salisbury doctrine had been challenged during the Blair/Brown years, and the Conservative leader in the Lords, Lord Strathclyde, had declared that, following the House of Lords Act of 1999, which removed all but 92 of the hereditary peers from the Lords, 'some of the implications of this convention need to be reviewed'.[3] The Liberal Democrats, who had not been a party to the Salisbury convention in 1945, went even further, arguing that while it might have been appropriate when the Lords were permanently dominated by one party, since that was no longer the case, it should be replaced by a new and more appro-

---

[1] Oral evidence to the Public Administration Committee, HC 555-i, 28 October 2010, qq 48, 36.
[2] Named after Lord Salisbury, the Conservative leader in the House of Lords.
[3] Lord Strathclyde, *New Frontiers for Reform* (Centre for Policy Studies, 2001) 26.

priate convention. As Lord McNally, the leader of the Liberal Democrats in the Lords, argued in a debate in the Lords on 26 January 2005, 'The Salisbury convention was designed to protect the non-Conservative government from being blocked by a built-in hereditary-based majority in the Lords. It was not designed to provide more power for what the late Lord Hailsham rightly warned was an elective dictatorship in another place against legitimate check and balance by this second Chamber.'[4] In a later debate he declared: 'I do not believe that a convention drawn up 60 years ago on relations between a wholly hereditary Conservative-dominated House and a Labour Government who had 48% of the vote should apply in the same way to the position in which we find ourselves today.'[5] He has described the 'traditional plea to the Salisbury convention' as 'the last refuge of legislative scoundrels'.[6]

Both Lord Strathclyde and Lord McNally became ministers in the new coalition. If the Salisbury convention was, as Lord Strathclyde and Lord McNally had suggested, designed for a house dominated by hereditary peers, and had been weakened by the House of Lords Act of 1999, it has, surely, been weakened still further by the advent of a coalition government whose agreement was the product of inter-party negotiations, rather than a party manifesto. In such a situation, the mandate argument enjoys even less plausibility than when Lords Strathclyde and McNally condemned it. Of course, the coalition government does enjoy the confidence of the House of Commons, the elected house; and the Lords, as an unelected chamber, ought to respect that. But it would not be surprising if some continued to argue that the Salisbury convention was falling into desuetude, and that the Lords should be more assertive in scrutinising the legislation emanating from the coalition. The advent of the coalition, therefore, might well lead to greater tensions between the two houses than has been the case in recent years.

The Programme for Government was complemented by a document published by the Cabinet Office in June on the institutional structure of the new government. This document began by making the somewhat contentious statement that there was 'no constitutional difference between a Coalition Government and a single party Government'. Nevertheless, it went on, 'working practices need to adapt to reflect the fact that the UK has not had a Coalition in modern times'. The document recorded that '[t]he initial allocation of Cabinet, Ministerial, Whip and Special Adviser appointments between the two Parties was agreed between the Prime Minister and the Deputy Prime Minister', and that the Liberal Democrats would have a share of such appointments roughly in proportion to their relative size vis-a-vis the Conservatives. Future nominations for Conservative ministerial appointments would be made by the Prime Minister, while future nominations for Liberal Democrat ministerial appointments would be made by the Deputy Prime Minister. Appointments themselves would continue to be made by the

---

[4] *Hansard* HL col 371 (26 January 2005).
[5] *Hansard* HL col 20 (17 May 2005).
[6] Cited in Philip Cowley, 'Parliament' in Anthony Seldon (ed), *Blair's Britain* (Cambridge University Press, 2007) 32–33.

Prime Minister, but only 'following consultation' with his deputy. Alterations to the allocation of portfolios during the lifetime of the coalition would have to be agreed by both the Prime Minister and his deputy. Dismissals would also have to be agreed by the two leaders. The doctrine of collective responsibility would continue to bind ministers, as with a single-party government, except where it was 'explicitly set aside'.

The structure of Cabinet committees and appointments to them would be decided by the two leaders acting together. The Liberal Democrats were to chair just two Cabinet committees, but all Cabinet committees were to have a chair from one party and a deputy chair from the other. There would in addition be a Coalition Committee, a formal committee of the Cabinet, co-chaired by the Prime Minister and the Deputy Prime Minister, with membership equally divided between the parties, whose function would be that of a dispute resolution committee, overseeing the implementation and operation of the Programme for Government. It would be quorate only if at least two members from each party in the coalition were present. There would also be an informal working group, called the Coalition Operation and Strategic Planning Group, consisting of four members, two from each party, 'to consider and resolve issues relating to the operation of the coalition agreement', and 'the longer term strategic planning of Government Business'. This Group would report 'as necessary to the Coalition Committee'. It would be co-chaired by the Minister of State at the Cabinet Office – a Conservative, and the Chief Secretary to the Treasury – a Liberal Democrat.

The Cabinet Office document might perhaps have been too sanguine in suggesting that there was 'no constitutional difference between a Coalition Government and a single party Government'. Under an uncodified constitution such as the British, it is never precisely clear which matters are 'constitutional' and which are not. But some of the differences between the working of a coalition and a single-party agreement are nevertheless quite striking, and amount, perhaps, to more than differences in 'working practices'.

The first point worthy of note is that the Prime Minister was chosen in part as a result of inter-party negotiations rather than directly by the electorate. This was obscured by the fact that the Prime Minister turned out to be the leader of the largest party, since the Liberal Democrats were perfectly happy to serve under David Cameron. Had Cameron been unacceptable to them, however, the Conservatives might well have come under pressure to change their leader. As we have seen, in the abortive negotiations between Labour and the Liberal Democrats, Gordon Brown was seen as an obstacle to coalition. A Labour/Liberal Democrat coalition, therefore – had one been formed – would almost certainly have come into existence under a new Labour leader, one whose arrival at No 10 would have been due to the exigencies of coalition, rather than the choice of the voters. Similarly, after the February 1974 general election, it was widely thought that Edward Heath might prove an obstacle to a Conservative/Liberal coalition. Indeed, recent papers released by the National Archives suggest that the Liberals had asked Heath to go, but that he had refused. For a coalition to have been possible in 1974, Heath might well have been required to resign, to be replaced by another Conservative whose arrival at No 10 would have been the outcome of the exigencies of coalition rather than the choice of the voters. If, in 2010, the leader of the Conservative Party had been unacceptable to the Liberal Democrats, and if the Liberal Democrats had insisted that they would only join a coalition with the Conservatives under another leader, it is perfectly possible that the Conservatives would have selected a new leader as the price of coalition. In a hung parliament, therefore, the Prime Minister may be chosen after the election through inter-party agreement rather than by the voters.

Second, not only did the Prime Minister have to subject himself to the approval of his coalition partners, but he was required to surrender his prerogative of choosing his Cabinet. Liberal Democrat Cabinet ministers were chosen by Nick Clegg, not by Cameron. No doubt Cameron could have objected to a particular Liberal Democrat, but it might have been difficult for him to insist upon an objection were Clegg to prove intransigent. The Prime Minister's power to insist upon the resignation of a Liberal Democrat minister is also limited by the exigencies of coalition. Admittedly the Coalition Agreement provides that it is the Prime Minister who appoints and dismisses ministers after consultation with his deputy. But, in practice, the Prime Minister would probably only be able to secure the resignation of a Liberal Democrat minister if he could obtain the agreement of Nick Clegg and other senior Liberal Democrats. It would be almost impossible for him to secure the dismissal of Clegg himself. It has been said that, under coalitions in Norway, '[a] communication from the Prime Minister to one of the coalition parties as to the effect that a cabinet minister is, for example, no longer *politically* suited to be the head of the ministry would indeed in most cases be interpreted as an open challenge to that party and consequently to one and all of its cabinet ministers in the coalition government'.[7] The same is likely to prove true in Britain, and it involves a significant weakening of the doctrine of individual ministerial responsibility. For, if the Prime Minister believed that a Liberal Democrat minister had been at fault in the administration of his department, or was inadequate in some other respect, he would not be able, as in a single-party government, to secure his resignation. The allocation of portfolios also was determined not by the Prime Minister but by the inter-party negotiations. The Prime Minister, with his Deputy, takes on the role of an inter-party mediator and conciliator, one of two joint arbiters of inter-party disputes. All this militates against strong Prime Ministerial government.

The coalition, therefore, implied a very significant reduction in the power of the Prime Minister as compared with the power he would have been able to exercise in a single-party majority government. It would be difficult for the Prime Minister of a coalition government to wield the overweening power that, it was alleged, both Margaret Thatcher and Tony Blair had been able to exercise. The coalition would prevent a renewal of the regime of prime ministerial power which

---

[7] Arne Solstad, 'The Norwegian Coalition System' (1969) *Scandinavian Political Studies* 161.

had, some suggested, been in operation during the reign of these two Prime Ministers. This reduction in the power of the Prime Minister reflected the weakened basis of his power in a hung parliament. The power of Margaret Thatcher and Tony Blair had rested largely on the fact that they had won landslide victories for their parties on manifestoes that had been stamped with their own personal imprint. There is a sense, therefore, in which it could be said that it was the voters who had conferred wide powers on both Margaret Thatcher and Tony Blair by giving them, under the first past the post electoral system, landslide majorities. The voters had, however, failed to confer such a majority, or indeed a majority of any sort, on David Cameron. Therefore, he would be unable to exercise the power that would go with a landslide majority. From this point of view, it was natural that Cameron should enjoy a much more limited power than his predecessors who had headed single-party governments with comfortable majorities. The Coalition Agreement reflected these realities of electoral and political power.

Had the coalition been wracked by inter-party disputes, the Coalition Committee might have seriously undermined the role of the Cabinet. In these circumstances, it could easily have become more important than the Cabinet, and Cabinet government might have come to be replaced by Coalition Committee government. In fact, however, in the first few months of government, the good feeling between the parties was such that the Coalition Committee needed to meet, in the words of Sir Gus O'Donnell, 'very rarely'.[8] It did not supersede the role of the Cabinet, which meets every week, as the ultimate authority in British government and which can, in theory at least, overrule the Coalition Committee. Nevertheless, a coalition does alter the basis of Cabinet government. A single-party Cabinet is composed of people who know each other well, and who have worked together in developing policy over many years. They already have a broadly common view, which is why they came together to be in the same party. A coalition Cabinet is quite different, being composed of a group of people brought together for the first time by a Prime Minister, without previous agreement on policy. A coalition Cabinet, then, becomes rather like an inter-departmental committee or Royal Commission, where people are brought together for the first time without a common background of tribal loyalty.

Therefore, when the honeymoon period of the coalition government is over, it is perfectly possible that the role of the Cabinet will change. Were there to be serious disagreements between the coalition partners, then the Coalition Committee could come to usurp the role of the Cabinet as a co-coordinating mechanism. Once the Coalition Committee had decided a matter in dispute between the parties, it would be very difficult for the Cabinet to unravel it. The needs of securing inter-party agreement would come to be superimposed upon the normal departmental conflicts between ministers, and the Coalition Committee rather than the Cabinet would come to be the key institution of government.

---

[8] Oral evidence to the Political and Constitutional Reform Committee, 4 November 2010.

The coalition government will, it seems, strengthen the Cabinet committee system. The Blair government was criticised by a Committee of Privy Counsellors, chaired by Lord Butler, a former Cabinet Secretary, in its Review of Intelligence on Weapons of Mass Destruction for 'the informality and circumscribed character of the Government's procedures which we saw in the context of policy-making towards Iraq'.[9] The term 'sofa government' was coined to describe these procedures, since crucial decisions seem, on occasion, to have been taken at informal meetings which were not minuted, and from which key ministers and officials were absent. The need for balance between the two parties probably makes such a form of government impossible in a coalition, even if the Prime Minister were to wish it. In Sir Gus O'Donnell's words, the cumulative effect of 'coalitionising everything' is 'to make sure it goes through a Cabinet Committee'. And Sir Gus predicted that '[i]n a coalition . . . we will have a lot more Cabinet Committee meetings and we have already had a lot more National Security Council meetings than we had in the past'.[10]

The Programme for Government provided, as we have seen, for the explicit abandonment of the doctrine of collective responsibility on the issue of the alternative vote. The two parties would be whipped to support the referendum but would take opposing views on the issue itself. There were further explicit 'agreements to differ' in the Coalition Agreement – on the issue of new nuclear power stations, to which the Liberal Democrats had been opposed; on the renewal of Trident; on married couples tax allowances and on university tuition fees. This last was particularly important for the Liberal Democrats: all Liberal Democrat MPs had made an explicit pledge, not only to vote against any increase in fees, but to work for their abolition entirely. Nick Clegg indeed was quite specific, saying, 'We will resist, vote against, campaign against, any lifting of the cap'. The Coalition Agreement accepted that, if the response of the government as a whole to the report of the Browne committee on higher education was 'one that Liberal Democrats cannot accept . . . then arrangements will be made to enable Liberal Democrat MPs to abstain in any vote'.

II. AGREEMENTS TO DIFFER

The 'agreement to differ' had first been introduced to hold together an earlier coalition, the National Government, in 1932, on the issue of free trade. Three Liberal Cabinet ministers had been allowed, not merely to abstain, but to speak and vote, both in the House of Commons and in the country, against the Import Duties bill, which imposed a tariff, being promoted by their Conservative coalition colleagues. The 'agreement to differ' was defended by Stanley Baldwin, Lord President of the Council and in effect deputy Prime Minister, as an expedient for a coalition, since '[t]he fate of no party is at stake in making a fresh precedent for

[9] HC 898, July 2004, para 611.
[10] Oral evidence to the Public Administration Committee, 28 October 2010, HC 555-i, q 43.

a National Government'. But, he went on to warn, '[h]ad the precedent been made for a party Government, it would have been quite new, and it would have been absolutely dangerous for that party'.[11] This agreement to differ, adopted as an expedient to avoid the resignation of the Liberal ministers, proved to be of merely temporary value; in September 1932, when the tariff was extended and imperial preference introduced on the basis of the Ottawa agreements, the Liberal ministers decided to resign after all. The 'agreement to differ' was something that proved impossible to renew. As the Liberal peer Lord Lothian insisted, 'You can't do it a second time'.[12]

The doctrine of collective responsibility came to be suspended twice in the 1970s, not by a coalition but by a single-party Labour government, first on the issue of whether the government should recommend acceptance of the renegotiated terms of Britain's continued membership of the European Community, as the European Union was then called, in the 1975 referendum; and secondly, in 1977, on the issue of direct elections to the European Parliament. On these occasions, in contrast with 1932, the freedom to dissent did not extend to parliamentary proceedings or official business; it applied only to votes in the Commons and speeches in the country. The precedents of the 1970s show that an 'agreement to differ' can be the product of a single-party government as well as a coalition, though it is no doubt far more likely to be necessary with a coalition government comprising parties with divergent views. The 'agreements to differ' of 2010 were significant as the first ever to be agreed *before* the formation of a government, as part of a Coalition Agreement, rather than *after* the formation of a government as an expedient to meet a new and unforeseen situation. To that extent, the 'agreements to differ' of 2010 are, from a constitutional point of view, more soundly based.

Agreements to differ provide for the suspension of the convention of collective responsibility for certain specific issues. This convention is perhaps as much a maxim of prudence as a fundamental constitutional principle. There seems to be no reason in principle why a Cabinet should not agree to suspend it on any issue. The Cabinet can collectively agree to suspend collective responsibility. When James Callaghan told the Commons in 1977 of the Cabinet's agreement to suspend collective responsibility on the issue of direct elections to the European Parliament, Margaret Thatcher, as Leader of the Opposition, challenged him as to whether the convention still applied to his government, only to receive the reply, 'I certainly think that the doctrine should apply, except in cases where I announce that it does not'.[13] It seems, therefore, that the doctrine can be suspended whenever the Cabinet agrees to do so. The New Zealand Cabinet Manual has, since 2008, accepted the legitimacy of the agreement to differ, and governments in New Zealand are therefore constitutionally free to waive the principle as and when they wish. The doctrine of collective Cabinet responsibility comes to be replaced by

[11] *Hansard* HC col 534 (8 February 1932).
[12] Thomas Jones, *A Diary with Letters* (Oxford University Press, 1954) 55.
[13] *Hansard* HC col 552 (16 June 1977).

that of collective Cabinet unanimity; or, as Baldwin put it in 1932, 'we have collective responsibility for the departure from collective action'.[14] In 1975, the Cabinet Secretary, Sir John Hunt, declared that collective responsibility was more than a convention: it was, he argued, 'a reality and important part of the constitution', but it had not been broken in 1975 over the European Community referendum 'because this was a decision by the Cabinet as a whole to waive collective responsibility on one particular issue for a limited time. It was not a decision which any minister took unilaterally.'[15]

The three occasions on which the doctrine was formally suspended were all for limited periods on what were hoped to be specific and transient issues, although the issue of the tariff in 1932 proved to be a running sore so that the agreement to differ only held the National Government together for nine months. There is no experience as yet of an agreement to differ on a continuing issue striking at the very heart of government policy.

On none of the occasions when agreements to differ were used did the device bring credit to the government that employed it. Instead, it merely advertised irreconcilable differences. During the election campaign of 1931, the National Government had sought to smother fundamental disagreement on tariffs by calling for 'a doctor's mandate' in its election manifesto. It left open the question of whether it would adopt a tariff or stick to free trade by declaring that all measures to remedy economic problems would be considered, 'not excluding tariffs'. In AJP Taylor's mordant words, the unity of the National Government 'was shown in practice by public declarations of disagreement over fundamental issues among the leading members of the government'.[16] It now appeared that the doctors could not agree on the proper treatment for the patient, and the Commons was to be treated in 1932 to the strange spectacle of the Liberal Home Secretary, Sir Herbert Samuel, denouncing the tariff policy put forward by his Conservative colleague, the Chancellor of the Exchequer, Neville Chamberlain, as likely to damage the national finances and lead to ruin. In 1975, ministers on each side of the European Community debate attacked the economic forecasts of their Cabinet colleagues, and indeed their economic competence. On both occasions, the government appeared to be in danger of making itself look ridiculous. Indeed, in 1932, the 'first impression' of one Conservative, when he heard of the 'agreement to differ', was that 'the whole world would rock with laughter at the fatuity of the proposal'.[17] Not only a government but any collegiate executive, whether a Board of Directors or the committee of a students' union, will make itself look ridiculous if it publicly advertises its disagreements. Any such body must therefore weigh up the benefits of employing an agreement to differ rather than trying to discover a compromise formula on which all can unite. It is surely advantageous

[14] *Hansard* HC col 535 (8 February 1932).

[15] Hugo Young, *The Crossman Affair* (Hamish Hamilton and Jonathan Cape, 1976) 84.

[16] AJP Taylor, *English History* (Oxford University Press, 1975 edn (orig 1965)) 321.

[17] John Barnes and David Nicholson, *The Empire at Bay: The Leo Amery Diaries, 1929–1945* (Hutchinson, 1988) 227.

if a coalition Cabinet can discover such a compromise formula. For the sanction on any departure from the convention of collective responsibility is not constitutional but political. It lies in the danger of public ridicule.[18]

III. THE COALITION AND THE CIVIL SERVICE

Although the constitutional principles defining the relationship between government and Parliament may not be altered by the advent of a coalition government, there are, nevertheless, considerable differences between the working of a coalition government and that of a single-party government. The central difference lies in the reduced power of the Prime Minister in a coalition government, and the special position of the Deputy Prime Minister, the leader of the minority party, and of the inter-party Coalition Committee brokering deals on difficult issues. A coalition government involves, therefore, considerable modifications to the traditional pattern of Cabinet government.

But, as well as modifying the role of the Prime Minister and the Cabinet, a coalition government also creates constitutional problems for a neutral, apolitical civil service. The first problem arises during the period of negotiating the coalition, and concerns the extent to which civil servants can assist in the negotiating process. On Friday 7 May 2010, the day after the election, Gordon Brown announced that he had asked the Cabinet Secretary to 'arrange for the civil service to provide support on request to parties engaged in discussions on the formation of a government'. An offer of support was in fact made, not only to the three parties involved in the negotiating process – Labour, the Conservatives and the Liberal Democrats – but also to the Democratic Unionist Party of Northern Ireland, Plaid Cymru and the SNP. This might perhaps be seen as an extension of the role of the civil service since 1964 in providing information on machinery of government issues to the opposition parties during the pre-election period, generally defined as beginning 18 months before the end of a parliament. During these pre-election discussions, the parties also outline their policy priorities so that the civil service has time to consider how they might be implemented. In the case of post-election negotiations, however, the role of the civil service would be restricted to one of providing 'logistical support, factual briefing and advice on constitutional processes on request to the parties'. 'The key principles' were that 'all parties involved will be treated equally; the process will be confidential; and support will cease when a government is formed unless any continuation is authorized by the Prime Minister'. Any factual material provided would be made available to all of the parties. But civil servants would not be present at the actual negotiations, and they would not offer 'advice to parties on negotiating tactics or positions'. Civil servants would not, therefore, play an active role in the negotia-

---

[18] See, on this issue in general, Philip Joseph, 'MMP and the Constitution' (2009) *New Zealand Journal of Public and International Law* 113, 119ff.

tions, for the negotiation of a new government was the responsibility of the politicians, not of the civil service. The civil service would take on the role of facilitator, not that of negotiator. Officials could answer queries on how much a proposed policy might cost, or what difficulties it might incur during the process of implementation; but not on whether the policy itself might be desirable; nor, without the permission of the party concerned, on the cost or difficulties of implementation of policies by one of its rivals.[19] The civil service indeed was in no position constitutionally to advise the parties to the negotiations. For until a new government was formed, its constitutional task was to advise the currently existing government led by Gordon Brown. In fact, the role of the civil service during the post-election negotiations seems to have been minimal and largely confined to that of providing logistical support.

Nevertheless, it will not always be easy to draw a clear distinction between providing information and giving advice. The boundary may not always be very precise. After the coalition was formed, there were critics who argued – unfairly in the view of the author – that officials had crossed that boundary by putting pressure on the parties – in view of the perilous financial situation, which required the rapid formation of a government with a stable majority in the House of Commons – to agree rapidly to a coalition, as opposed to a minority government.

Once a coalition government has been formed, it is able to receive civil service advice; but the civil service must restrict itself to the giving of advice. It must not get involved in political negotiations between the partners to the coalition and must keep outside the process of internal deal-making. Yet when tensions arise between the two parties in the coalition, this boundary may not be wholly clear. There may be a particular problem for civil servants advising a minister from the minority party if they suspect that the policy of their minister is not that of the government as a whole. That problem can of course also arise with an ideologically divided single-party government, as it did during the 1970s, when civil servants advising Tony Benn, first as Industry Secretary and then as Energy Secretary in the 1974–79 Labour government, often faced the dilemma of reconciling their obligations to their minister with their obligations to the government as a whole. For they felt that the policies which Benn was advocating and pursuing were not always those of the government.[20] Recent single-party governments have also been, to a certain extent, coalitions. John Major's government was a coalition between europhiles and eurosceptics, Tony Blair's between New and Old Labour. It will not, therefore, be a new experience for civil servants to reconcile their duty to advise ministers individually with their duty to the government collectively. But the problem of reconciling the two obligations, although it can arise in a government of any sort, could become more acute with the advent of coalition

[19] 'Civil Service Support to Coalition Negotiations', www.cabinetoffice.co.uk. There was a precedent for civil service involvement with opposition parties in the devolved bodies in Scotland and Wales, where every election so far has resulted in a hung parliament.

[20] See eg Aoife Collins, 'The Cabinet Office, Tony Benn and the Renegotiation of Britain's Terms of Entry into the European Community, 1974–1975' (2010) *Contemporary British History* 471–91.

government, when inter-party conflict may come to threaten the operation of the Cabinet as a unity.

The Cabinet Office some years ago produced guidelines to regulate contacts with leaders of the opposition parties during the pre-election period. Perhaps similar guidelines should also be produced to regulate the relationships between civil servants and ministers in a coalition government.

IV. TYPES OF COALITION

In a radio broadcast on 14 September 2010, the former Labour deputy leader, Roy Hattersley, author of a recently published book on Lloyd George, argued that there were three kinds of coalitions. First, there were coalitions of conviction, such as the Conservative/Liberal Unionist coalition of 1895, which was formed to resist Irish Home Rule. Second, there were coalitions of necessity, such as the war-time Lloyd George coalition of 1916 and the Churchill coalition of 1940. Finally, there were coalitions of convenience. Hattersley argued that once the First World War was over in 1918, the Lloyd George coalition became a coalition of conveni-ence and no longer one of necessity, for the general election of 1918 gave the Conservatives an overall majority in the Commons, and they could therefore have governed alone without Lloyd George or his Coalition Liberals. There was no longer, in Hattersley's view, any overriding national menace which necessitated the continuation of the coalition. Hattersley claimed that the 2010 coalition was also a coalition of convenience, even though no single-party majority government was possible, since there was so little ideological sympathy between the two par-ties comprising the coalition, and since the Liberal Democrats had broken their electoral pledges in order to join the coalition. The Liberal Democrats and Conservatives would no doubt respond that the 2010 coalition was a coalition of necessity, since the fiscal crisis made it absolutely essential that Britain had a strong government with a majority capable of eliminating the deficit.

As we have seen, the Conservative/Liberal Democrat coalition was formed in part as a result of ideological sympathy, in part for reasons of parliamentary arith-metic, and in part for purely contingent reasons. Yet it could have lasting results. For the decision by the Liberal Democrats to form a coalition with the Conservatives seems to bring to an end the project of realignment of the Left, begun by Jo Grimond in the 1950s, and continued by David Steel in the 1970s and by Paddy Ashdown in the 1990s. It will be difficult for the Liberal Democrats to continue to maintain that they are a party of the Left, or that they could become part of a new progressive alliance.

It is possible that the Liberal Democrats will once again become, as they were in the immediate post-war years under Clement Davies – Jo Grimond's predecessor as leader from 1945 to 1956 – not an anti-Conservative party, but an anti-Labour party. In the early 1950s, co-operation between the two parties was very close. In 1949, a Gallup poll asked Liberal voters how they would vote in the absence of a

Liberal candidate in their constituency. The answer was two to one in favour of the Conservatives.[21] During the 1950 general election campaign, when Clement Davies complained that candidates indistinguishable from Conservatives were running under the label 'National Liberal' or 'Liberal and Conservative', Churchill replied, 'I have not heard . . . of any candidate who is standing as a Liberal-Socialist . . . [N]o one can be at once a Socialist and a Liberal.'[22] In the 1951 general election, there were various local electoral pacts between the Liberals and the Conservatives without which the Conservatives might well not have been returned to government. Winston Churchill, the Conservative leader, even went so far as to speak for a Liberal candidate, Lady Violet Bonham Carter, in the Colne Valley constituency in which no Conservative was standing; and, after the election, Churchill offered the Liberals participation in a coalition, which the Liberals declined. But only one of the six Liberal MPs returned in that election had won his seat against Conservative opposition, and that was Jo Grimond in the far-flung and highly untypical constituency of Orkney and Shetland. The Liberal Party seemed near extinction and had become dependent on the Conservatives for its very existence.

In the 2010 coalition, the Liberal Democrats discovered, perhaps to their surprise, some degree of fellow-feeling with the Conservatives, and the early months of the coalition were marked by a remarkable degree of harmony between the two parties. David Cameron proved an emollient Prime Minister, as MacDonald and Baldwin had been when leading the National Government coalition in the 1930s; and he exuded the good feeling necessary to soften conflict. Such conflict as did occur tended to be between Conservative ministers rather than between Conservatives and Liberal Democrats. Even so, there seemed much less factionalism in the Cameron government than there had been in either the Blair or Brown administrations. The two parties to the coalition found no difficulty in agreeing to a programme of public expenditure cuts to eliminate the deficit, the Liberal Democrats displaying all the zeal of the convert. The two parties seemed to share a greater commitment to civil liberties than Labour had exhibited. They agreed that Britain under Labour had become over-centralised, and accepted, in theory, that powers should be restored to local government – although some of their proposals such as those for 'free schools' outside local authority control, and for directly elected police commissioners, would have the effect of weakening local government. David Cameron, in what seemed like an implied rebuke to Margaret Thatcher, insisted that there was such a thing as society but that it was not the same as the state. His idea of the Big Society, in which a greater role would be played by local institutions and voluntary bodies, dovetailed well with the traditional Liberal Democrat belief in decentralisation in a way that a more purely Thatcherite approach would not have done. There were, admittedly, areas where the two parties disagreed, but it seemed that these could be finessed more

---

[21] David Cowling, 'Is there a Progressive Electorate?' in Neal Lawson and Neil Sherlock (eds), *The Progressive Century: The Future of the Centre-Left in Britain* (Palgrave, 2001) 57.

[22] David Butler (ed), *Coalitions in British Politics* (Macmillan, 1978) 96.

easily than had been imagined before the election. Perhaps there was even coming to be a degree of ideological convergence between the two parties – an ideological convergence between two hitherto opposed political traditions.

One newly elected Conservative MP, Nick Boles, in a book published shortly after the election, claimed that there was indeed such a convergence, detecting 'a shared sense of direction' in the coalition, and arguing that this should be cemented by an electoral pact. Boles was, like most Conservatives, opposed to the alternative vote, but were it to be endorsed in the referendum, to be held in May 2011, then, in his view, the introduction of preferential voting would provide a wonderful opportunity for the two parties to co-operate. For the Conservatives could then urge their supporters to give their second preferences to the Liberal Democrats, while Liberal Democrat voters would be urged to give their second preferences to the Conservatives. If the referendum was, however, lost, as Boles hoped, then, although co-operation would be more difficult to achieve, it could still be possible through mutual withdrawal of candidates, as occurred in the 'coupon' election of 1918 and the general election of 1931. Conservatives could withdraw in constituencies that were hopeless for them, and urge their supporters to vote for the Liberal Democrats, while Liberal Democrats could do the same in constituencies which were hopeless for them.[23] This call was echoed by a far more powerful voice, Sir John Major, the former Conservative Prime Minister, in his Churchill lecture at Cambridge on 26 November 2010. Major expressed the hope that 'some way can be found to prolong co-operation beyond this Parliament'. He went on:

> It may be that a temporary alliance will turn into a mini realignment of politics. After all, in a world that is changing so comprehensively, why should politics not change too? Neither Party will admit that possibility at present, not least because it would upset their core vote but – if events turn out well for the Coalition – I, for one, would not be surprised at that outcome.

Major then drew an explicit comparison with 1951, when the Liberals had been 'saved as a Parliamentary force . . . by the Conservatives not opposing five of its MPs: progressive co-operation is nothing new. It can be done – if it is in the interests of the Country, it may need to be done again.' Nevertheless, few Conservatives or Liberal Democrats defended the coalition in ideological terms. Most Liberal Democrats, in particular, were careful to insist that they had not become ideological allies of the Conservatives, and had no intention of concluding an electoral pact with them, much less merging, as predecessor groupings from the Liberal Party had done in the past – the Liberal Unionists in 1912, and the National Liberals in 1968. The Liberal Democrat perspective was somewhat different. For most Liberal Democrats, coalition with the Conservatives did not indicate any ideological convergence. Instead, so they argued, they were merely doing what was necessary to make a multi-party system work. In forming a coalition with the

---

[23] Nick Boles, *Which Way's Up: The Future for Coalition Britain and How to Get There* (Biteback, 2010) 131–32.

Conservatives, the Liberal Democrats were, according to this view, doing what was normal in Continental political systems where proportional representation generally leads to hung parliaments. In such situations, two or more parties are able to co-operate for a limited period on an agreed programme, while retaining their separate identities, and without intending to merge or to secure any fundamental realignment of parties. The Liberal Democrats have already competed with the Conservatives in a by-election, and they will take opposing views in the referendum on the alternative vote in May 2011. It is possible that elections to the devolved bodies in Scotland and Wales, following elections to them in May 2011, will yield Labour/Liberal Democrat coalitions. Therefore there may come to be different coalitions at different levels of government, as there often are in Germany. Inter-party co-operation rather than ideological convergence is, from the Liberal Democrat perspective, the watchword of the coalition.

When the next general election comes, according to this view, it is possible that the two parties will go their separate ways, fighting the election as independent and competing parties, with conflicting views concerning the future direction of the country. Many Liberal Democrats hope that the general election of 2010 will inaugurate a new co-operative style of politics, in place of the adversarialism which, they believe, has had deleterious effects in British politics for too long. After the next election, depending upon the electoral arithmetic and the stances of the parties, the Liberal Democrats will, so they would argue, reconsider their position. They might find it perfectly possible to form an alliance with Labour rather than with the Conservatives. They would become, as it were, serial monogamists, a hinge party, willing to trade their position with either of the other two in the hope of eventually achieving their cherished goal of proportional representation. The first step to achieving that end would be the alternative vote, which the Liberal Democrats hope might prove a prelude to proportional representation. The Liberal Democrats hope that the general election of 2010 will be the harbinger of a new style of politics in which coalition government becomes the norm not the exception, and in which they will be able to play a pivotal role, as the Free Democrats, their German counterpart, have done. The Free Democrats have been in power in Germany for all but 10 of the 62 years of the Federal Republic's existence, even though their average vote, at around 9%, is far lower than the Liberal Democrats have secured in recent years. The Belgian and Dutch Christian Social parties and the National Religious Party in Israel have similarly benefited from enjoying a pivotal position in their respective political systems.

Yet the Liberal Democrats could hardly, having spent five years with the Conservatives, then declare at the general election a policy of equidistance between the major parties. Nor could they easily attack the Conservatives in an election campaign, for the voters would rightfully ask, 'If the Conservatives were governing so badly, why did you remain in coalition with them?' Therefore, a little-noticed corollary of the Liberal Democrat argument for a principled coalition of co-operation is that the party should leave the coalition some time before the next general election in order to re-establish an independent identity and the freedom of action needed to choose between the major parties. That apparently is also the view of David Steel, the former Liberal leader, who told Clegg that 'he must have a fixed end to any agreement and an exit strategy . . . Steel's advice was that Clegg must think how to get out of the coalition before a general election so that the party could reassert its own identity in plenty of time.'[24] In Germany, in 1982, the Free Democrats switched from the Social Democrats to the Christian Democrats in the middle of a parliament, a switch that was to be validated after the event by the general election of 1983.

The Liberal Democrats would probably argue that there is a fourth type of coalition, in addition to the three identified by Roy Hattersley. They would deny that the coalition formed in 2010 was a coalition of convenience. Instead, so they might suggest, it was a coalition of co-operation, whereby two parties, with different political views, agree to co-operate for limited purposes and for a limited period of time in order to ensure effective government. Were Britain to be entering an era of multi-party politics, such coalitions of co-operation might well become a regular part of the political landscape. For they offer one answer to the question of how Britain is to be governed when the voters refuse to entrust one party with an overall majority.

---

[24] Rob Wilson, *5 Days to Power: The Journey to Coalition Britain* (Biteback, 2010) 138.

4

'England Does Not Love Coalitions'

I. COALITIONS IN PEACETIME

IN DECEMBER 1852, the Chancellor of the Exchequer, Benjamin Disraeli, faced the defeat of his budget by what he regarded as a 'coalition'. He remained defiant. 'The combination may be successful,' he declared. 'A Coalition has before this been successful. But Coalitions though successful have always found this, that their triumph has been brief.' And then he concluded with his famous assertion. 'This too, I know, that England does not love Coalitions.'

Whether Britain does or does not love coalitions, she has had her fair share of them. Since 1895, there have been three peacetime coalitions – the Unionist coalition of Conservatives and Liberal Unionists, which ruled from 1895 to 1905, the Lloyd George coalition, which lasted from 1918 to 1922, and the National Government, formed in 1931, which lasted until 1940 when it was superseded by an all-party wartime coalition led by Winston Churchill, which was, as AJP Taylor has suggested, 'more than a coalition', since it was 'in the unique position of commanding the almost unanimous allegiance of both parliament and country'.[1]

The Unionist coalition was formed in 1886, when 93 Liberals voted to defeat Gladstone's bill providing for Home Rule for Ireland. These Liberals rapidly formed themselves into a separate party and called themselves Liberal Unionists. Gladstone's government of 1886 was followed, until 1892, by a purely Conservative administration, the Liberal Unionists preferring to offer support from outside the government. But, after the interlude of a short Liberal administration which lasted from 1892 to 1895, the Liberal Unionists joined the Conservatives in a coalition and fought the 1895 election on that basis.

The Lloyd George coalition was formed in 1916 in order to prosecute the war more effectively. This coalition also split the Liberals, with one wing supporting Lloyd George and the other remaining with the deposed Liberal Prime Minister, Asquith. But the Lloyd George coalition was supported by the Conservatives and, until 1918, by Labour. When the war came to an end in November 1918, Lloyd George decided to call an immediate general election, and to fight it as leader of those Liberals who supported him, in co-operation with the Conservatives. Labour, however, decided to fight the election as an independent party. In 1920, the Lloyd George Liberals formed a separate party, calling themselves the Coalition

---

[1] AJP Taylor, '1932–1945' in David Butler (ed), *Coalitions in British Politics* (Macmillan, 1978) 74.

Liberals, but the party never really established deep roots except in Wales. Indeed, it could not become a national party since it could not challenge the Conservatives, who held the majority of House of Commons seats. The Coalition Liberals were, therefore, 'a Liberal party called into existence by an anti-Liberal pact. They had no raison d'etre . . .'[2] So the coalition was 'less of a coalition between one party and another than one between a party and a Prime Minister whose party resources, outside his native land [Wales] were minimal'.[3] The Lloyd George coalition came to an end in 1922 when a meeting of Conservative MPs at the Carlton Club decided to fight the next general election as an independent party.

The National Government of 1931 was formed following a financial crisis which split Ramsay MacDonald's minority Labour government. The Cabinet could not agree on an economy programme which included a 10% cut in the standard rate of unemployment benefit. Although the majority supported the cut, the opponents included such heavyweight figures as the Foreign Secretary and the Home Secretary, making it impossible for the Labour government to continue. MacDonald then formed a National Government, supported by the Conservatives, the Liberals, and a small number of Labour MPs, including three other members of the outgoing Labour Cabinet. The Liberals supporting the National Government were divided into two groups, which became separate parties – the independent Liberals, led, in the absence of Lloyd George through illness, by Sir Herbert Samuel, who stood by the party's traditional belief in Free Trade; and the Liberal Nationals, led by Sir John Simon, who were prepared to accept Conservative proposals for a revenue tariff to combat the slump.

When it was formed, the National Government was described by MacDonald as 'not a coalition, but a co-operation between individuals who are banded together to avoid the disaster [of financial collapse]. No parties are involved in it, and as soon as the country gets on an even keel again, the Government will cease to exist.' One of the members of the Cabinet, Sir Samuel Hoare, described it as 'an emergency Committee of Public Safety'.[4] It was intended to be a short-lived government formed simply to resolve the financial crisis. It was not intended that it would fight a general election as a National Government. That, however, was precisely what it came to do, in October 1931, just two months after it was formed.

The National Government seemingly comprised four parties – the Conservatives, the National Labour Party (as the supporters of MacDonald were now calling themselves), the Liberals, and the Liberal Nationals. Of these parties, only the Conservatives and the Liberals had any genuine independent existence, but only the Conservatives had the resources to put up sufficient candidates to form a government on their own. The Liberals fought just 112 seats, partly because they had withdrawn in some constituencies in favour of the Conservatives, but more because they lacked the financial resources to fight on a wider front. The National Labour party fought just 20 seats. It made no pretence of being a national party.

---

[2] Trevor Wilson, *The Downfall of the Liberal Party, 1914–1935* (Collins, 1966) 156.
[3] 'Kenneth O Morgan '1906–1924' in Butler (n 1) 45.
[4] Lord Templewood (Sir Samuel Hoare), *Nine Troubled Years* (Collins, 1954) 22–23.

'The real fact', according to one commentator, 'was that the National Labour Party did not exist; there were individual members of the Labour Party who were supporters of the prime Minister, but they had no organization in the constituencies';[5] while the Liberal National Party, which fielded just 41 candidates, was, according to one of its whips, 'never intended to be permanent'.[6] Of the 35 seats which the Liberal Nationals won in the 1931 general election, only four were won in competition with the Conservatives. Although the coalition lasted until 1940, its character was altered in September 1932, when the Liberals, led by Sir Herbert Samuel, resigned from the government on the issue of free trade. The other parties remaining in the coalition – National Labour and the Liberal Nationals – were satellites dependent upon the Conservatives for their existence, and the coalition was now predominantly 'a Conservative Government which happened to have a non-Conservative at its head and a number of other non-Conservatives attached to it'.[7]

There are, therefore, three precedents for Conservative/Liberal coalitions. There are none for a Labour/Liberal coalition. But the Liberals have supported minority Labour governments from the outside, in 1924, 1929–31 and, during the period of the Lib-Lab pact, in 1977–78.

The three peacetime coalitions were advocated partly by those who deplored the divisiveness of party spirit, and sought to put 'country before party'.[8] Joseph Chamberlain summed up the spirit of the coalitionists when, in 1894, he called for 'a great national and patriotic party, a party that will put country before the interests of any faction . . . a Government which really represents the strength and the best intelligence of the British people'.[9] This aim was not achieved. The peacetime coalitions did not succeed in rising above faction. Indeed, they aroused powerful opposition in the House of Commons. The coalitions sought to realign the parties. They did not succeed either in transcending party or in abolishing party warfare.

There are fundamental differences between the three peacetime coalitions since 1895 and that formed in 2010. The first is that past coalitions were formed *before* general elections, not after them, and were, in each case, endorsed by the voters with landslide majorities. In 1895, 1918 and 1931, the coalitions went to the country as coalitions, and the electors knew what combination of parties they were voting for. In 2010, by contrast, the voters would have had to guess which coalition would be formed if there were to be a hung parliament. Many would have guessed wrong. But, because no voter was given the chance to endorse the 2010 coalition, it lacks the legitimacy of its three predecessors.

[5] Tom Stannage, *Baldwin Thwarts the Opposition: The British General Election of 1935* (Croom Helm, 1980) 32.

[6] Henry Morris-Jones, *Doctor in the Whips' Room* (Hale, 1955) 87.

[7] David Marquand, *Ramsay MacDonald* (Jonathan Cape, 1977) 731.

[8] See GR Searle, *Country Before Party: Coalition and the Idea of 'National Government' in Modern Britain, 1885–1987* (Longman, 1995).

[9] ibid, 41.

The second difference between the three earlier coalitions and that of 2010 is that the earlier ones were unnecessary on strictly parliamentary grounds, in that on each occasion the Conservatives had enough seats to govern on their own. In 1895 the result of the election was as follows:

	Seats
Conservatives	341
Liberal Unionists	70
Liberals	177
Irish Nationalists	82
Total	670

The Conservatives had won an overall majority and no longer needed their Liberal Unionist allies.

The Lloyd George coalition, when formed in 1916, was a coalition of necessity, in that no single party enjoyed a majority in the Commons, and no general election was possible in wartime. But the general election of 1918 gave the Conservatives an overall majority:

	Seats
Conservatives	335
Irish Unionists	25
Independent Conservatives	23
Lloyd George Liberals	133
Labour supporters of coalition	10
Liberals	28
Labour	63
Irish Nationalists	7
Sinn Fein	73
Others	10
Total	707

The Sinn Fein MPs did not take their seats in the Commons, and so the effective size of the House was 634, giving the Conservatives an overall majority.

When it was formed, the National Government did not enjoy a single-party majority. In what was effectively a vote of confidence on 8 September 1931, it gained 311 votes to the opposition's 250, in a House of 615 MPs – its supporters, including the two tellers, comprising:

	Votes
Conservatives	243
Liberals	53
Labour	12
Independent	3
Total	311

But the general election held on 27 October yielded a landslide Conservative majority.

	Seats
Conservatives	473
National Labour	13
Liberal Nationals	35
Liberals	33
Independent Liberal	4[10]
Labour	52
Others	5
Total	615

The 2010 coalition, therefore, is the first to owe its existence to the lack of a parliamentary majority. That of course alters the dynamics of coalition. In the coalitions of 1895, 1918 and 1931, the non-Conservative parties were expendable; and in 1922 the Coalition Liberals were in fact expended, while in 1932, the Samuelite Liberals were expended. Further, two of the coalitions – those of 1918 and 1931 – were led by members of minority parties, rather than by the leader of the majority party, the Conservatives. Therefore, they too were expendable. In November 1918, Bonar Law, the Conservative leader, had advocated continuing the coalition with the Liberals by telling his MPs: '[B]y our own action we have made Mr Lloyd George the flag bearer of the very principles upon which we should appeal to the country. It is not his Liberal friends, it is the Unionist Party [ie the Conservatives] which has made him Prime Minister and made it possible for him to do the great work that has been done by this Government . . .'[11] The implication was that, just as the Conservatives had made Lloyd George Prime Minister, so, in due course, they could unmake him; and it would be natural for the Conservatives to ask why it was that, as the majority party, they did not supply the Prime Minister. That was a prime motive for the collapse of the coalition in 1922. After 1932, similarly, the Conservatives might have been able to replace Ramsay MacDonald with one of their own, but Baldwin, a consensual and emollient leader, refused to have any truck with suggestions that MacDonald be deposed.

The coalition of 2010 is of course a great contrast. The Prime Minister is the leader of the largest party, the Conservatives; and, by contrast with previous coalitions, the Liberals are not expendable. Were the Liberal Democrats at any time to leave the coalition and vote against the Conservatives, the Conservatives would be out of office. To this extent, the electoral and political facts therefore favour the coalition more than they did its three predecessors.

The preceding three peacetime coalitions owed their existence not to a hung parliament but to a sense that there were political issues which transcended traditional party lines. Certainly Irish Home Rule was seen by the two Unionist parties – the Conservatives and the Liberal Unionists – as such an issue. In 1931, the need

[10] These independent Liberals were a small family group headed by Lloyd George, who had opposed the National Government's decision to call an election. They had fought the election as opponents of the government.

[11] Robert Blake, *The Unknown Prime Minister: The Life and Times of Andrew Bonar Law, 1858–1923* (Eyre and Spottiswoode, 1955) 387–88.

to secure economies in the budget was another. In 1918 there was no such specific issue, but there was a new mood after the war which, so advocates of the coalition believed, justified the coming together of those who had hitherto been antagonists. That mood had two components, one positive, the other negative. The positive component was the desire to deal with a new post-war world in which older issues such as free trade, Irish Home Rule and the disestablishment of the Church of Wales would no longer be relevant. A new party alignment should therefore be created to meet the conditions of a new political era. 'Why,' Winston Churchill asked in an election speech in November 1918, 'if men and women of all classes, all parties, are able to work together for five years like a mighty machine to produce destruction, can they not work together for another five years to produce abundance?'[12] The Cabinet Conclusions in June 1920 were to declare: 'The only justification for the existence of the present form of Government was that it attempted to hold the balance evenly and fairly between all classes of the community.'[13] There was, one historian of the coalition believes, 'a yearning for unity in 1919–20 in Britain and the Coalition came near to expressing it'.[14] The coalition did indeed, according to the social theorist WG Runciman, succeed in transforming an unreconstructed capitalist society into a regulated one, a more radical transformation than that achieved by Attlee's 1945 administration; in Runciman's view, it was the only major social transformation to occur in the twentieth century.[15]

In international affairs, too, it was hoped that the end of the war would herald a new era in which, in place of national conflicts, disputes would be settled by the League of Nations. One supporter of the Lloyd George coalition went so far as to suggest that the coalition was 'the natural corollary to the League of Nations'.[16] A historian of the coalition suggests that 'above all through Lloyd George himself, [it] offered some kind of vision of social harmony and international conciliation which many young men and women entering politics in 1919 found neither ignoble nor undeserving of support. The coalition tried to seize the opportunity, fleeting though it was, to take advantage of the war years and to create a middle way for a nation at peace with itself and in fruitful collaboration with its allies.' It sought to 'harness political consensus to positive ends'.[17]

But there was also a negative element, which conflicted somewhat with the positive. This negative element was characterised by fear – fear of the trade unions, fear of a general strike, and, above all, fear of 'Bolshevism', sometimes equated,

---

[12] Martin Gilbert, *World in Torment: Winston S Churchill, 1917–1922* (Minerva, 1990 (orig 1975)) 171.

[13] Cited in Kenneth O Morgan, *Consensus and Disunity: The Lloyd George Coalition Government 1918–1922* (Clarendon Press, 1979) 43. This book offers by far the best analysis of the Lloyd George coalition.

[14] ibid, 190.

[15] WG Runciman, *A Treatise on Social Theory, vol III: Applied Social Theory* (Cambridge University Press, 1999).

[16] OF Maclagan, *Coalition Government* (Purbrook and Eyres, 1920) 6.

[17] Morgan (n 13) 375.

odd though it may seem today, with the Labour Party. But, following the Russian revolution in 1917, and Communist risings in many of the countries of central and eastern Europe, there was a feeling, however misplaced, amongst members of the governing class – few of whom had any close understanding or knowledge of the labour movement – that Britain too might be on the brink of revolution, and that the forces of order should combine together to defeat this threat. In February 1920 the Deputy Cabinet Secretary, Thomas Jones, recorded a meeting of Lloyd George with his advisers at which the Home Secretary 'outlined his proposals to raise a special temporary force of 10,000 soldiers for the national emergency', the existing police force being inadequate. 'There are', the Food Controller insisted, 'large groups preparing for Soviet government'. Walter Long, First Lord of the Admiralty, was worried that '[t]he peaceable manpower of the country is without arms. I have not a pistol less than 200 years old.' Bonar Law, the Conservative leader, summed up the discussion, saying, '[a]ll weapons ought to be available for distribution to the friends of the Government'. Sir Auckland Geddes, President of the Board of Trade, 'pointed to the universities as full of trained men who could co-operate with clerks and stockbrokers. (During the discussion Bonar Law so often referred to the stockbrokers as a loyal and fighting class until one felt that potential battalions of stockbrokers were to be found in every town.)'[18]

With the end of the post-war boom, however, the perils of 'Bolshevism' gradually came to recede, while the threat of a general strike also receded after 'Black Friday' in 1921, when Lloyd George skillfully took advantage of divided counsels in the trade union leadership to undermine union solidarity. As post-war disillusionment set in, the positive impulse behind the coalition weakened and it began to look like little more than an anti-socialist front. But, if that was all it was, why was coalition needed at all? Would not the aims of anti-socialism be best secured by a purely Conservative government with a Conservative Prime Minister?

The general elections of 1895, 1918 and 1931 all resulted in landslide victories for the coalition, and there can be little doubt that coalitions have benefited the Conservative Party, the dominant element in all three, more than they have benefited their Liberal partners. The Conservatives would probably have won the elections of 1895, 1918 and 1931 even without the aid of their coalition partners, but their partners strengthened them, enabling them to win seats in areas that were not naturally Conservative. As late as 1965, John Nott, who was to be a minister in the governments of Edward Heath and Margaret Thatcher, came to be 'selected as the National Liberal and Conservative candidate for St Ives . . . not the Conservative candidate . . .. I was told by the local association that St Ives could not be won by a Conservative – but that as the National Liberals had supported the Conservatives and had done so since 1931, I should not fret about the label.' Nott did not drop the National Liberal label until the general election of 1974, even though the party wound itself up in 1968. The accumulated funds of the party, amounting to

---

[18] Keith Middlemas (ed), *Thomas Jones: Whitehall Diary, vol 1, 1916–1925* (Oxford University Press, 1969) 99–101.

£50,000 were then given to the Conservatives, 'who, of course, blew it in an afternoon on some futile advertising campaign'.[19]

Support from Liberals and others helped to give the Conservatives a 'national' appeal over and above their purely party appeal. The landslide victories of Conservative-dominated coalitions in 1918 and 1931 were assisted by the fact that they were led by leading figures from other parties – Lloyd George and Ramsay MacDonald – who were saying that their former parties – the Liberals in Lloyd George's case and Labour in MacDonald's – were irresponsible and could not be trusted with power. Similarly, in 1895, Conservative dominance was assisted by another non-Conservative, Joseph Chamberlain, who, although not Prime Minister, was the leading figure in the Unionist coalition. Both Chamberlain and Lloyd George were, however, disruptive personalities and in large part responsible for breaking up the coalitions in which they were the dominant figures. In 1903, Joseph Chamberlain's tariff reform campaign split the Unionist coalition and made possible the Liberal landslide of 1906. Lloyd George was, as Stanley Baldwin declared at the meeting of Conservative MPs at the Carlton Club in 1922, 'a great dynamic force', and such a force, Baldwin insisted, was a 'very terrible thing'. There is indeed a striking contrast between Baldwin and Lloyd George. In the 1930s, Baldwin was to prove an emollient leader of the National Government. Peacetime coalitions, if they are to be successful, need emollient personalities at their head rather than great dynamic forces. For the 2010 coalition to be a success, David Cameron must prove himself a Prime Minister in the mould of Baldwin rather than Lloyd George.

The coalition government of 2010 is intended as a recognition of multi-party politics which the Liberal Democrats hope will prove a permanent part of the constitution. Earlier coalitions, however, implied no such recognition. On the contrary, they proved to be steps towards realignment and the restoration of a two-party system – in each case a two-party system in which the Conservatives were to enjoy a hegemonic position, so that they became the natural party of government. They secured this position with the aid of leaders who, however one chooses to describe their political position, were in no sense Conservatives – Joseph Chamberlain, Lloyd George and Ramsay MacDonald. 'The last purely Conservative government', declared Harold Macmillan in 1975, perhaps with tongue in cheek, 'was formed by Mr Disraeli in 1874 – it is the fact that we have attracted moderate people of Liberal tradition and thought into our ranks which makes it possible to maintain a Conservative government today. A successful party of the Right must continue to recruit its strength from the centre and even from the left centre. Once it begins to shrink into itself like a snail it will be doomed.'[20]

Coalitions have been of much less benefit to the Liberals. The Liberals entered each of the three peacetime coalitions as a disunited party. The coalition of 1895 was the product of Liberal disunion. The coalition of 1918 caused Liberal

---

[19] John Nott, *Here Today, Gone Tomorrow: Recollections of an Errant Politician* (Politico's, 2002) 125–26.
[20] Harold Macmillan, *The Past Masters* (Macmillan, 1975) 18–19.

disunion. The coalition of 1931 widened Liberal disunion. After two of the coalitions, one wing of the Liberal Party came to merge with the Conservatives – the Liberal Unionists in 1912 and the Liberal Nationals in 1968.

Lloyd George had also hoped to merge his Coalition Liberals with the Conservatives, and in 1920 he proposed fusion, a proposal that has been called 'the boldest attack that has ever been attempted on the separate identity of the party organizations since their origins in the late nineteenth century'.[21] The Conservatives were perfectly happy to accept fusion, and *The Daily Mail* declared that '[t]he formation of a new Centre Party . . . in place of the existing Coalition' was 'a certainty in the very near future'. A programme was drafted for the new party which would be called, perhaps rather unpromisingly, the 'United Reform Party'.[22] The Conservatives, remarkably, were even willing to accept Lloyd George as leader of the fused party. But it was not to be. Surprisingly, it was the Coalition Liberals who objected. They were determined to preserve their Liberal identity. The two parties were, accordingly, to remain separate. Once fusion had failed, the Lloyd George coalition 'always had an air of impermanence. It had been unable to evolve from its earlier stage of party competition; it was all trees and no wood. It seemed inevitable that at some future stage its basic components, the party machines, would reassert themselves and show up the basic fragmentation within the Coalition.'[23] After the Lloyd George coalition broke up, the two wings of the Liberal Party – the Asquithian and the Lloyd Georgian – were briefly reunited, but in 1931 the party split again.

After the National Government was established, there was also much talk of realignment between Conservatives and Liberals. Neville Chamberlain argued in favour of 'that fused Party under a National name which I regard as certain to come'. For '[a] National Party [would] get rid of that odious title of Conservative which has kept so many from joining us in the past'. He was supported by his party leader, Baldwin, who hoped that it might prove possible 'to change the title of our Party to National', since little would soon 'really [divide] us from the great bulk of the liberals'.[24] Chamberlain correctly predicted that the 1931 coalition would 'split it [the Liberal Party] from top to bottom, and [would] end it, the two sections going off in opposite directions; and bring us back nearly to the two-party system'.[25] The Liberals split off from the National Government in 1932, while the Liberal Nationals, whom Lady Violet Bonham Carter, the daughter of Asquith, was to call 'Vichy Liberals',[26] did eventually fuse with the Conservatives, so leading to the restoration of a two-party system.

---

[21] David Close, 'Conservatives and Coalition after the First World War' (1973) *Journal of Modern History* 243.

[22] Searle (n 8) 128–29.

[23] Morgan (n 13) 188.

[24] Searle (n 8) 182.

[25] David Dutton, *Liberals in Schism: A History of the National Liberal Party* (IB Tauris, 2008) 36. The Liberal Nationals altered their name to National Liberals in 1948.

[26] David Dutton, *A History of the Liberal Party in the Twentieth Century* (Palgrave Macmillan, 2004) 147. This is by far the most useful history of the party in the twentieth century.

Lady Violet was to sum up the Liberal experience of coalition with the Conservatives when in 1955 she told Lord Samuel, Liberal leader in the Lords (the former Sir Herbert Samuel, who had preserved Liberal independence in 1932 by resigning from the National Government):

> Joe Chamberlain became the mainspring of Protection and Imperialism; Lloyd George sold the Liberal Party to the Tories in 1918. Such things are possible for so-called Radicals. – impossible for any Liberal – you – my father – Edward Grey.[27]

The coalitions of 1918 and 1931 helped to ruin the Liberal Party. On both occasions, fear of 'socialism' and 'Bolshevism' drove them into the arms of the Conservatives. 'Coalitions between two unequal parties', David Butler has argued, 'can turn out to be like the relationship between the tiger and the young lady of Riga'.[28] Both coalitions confirmed the fragmentation of the Liberals and proved to be stages on the way to the development of a two-party system in which the Liberals were to have no place. On each occasion, the Liberals found it impossible to maintain a secure identity. They found themselves the victims of the binary assumptions that lay behind British politics. Left-leaning Liberals regarded the Conservatives as the enemy; Right-leaning Liberals, such as Winston Churchill in the 1920s and the Simonites in the 1930s, regarded Labour as the enemy. British politics since the 1930s has been based on binary assumptions. These assumptions would be undermined by proportional representation, which the Liberals have supported since 1922, though they had opposed it when in government. The alternative vote, by contrast, could well confirm them, as it has done in Australia.

Talk of realignment under previous coalitions was not entirely empty. The coalitions of 1918 and 1931 did help to secure realignment, in the sense that they made it possible to resolve old issues, and allowed governments to adapt to new concerns. They were a means of allowing the party system to accommodate itself to social change. The 1918 coalition enacted the Representation of the People Act, which provided for female suffrage – a measure of great contention before 1914 – as well as universal male suffrage. The coalition also ensured that post-war politics was not wracked by Irish home rule, as pre-war politics had been. The coalition secured an Irish settlement, admittedly after a terrible attempt at repression with the 'Black and Tans', and it is possible that only a coalition could have achieved a settlement. A purely Conservative government would have been unwilling to grant Irish self-government, while a purely Liberal government would not have been able to secure Conservative acquiescence to a settlement which they would have regarded as a surrender to terrorism. One defender of the coalition claimed: 'In such an act as the Representation of the People Act and in the Irish settlement it [the coalition] has achieved an agreement between hitherto opposed parties which some old Liberals would not have deemed possible.'[29]

---

[27] John Bowle, *Viscount Samuel: A Biography* (Gollancz, 1955) 357.
[28] David Butler (ed), *Coalitions in British Politics* (Macmillan, 1978) 118.
[29] Maclagan (n 16) 8–9.

The National Government, similarly, was able to ensure a degree of consensus over the progress of India towards self-government. By contrast with Ireland between 1885 and 1914, India did not become a matter of party contention. It might have done so had a party government, whether Labour or Liberal, been in power, while a purely Conservative government would have found it more difficult to resist the hostility to Indian self-government of the right wing of the party, powerfully led as it was by Winston Churchill. Indeed, Sir Samuel Hoare, Secretary of State for India, and responsible for steering Indian self-government onto the statute book against the vehement opposition of Churchill and the diehards, admitted that 'nine out of ten Conservatives wish me to do nothing at all'.[30] Another leading member of the National Government, Neville Chamberlain, insisted that there was no need to sympathise with him 'on not having a Conservative Government, since I have got just as much out of the present composite team as I wanted; and if I had owed my support to an extreme right-wing, I might have found them much more difficult to control'.[31] Perhaps David Cameron feels the same.

All three peacetime coalitions, then, have involved the Conservative Party and elements of the Liberal Party. But the coalition of 2010 is the first in which the Conservatives have formed a government with a united Liberal party. It was perhaps an under-estimated triumph for Nick Clegg to be able to bring a united Liberal Democrat Party into a coalition with the Conservatives, a party hitherto regarded with great suspicion by many Liberal Democrats.

II. ELECTORAL PACTS

Each of the three previous coalitions faced the problem of how they could maintain at the hustings the co-operation that they had enjoyed in government. 'We cannot go on as we are,' Bonar Law told Balfour in 1920, 'that is with the United Party in the House of Commons, but with no such union in the constituencies.'[32] The 1895 Unionist coalition found this problem comparatively easy to resolve since the electoral support of the Liberal Unionist leader, Joseph Chamberlain, was regionally concentrated in his fiefdom of the West Midlands. There seemed to be a genuine element of complementarity to Conservative and Liberal Unionist support. The Conservatives could not hope to make successful incursions into the West Midlands, while the Liberal Unionists were unlikely to make much impact in those rural areas where Conservative support was entrenched. Matters were more difficult, however, with later coalitions, and also with the Liberal/SDP Alliance, formed in 1981, which sought to divide constituencies between them in the two general elections which they fought, in 1983 and 1987, so as not to split their vote. Past coalitions have sought to deal with this problem of securing co-operation in the constituencies in a variety of different ways.

[30] Nick Smart, *The National Government, 1931–1940* (Macmillan, 1999) 65.
[31] Dutton (n 25) 64.
[32] Morgan (n 13) 184.

In 1918, the leaders of the coalition, Lloyd George for the Liberals and Bonar Law for the Conservatives, issued a 'coupon' to those candidates officially approved by the coalition. It appears, although there were of course no opinion polls at that time, that public opinion was veering strongly towards the Conservatives. The Liberals were therefore very much on the defensive, and Lloyd George did well to secure as many as 159 coupons for his Liberal supporters. 322 Conservatives were given the coupon, and a further 41 Conservatives were returned unopposed. Of the other 81 Conservatives who stood, 36 sat for Irish constituencies which were not included in the coupon scheme, while a further 22 Conservatives were either offered the coupon and refused it, or stood in constituencies where there was no official coalition candidate at all. That left 23 constituencies where the local Conservative association put up a candidate in defiance of the official couponed nominee.[33]

The general election of 1918 proved a triumph for the coalition. Indeed, '[w]hen the votes were counted it seemed that candidates who had received the coupon had been given something very much like a complimentary ticket to Westminster'.[34] In addition to the 41 Conservatives returned unopposed, 294 of the 322 couponed Conservatives were successful, likewise 133 of the 159 Liberals. But, of the 45 un-couponed Conservatives who stood, 23 were successful – nearly as many as the independent Asquithian Liberals, who returned just 28 MPs to the Commons. Conservatives actively denied the coupon were, therefore, 'every bit as successful as those who received it', the function of the coupon being primarily to spare Liberals from Conservative attack. The Conservatives hardly needed it, since they were much less fearful of attack from the Liberals, who were already a declining force.[35]

In 1931 there was no centrally directed coupon, and no national agreement between party headquarters on which parties should contest which seats. It was nevertheless vital that, wherever possible, a single 'National' candidate be selected to oppose Labour, for in the 1929 general election Labour had won 123 of its 288 seats on a minority vote, and there had been 447 three-cornered fights. Again, the initiative lay with the Conservatives, who were thought to be on course for a large majority. The other parties were to a large extent dependent upon their generosity. As in 1918, they needed protection from Conservative attack. The Conservatives were the patrons, and the other parties their clients. Ramsay MacDonald hoped that partisan concerns could be put aside, and suggested to Baldwin, the Conservative leader, that 'the Party in possession ought to claim the national candidature, so that no partisan advantage may be gained from the national crisis'. MacDonald feared, however, that the Conservatives were seeking an absolute majority for themselves. 'They are keeping as many Liberal and my Labour friends out of constituencies, as they can . . . Never let it be said that the Tory machine had

---

[33] JM McEwen, 'The Coupon Election of 1918 and Unionist Members of Parliament' (1962) *Journal of Modern History* 295.

[34] ibid.

[35] Wilson (n 2) 179, 181.

a glimmering of national duty and sacrifice.'[36] Baldwin, however, appeared to believe that it was legitimate for a Conservative to oppose a Liberal, other than a Liberal National, in any constituency except where a minister was defending his seat. In the end, while 30 Conservative ministers were unopposed by Liberals, five Liberal ministers found themselves opposed by Conservatives.[37] Baldwin summed up his party's position when he told Sir John Simon, leader of the Liberal Nationals:

> While I can give no guarantee that will bind individual constituencies, for democracy is a reality in the Conservative Party and each constituency is a law until itself, I, as leader of the Party, and the Chairman who directs the Conservative Party Headquarters, will exercise all the influence and authority we possess to see that those who play a patriotic part receive the full support of our party in the constituencies they now represent.[38]

The Conservatives did in fact exert pressure on a number of constituencies, but co-operation depended primarily upon local constituency opinion. Agreement was, however, often reached at the local level, owing to a strong feeling that the Labour Party's programme was dangerously profligate and would lead the country to financial disaster. The general election, on this view, was not about old political issues such as free trade versus protection, but about the danger of financial collapse and 'socialism'. Therefore it was the duty of all patriotically inclined people to co-operate to ensure that Labour faced just one 'National' candidate.

Conservatives were, however, much more willing to withdraw in favour of Liberal Nationals, where there were 35 withdrawals, than in favour of Liberals, where there were just 19 withdrawals. There were 81 constituencies where Conservatives and Liberal supporters of the National Government fought each other, but only four where Conservatives and Liberal Nationals fought each other. Nevertheless, there was a considerable degree of co-operation. Whereas in 1929 there had been 447 three-cornered fights between the major parties, in 1931 there were just 79, and in only 14 of these were Labour candidates incumbents. In few of the seats where there was more than one candidate supporting the National Government was there a real danger of a split vote handing victory to Labour. Indeed, after the election, the Conservative National Agent declared that there was only one constituency – Walthamstow West – where a split in the National vote had prevented the Conservatives from winning a seat. Of the 190 Conservative gains, around half of them had been won by Labour in 1929 on a minority vote. It was this factor – elimination of the split opposition to Labour rather than a collapse in the Labour vote – that was primarily responsible for the catastrophic fall in the number of Labour seats between 1929, when the party had won 288, and 1931, when it won only 52. The average Labour vote per opposed candidate in 1929 had been 14,692; in 1931 it was reduced to 13,064.[39] But in 1929 there had been only 102 straight fights, whereas in 1931 there were 409.[40] So, 'faced with a

---

[36] Dutton (n 25) 50.
[37] Stannage (n 5) 17–18, 20–21.
[38] ibid, 32.
[39] Nick Smart, 'Constituency Politics and the 1931 Election' (1994) *Southern History* 143.
[40] Stannage (n 5) 24.

fourfold increase in the number of straight fights in comparison with 1929, Labour was effectively "couponed" in 1931 despite the absence of coupons'.[41] Of the 190 seats that the Conservatives gained from Labour, precisely half of them – 95 – had been won by Labour on a minority vote in 1931.[42] By 1935, when the Liberals had left the government, co-operation was even better than it had been in 1918, and no Liberal National or National Labour candidate was opposed anywhere by a Conservative. Paradoxically, the National Government, a coalition, inaugurated a trend towards a two-party system in place of the three-party politics of the 1920s – a two-party system in which straight fights became the norm and Liberal candidates came to be seen as spoilers.

The Liberals and the SDP faced a similar problem of seat allocation for the 1983 and 1987 general elections. There was in effect a coupon on both occasions, reached by agreement after somewhat prolonged and difficult negotiations between the national headquarters of the two parties. In 1983 there were only three seats where Liberals and SDP candidates stood against each other. In 1987 there were none, a remarkable achievement.

The fundamental problem which faces political parties in seeking an agreement on an electoral pact is that it cannot be imposed from above by central party headquarters, but requires acquiescence at constituency level. Local constituency parties are autonomous bodies, and, while they may be influenced by the wishes of central headquarters, strong pressure is likely to prove counter-productive. Indeed, the more the parties have developed as membership-based mass organisations, the more constituency parties have grown to resent interference in their affairs by their party leaders.

This means that an electoral pact involving reciprocal withdrawal of candidates cannot be imposed by party leaders alone; it must be agreed by local constituency parties. Local parties regard selecting a candidate as their raison d'etre, their reward for the many hours that they spend voluntarily delivering campaign material and undertaking similarly mundane tasks. A Liberal candidate asked to stand down in favour of one from the SDP made the following *cri de coeur* at a meeting of the SDP's Council for Social Democracy at Great Yarmouth in 1982.

> Seven years ago when I became prospective parliamentary candidate for this constituency, we sold a home we all dearly loved, to move to live in the constituency; our youngest left her school and all three children eventually went to school locally. My wife changed her job to teach in the local comprehensive school and we accepted the upheaval because we both believed that for me the only way to nurse the constituency was to live in it and become part of it.[43]

His comments can stand for all those asked to stand down in favour of candidates from coalition partners.

---

[41] Smart (n 39) 144.

[42] ibid, 145.

[43] Jeremy Josephs, *Inside the Alliance: An Inside Account of the Development and Prospects of the Liberal/SDP Alliance* (John Martin, 1983) 155.

When local party feelings are strong, an agreement by party headquarters may simply be ignored. An unofficial local candidate might appear, even if not supported by central headquarters, so that the views of the party can be heard in the constituency. That is what happened to Asquith in the general election of 1918. Out of respect for him, the Lloyd George coalition did not issue any 'coupon' in his constituency of East Fife. This meant that Asquith would not be opposed by an official Conservative candidate. But the local Conservatives decided to ignore this edict from the centre and they put up Captain Sir Alexander Sprot – a baronet with a distinguished war record, though otherwise unknown – to fight the seat. Although he had not received the 'coupon', Sprot defeated Asquith in the seat that he had held since 1886. Indeed, as we have seen, in the general election of 1918, of the 45 un-couponed Conservatives who fought, 23 were returned.[44]

Even if an electoral pact can be agreed, and there are no unofficial local candidates, it does not follow that the electors will follow the dictates of party headquarters. At the next election, it is possible that the Conservatives will, in constituencies where they have no chance, withdraw their candidate, and ask their supporters to vote for their Liberal Democrat coalition partners. But Conservative supporters might decline to take that advice and vote UKIP instead. Similarly, Liberal Democrat voters, in constituencies in which the Liberal Democrat candidate has been withdrawn, might ignore an injunction to support the Conservative candidate, and vote Labour or Green instead.

Lord Hailsham, whilst Chairman of the Conservative Party from 1957 to 1959, was frequently enjoined to seek a pact with the Liberals to avoid splitting the anti-socialist vote. But the difficulties were formidable.

> I could think of no more certain way for a party in office to ensure its own defeat than to be seen to make an arrangement of this kind before holding an election. . . . It must be remembered that, on the withdrawal of either a Liberal or Conservative candidate, the votes he would otherwise have won are not automatically transferred. A number of voters would abstain in disgust. A number of Liberals would certainly vote Socialist in the absence of a Liberal candidate . . .

Reciprocal withdrawal would be impossible unless

> there was already a feeling of cordiality sufficient to make the association lined up for sacrifice willing to withdraw its candidate. Such feelings of self-sacrifice cannot normally be imposed from above and, on the level of constituency organisations, nothing can be more disheartening or destructive for years afterwards of morale than such a request coming from national headquarters. Finally, and most ludicrous of all, if all went through up to this point, in a number of cases at least, no sooner would the official candidate be withdrawn than out of the undergrowth an unkempt John the Baptist type figure would emerge calling himself, as the case might be, an Independent Liberal or Conservative, or in the case of some Welsh and Scottish constituencies, a Nationalist and carry off all the votes which had been bargained and sold as a result of the arrangement.[45]

---

[44] McEwen (n 33) 295.
[45] Lord Hailsham, *The Door Wherein I Went* (Collins, 1975) 174–75.

The supporters of a political party are not like members of a disciplined army whose votes can be transferred as their party leaders wish. For them to be willing to transfer their votes, some overriding reason is needed. That reason could be found in 1895 in the desire to defeat Home Rule; in 1918 in the desire to defeat candidates who had shown themselves 'unpatriotic' during the war; and in 1931 to ensure that the pound was not destroyed by the financial crisis and the supposed profligacy of the Labour Party. On each occasion, the nation needed to be saved from opponents who had in some subtle sense ceased to be a part of it. It was this 'national' appeal that made electoral pacts possible. Such pacts, if they are to be successful, must go with the grain both of constituency opinion and of public opinion.

III. GRASS-ROOTS HOSTILITY TO COALITIONS

A coalition will last only so long as its overriding purpose is seen to transcend everyday party battles. As soon as that ceases to be the case, the coalition will collapse. What is remarkable about the Lloyd George coalition is how quickly it ended after its landslide victory in the election. In 1918, it was difficult to believe that it would prove anything but permanent. Indeed, Lloyd George's popularity at the end of the war was so great that Bonar Law, the Conservative leader, said – 'He can be Prime Minister for life if he likes'.[46] Yet just four years later it collapsed and Lloyd George was never to hold office again. The National Government lost the support of the Liberals, the one genuinely independent non-Conservative element in the coalition, just one year after winning, in 1931, the largest electoral landslide ever enjoyed by any administration in British history,

In each case, the fundamental purpose animating the coalition had disappeared. In 1918, as we have seen, that fundamental purpose was both positive – the desire to create a new order out of the ruins of war – and negative – the desire to combat 'Bolshevism'. But, by 1922, these were no longer such pressing considerations, with the ending of trade union militancy after Black Friday in 1921. The idealism that had animated many of the early supporters of the coalition had dissipated as post-war disillusionment set in. The Conservatives were thought by many to be too dominated by shady business interests and with weak leadership, while Lloyd George had become widely distrusted because of the whiff of corruption that surrounded his government, culminating in the scandal of the sale of honours. One wag described the coalition as 'a deal between a flock of sheep led by a crook [the Coalition Liberals] and a flock of crooks led by a sheep [the Conservatives]'.[47] It began to look as though the coalition had no purpose except to perpetuate itself. That was not a purpose that could animate either the voters or the party members, whose support was needed for it to continue and flourish.

---

[46] Hugh Purcell, *Lloyd George* (Haus, 2006) 73.
[47] Michael Kinnear, *The Fall of Lloyd George* (Macmillan, 1973) 4.

There was a feeling on the part of many Conservatives that a return to party government was overdue. 'In the last analysis, what Tories came to want in the spring and summer of 1922 was a reassertion of the autonomy of party, for its own sake.'[48]

In 1931 the primary concern, amounting almost to panic in the minds of many party leaders, was to restore the national finances. To that aim, all other concerns were subordinate. Therefore, although the Liberals and Conservatives differed on the issue of free trade versus protection, they could join together in an emergency government whose overriding purpose was to balance the budget. To help secure this overriding purpose, the Conservatives were willing to make compromises to retain the Liberals and so preserve the 'National' character of the government. By 1932, however, the national finances seemed to have been restored, and the older issue of free trade reasserted itself. By that time, the Conservatives were prepared to continue working with the Liberals only if the Liberals were prepared to abandon free trade; but that, for the Liberals, meant abandoning the main principle that kept them alive as a party and distinguished them from the Conservatives. With the crisis seemingly over, they saw no further need to compromise their principles.

In 1922, the revolt that destroyed the coalition came from the Conservative grass-roots, not from the leadership. Many historians have emphasised the meeting of Conservative MPs at the Carlton Club in October 1922 which voted against the continuation of the coalition as the crucial factor in its downfall. But the coalition was almost certainly doomed, whatever MPs thought. It was being repudiated by Conservative constituency associations who were adopting candidates opposed to its continuation. These candidates were opposed to the policy of the leadership, but they could not be repudiated by the leadership since they had been chosen by entirely proper procedures and were, therefore, official Conservative candidates. By the time of the general election of 1922, over 180 Conservatives opposed to the coalition had been chosen as candidates by their constituency associations.[49] It was this grass-roots Conservative revolt that ensured the downfall of the coalition, for if the party leadership ignored it, then it would be the leadership that would be repudiated, not the candidates. The Conservative leader, Austen Chamberlain, who had replaced Bonar Law in 1921, when the latter had retired due to ill-health, lacked his predecessor's authority and understanding of the party's grass-roots. It was he and not the rebels who called the meeting at the Carlton Club. He did so in order to pre-empt the forthcoming Conservative Party conference at which the view of the constituency parties would be dominant. He wrote to the Lord Chancellor, Lord Birkenhead, 'I am not sure that it may not now be necessary to call a Party meeting and to tell them bluntly that they must either follow our advice or do without us, in which case they must find their own Chief and form a Government *at once*. They would be in a d--d fix.'[50] As a former

---

[48] Morgan (n 13) 355.
[49] ibid, 342.
[50] Blake (n 11) 451, emphasis in original.

Liberal Unionist, Chamberlain hoped that the Coalition Liberals would follow the Liberal Unionist example in fusing with the Conservatives. But the moment had passed, and Chamberlain was foolish to ignore the grass-roots pressures in his party and to invite a confrontation with Conservatives in the constituencies and the House of Commons.

Chamberlain tried to maximise his chances of success by inviting only MPs to the meeting at the Carlton Club, and not Conservative candidates, so many of whom had already repudiated the coalition. But these were misguided tactics. For, if the Carlton Club meeting had voted to continue the coalition, then the Conservatives might have suffered a split such as that which occurred after the repeal of the Corn Laws in 1846. They might have remained in the wilderness and been shattered as a party of government, as they were after 1846. That was the explicit analogy drawn by Bonar Law, Chamberlain's predecessor as Conservative leader, called out of retirement to express the views of the grass-roots of the party and repudiate the coalition. He drew a comparison with 1846, and declared that continuation of the coalition would split the party. 'The body that is cast off will slowly become the Conservative Party, but it will take a generation before it gets back to the influence which the Party ought to have.'[51]

The rejection of the coalition was inevitable, whatever happened at the Carlton Club. When asked 'What is going to happen?' as he ascended the steps of the Carlton Club, one leading Conservative answered, 'A slice off the top.'[52] What he meant was that local constituency parties had already decided against the coalition. The only issue was whether the leadership was prepared to respect that decision. If, as turned out to be the case, it was not, it would be repudiated. For there were available alternative Conservative leaders who were willing to represent the decision made by the constituency associations – men such as Bonar Law, and the hitherto unknown Stanley Baldwin, a junior Cabinet minister in the coalition and seemingly of no great weight. In fact, most of the MPs had made up their minds to end the coalition before the Carlton Club meeting, and at the meeting it was repudiated by 187 votes to 87.[53] Every major figure in the party organisation voted against the coalition.[54]

Pressure from the grass-roots also played an important role in the Liberals' decision to leave the National Government in 1932. Liberal Party members in the country had been sceptical of 'the agreement to differ' and the 1932 conference of the National Liberal Federation condemned it. After Liberal ministers resigned from the government in September 1932 in protest at the imperial tariff, which resulted from the Ottawa agreements, they nevertheless continued to sit on the government benches – an odd compromise with echoes perhaps of the 'agreement to differ'. Liberal MPs defended their position by saying that they would

---

[51] ibid, 457.
[52] Robert Rhodes James, *Memoirs of a Conservative: JCC Davidson's Memoirs and Papers, 1910–37* (Weidenfeld and Nicolson, 1969) 127.
[53] See Kinnear (n 47) ch 6.
[54] Morgan (n 13) 356.

continue to support the government on 'National' issues while opposing it when it acted in a partisan Conservative Party manner. They were continually pressed to end this illogical compromise by local Liberal constituency associations and by the National Liberal Federation, which declared in 1933 that the 'appropriate place' for the Liberals 'is on the opposition benches'.[55] Lloyd George, who had declared himself independent of the Liberal Party since the 1931 general election, said that the undignified position of the Liberals resembled that of a cat that 'has pushed its head into a cream jug and cannot get it out without either breaking the jug or having someone pull it out by the tail. It is the latter process that is going on at the moment and I hope it will succeed.'[56] The Liberals duly went into opposition in November 1933, giving as their reason the government's dilatoriness in pursuing disarmament, an odd excuse to choose 10 months after Hitler's ascent to power.

The 2010 coalition has attempted to cement itself in office by declaring that it will not go to the country until 2015. It lacks the negative element of fear that, for a short time at least, held together the coalitions of 1918 and 1931 – fear of 'Bolshevism' in 1918, and fear of Labour profligacy in 1931. However, as the history of past peacetime coalitions shows, the longevity of the coalition depends not only or even mainly upon the views of party leaders or MPs, but on opinion at the grass-roots. Historically, coalitions have come under pressure from below, not from the top. If the Conservative/Liberal Democrat coalition of 2010 comes to a premature end, this is more likely to be the result of grass-roots pressure than a calculated decision of the leaders or the MPs. The first signs of Liberal Democrat unease were to appear at the end of 2010 over the issue of higher tuition fees for students in universities. All of the Liberal Democrat MPs had pledged themselves to vote against any increase. But they had also endorsed the Coalition Agreement, which took priority over their pledges, and Liberal Democrat ministers supported the proposals of the Browne committee, which involved a tripling of tuition fees. The lead minister putting forward this proposal was Vince Cable, the Business Secretary, whose department is responsible for the universities, which absorb around one-third of its budget. There was much hostility to this policy amongst Liberal Democrat voters, especially amongst students. The National Union of Students had advised its members to support the Liberal Democrats in the election precisely because of the party's stance on student fees. The Coalition Agreement, as we have seen, gave Liberal Democrat MPs the right to abstain on any Commons vote if they could not accept the Browne proposals. But their colleagues in government had accepted them, and Cable would have become an object of ridicule had he abstained on a policy which he was himself presenting.

Liberal Democrat pressures against the coalition could prove particularly strong in Scotland, where the unpopularity of the Scottish Conservatives might prove contagious, so that association with them causes electoral damage to the

---

[55] Wilson (n 2) 376.
[56] Bernard Wasserstein, *Herbert Samuel: A Political Life* (Clarendon Press, 1992) 360.

Liberal Democrats. Elections to the Scottish Parliament in 2011 could nevertheless result in a Liberal Democrat coalition with Labour, as occurred between 1999 and 2007. Liberal Democrats are insouciant about different coalitions at different levels of government, and these are indeed frequent in Germany. But a Liberal Democrat/Labour government in Scotland could put pressure on Liberal Democrat MPs representing Scottish seats at Westminster to end the coalition.

The history of previous coalitions tends to confirm Disraeli's view that 'England does not love coalitions', though the experience of devolution shows that they may be loved more in Scotland and Wales. Coalitions can be cohesive and enjoy a solid basis in wartime – as with the Lloyd George coalition between 1916 and 1918 and the Churchill coalition from 1940 to 1945 – since there is an overriding national purpose until the war ends. In peacetime, however, history shows that 'they tend to be uneasy, nervous and insecure after the situation which produced them has been solved or has gone away'.[57] It is for this reason that, as Disraeli foresaw, although coalitions might enjoy some triumphs, 'their triumph has been brief'. Many Liberal Democrats would argue that we are now entering an era of coalition government under quite different conditions from those that attended the formation of earlier coalitions. That may indeed be the case. It remains to be seen, however, whether experience of coalition government under the new conditions of the twenty-first century will serve further to confirm Disraeli's famous aphorism or to refute it.

[57] Robert Blake, '1783–1902' in Butler (n 28) 24.

5

Electoral Reform and the Alternative Vote

I. REDUCING THE NUMBER OF MPS

A CCORDING TO THE Coalition Agreement, 'Our political system is broken. We urgently need fundamental political reform, including a referendum on electoral reform, much greater co-operation across party lines, and change to our political system to make it far more transparent and accountable.' This belief that the political system is 'broken' is in large part a reaction to revelations of the abuse of expenses of 2009. In the Third Reading debate on the Parliamentary Constituencies and Voting Bill, the Deputy Prime Minister, Nick Clegg, declared: 'I am sure I do not need to remind Members of the damage that was done by the expenses scandal, which lifted the lid on a culture of secrecy, arrogance and remoteness, right at the heart of the democracy. The coalition Government are determined to turn the page on that political culture and give people a political system they can trust.'[1]

In July 2010, the government published two major bills providing for constitutional change with regard to House of Commons elections. In addition it committed itself to a wholly or mainly directly elected House of Lords, which is discussed in Chapter 7; a Localism bill, decentralising power and redistributing it to local authorities and local communities; and a European Union bill, requiring a referendum before any further treaty amendments or significant transfers of power to the European Union would be ratified, and reiterating that Parliament was sovereign.

Of the two major constitutional reform bills, the first, the Fixed-Term Parliaments Bill, proposed fixed parliamentary terms of five years, and is discussed in Chapter 6. The second, the Parliamentary Voting System and Constituencies Bill, provided for three reforms. They were:

a. a reduction in the number of MPs from 650 to a fixed number of 600;

b. a new set of rules to be used by the Boundary Commissions to ensure greater equalisation of constituency boundaries, and more frequent boundary reviews; and

c. a referendum on the alternative vote method of election to the House of Commons, to be held on the first Thursday of May in 2011.

[1] *Hansard* HC col 802 (2 November 2010).

This bill represented a compromise between the two parties in the coalition. The Conservatives were against any change in the electoral system. But they were prepared to accept a referendum on the alternative vote, though not proportional representation, provided that they could campaign for a 'No' vote and that provision was made for equalising constituency boundaries, so reducing the bias against them in the electoral system. The Liberal Democrats sought a referendum on proportional representation, but, that being unattainable because of Conservative hostility, they were prepared to settle for the alternative vote.

A reduction in the number of MPs had, however, been proposed in both the Conservative and Liberal Democrat election manifestoes. This was a reaction to the expenses scandal of 2009. Because MPs were abusing the system, it was felt that the fewer of them there were, the better. In addition, reducing the number of MPs would help to save public money. The Conservatives proposed in their election manifesto a reduction by 10% to 585 MPs, arguing that Britain had one of the largest legislatures in the democratic world – 650 MPs, as compared, for example, with just 440 members of Congress in the United States and 545 in the lower house in India. The Liberal Democrats had proposed a reduction to 500, but in the context of the introduction of proportional representation. The Coalition Agreement gave no specific figure but declared that there should be fewer and more equal sized constituencies. It is not clear how the proposal to reduce the number of MPs to precisely 600 was arrived at. The Deputy Leader of the House, David Heath, declared, '[t]he figure is not magical; it is simply an arbitrary figure that reduces the size of the House in a way that I believe is consistent with the public mood and the needs of this House'.[2] The number of parliamentary constituencies will, however, remain capped at this figure, and this prompted opposition spokesmen to speak of a tyranny of arithmetic.

In 1950 the House of Commons contained 625 MPs. By 2010 it had grown to 650 MPs, despite the existence of the devolved bodies, which were not only responsible for most of the matters which had previously been the responsibility of the Secretaries of State for Scotland and Wales – they had also taken over many of the constituency responsibilities of Scottish and Welsh MPs. Nevertheless, the idea of reducing the number of MPs seems a perverse reaction to the expenses scandal. Population growth and the lowering of the voting age to 18 means that the average MP represents a far larger constituency today than in 1950. In 1950 the total electorate was 34,412,255. By 2005 it had grown to 45,610,369, an increase of around 30%. In 1945 the average MP represented a constituency of around 66,000; today the figure is around 96,000; following the reduction it will be around 105,000 – a 60% increase since 1945. There will therefore be a considerable increase in the workload of MPs. Moreover, constituents today are far more demanding of their MP than they were 60 years ago in an era of deference, when many MPs visited their constituency only infrequently. In the 1930s, one MP's 'conscientious approach to local interests in Lanark puzzled Collins

---

[2] *Hansard* HC col 1056 (20 October 2010).

[Sir Godfrey Collins, Secretary of State for Scotland, 1932–36]'. Asked how often he visited his constituency in Greenock, Collins replied, 'Five times in thirty years.'[3] Clement Attlee refused to conduct a constituency surgery on the ground that it dealt with local matters, whereas his task was to concern himself with matters of high policy at Westminster. In the 1950s, Hugh Gaitskell, Shadow Chancellor and then Leader of the Opposition, received just 20 letters a month from constituents. One of his colleagues, Charles Pannell, the MP for West Leeds, never held a constituency surgery at all.[4] It is unlikely that there are any MPs who do not hold constituency surgeries today. They have become, in effect, ombudsmen for their constituents, acting as intermediaries in their dealings with an increasingly complex administrative structure. Therefore, any reduction in the number of MPs could lead to greater alienation amongst those who find themselves lost amidst the thickets of modern bureaucracy.

If there are fewer MPs, but the number of ministers remains the same, then legislative scrutiny will be weaker. Even without the proposed reduction in the number of MPs, there would be a strong case for reducing the statutory maximum number of ministers entitled to sit and vote in the House of Commons. In 1900, when Britain ruled an Empire covering a quarter of the world, there were just 60 ministers. By 1950 this had increased to 81, and by January 2010, 119. While the Cabinet increased only from 19 in 1900 to 23 in 2010, the number of ministers below Cabinet rank increased from 41 in 1900 to 96 in 2010. Over a quarter of Conservative and Liberal Democrat MPs were ministers. A further 32 MPs were Parliamentary Private Secretaries, placemen, required always to support the government. The average cost of each minister, including secretaries, offices etc, is apparently around £500,000, as well as 'tying down a lot of civil service resources'.[5] The former Cabinet Secretary, Lord Turnbull, told the Commons Public Administration Committee in January 2010 that the number of ministers could be reduced by 50%. Chris Mullin, a former MP, wrote in his diaries of his time as a junior minister in the Department for Environment, Transport and the Regions: 'My existence is now [after four months as a minister] almost entirely pointless . . . [W]ith hand on heart I can say that I have less influence now over government policy than at any time in the last eight years. The only possible excuse for doing this is the hope that it will lead to something better.'[6] In addition to ministers on the government side, there are a roughly equivalent number of MPs on the Opposition Front Bench who are bound by the collective responsibility of decisions made by the official Opposition. The payroll vote, the vote of Disraeli's Tadpoles and Tapers, has become far too high. In consequence, there are too few MPs able to speak their minds.

[3] DR Thorpe, *Alec Douglas-Home* (Sinclair Stevenson, 1996) 54. I am grateful to Richard Thorpe for this reference.

[4] Philip M Williams, *Hugh Gaitskell* (Jonathan Cape, 1979) 380; Brian Brivati, *Hugh Gaitskell* (Richard Cohen, 1996) 158.

[5] House of Commons Public Administration Select Committee, *Too Many Ministers?*, 9th Report 2009–10, HC 457, para 16.

[6] Chris Mullin, *A View from the Foothills: The Diaries of Chris Mullin* (Profile Books, 2009) 43–44.

In a speech to the Institute for Government in January 2010, Nick Clegg proposed that, in addition to a reduction in the number of MPs to 500, the number of ministers in both houses should be cut to 73. Nevertheless, on 25 October 2010, the coalition government resisted an amendment to reduce the statutory maximum number of MPs in the Commons under the House of Commons Disqualification Act and the Ministerial and Other Salaries Act, both of 1975, from 95 to 87, directly reflecting the percentage reduction in the number of MPs. The amendment was supported by just 22 Conservatives and one Liberal Democrat. But David Heath, Deputy Leader of the House of Commons, did declare, in resisting the amendment, that 'it is likely that at some stage in the future we will reduce the number of Ministers'.[7]

II. MORE FREQUENT BOUNDARY REVIEWS

The second change proposed by the coalition and embodied in the Parliamentary Voting System and Constituencies Act proposes new rules to be used by the Boundary Commissions. The current rules, originally established in 1944 in the House of Commons (Redistribution of Seats) Act, and subsequently amended and consolidated in various later Acts of Parliament, provide for Boundary Commissions for England, Scotland, Wales and Northern Ireland. Commissioners are required to define an electoral quota for their territory by dividing the total number of electors by the number of constituencies. Largely for historical reasons, there is a different electoral quota for each of the four territories in the United Kingdom. In 2010 the average constituency electorate in each of the four territories was:

England	71,882
Scotland	65,498
Northern Ireland	63,101
Wales	56,545

Once the Commissioners have defined a quota, they are then required to make recommendations for constituency boundaries according to a complex set of rules, which, so some have argued, are in fact contradictory. The rules, it has been said, are 'ambiguous and unclear, and so invite inconsistency in treatment'.[8] At a meeting at the Electoral Reform Society on 4 November 2010, Professor Ron Johnston, the country's leading authority on the Boundary Commissions, pronounced that they operated on the basis of 'a ragbag of inconsistent rules'. Equality of constituencies is just one of these rules: rule 5 declares that '[t]he electorate of any constituency shall be as near the electoral quota as is practicable', but

---

[7] *Hansard* HC col 129 (25 October 2010).

[8] DJ Rossiter, RJ Johnston and CJ Pattie, *The Boundary Commissions: Redrawing the UK's Map of Parliamentary Constituencies* (Manchester University Press, 1999) 400. This book gives an exhaustive account of the system for redrawing constituency boundaries before 2010.

this rule is not given primacy. There are in consequence large local variations in constituency size. Once the Commissions have published their conclusions, there is provision for a public inquiry if a local authority or more than 100 electors object to a particular recommendation. The process is time-consuming, and the last boundary review in England took seven years to complete. In consequence, even after a boundary review, constituency sizes fail to register recent population changes. In 2010, for example, the electoral register was based on figures from the year 2000. Because population movement is in general from Labour-voting inner cities to the Conservative-voting rural areas and the more marginal suburbs, deficiencies in the boundary review process work to the disadvantage of the Conservatives.[9]

The Parliamentary Voting System and Constituencies Act seeks to secure equal constituencies, an ideal first put forward by the Chartists nearly 200 years ago. It provides that, instead of quotas for the four territories of the United Kingdom, there will be a single quota for the whole country, and primacy will be given to the rule that every constituency must have an electorate within just 5% of the quota.[10] Public inquiries are to be abolished, but the period of public consultation is to be extended from four to 12 weeks. The first review under the rules will be completed by October 2013, which is 18 months before the end of the 2010 parliament and the proposed date of the next general election. But the review will be based on the December 2010 electoral roll, and therefore, if the next election is held in 2015, the boundaries will still be over four years out of date. Subsequent reviews are to be completed at five-year intervals, so that each review will occur 18 months before the date of the election if Parliament runs its full term.

There can be no obvious objection to the Act on grounds of equity. But the more frequent boundary reviews are likely to disadvantage small parties which depend upon local connections or an incumbency effect, as well as independents, such as Dr Richard Taylor, MP for Wyre Forest between 2001 and 2010, who based his electoral campaign on the need to save a local hospital in Kidderminster threatened with closure. 'Constituencies', James Callaghan declared, as Home Secretary in 1969, 'are not merely areas bounded by a line on a map; they are living communities with a unity, a history and a personality of their own.'[11] The old rules provided for community feeling; the new ones give primacy to the aim of numerical equality. But it may be that voters would prefer to be under-represented rather than abandoning strong community ties in the interests of 'the tyranny of arithmetic'. An opposition spokesman, Chris Bryant, has argued that '[a] system that delivers mathematical perfection may be aseptically clean, and please the tidy utilitarian and the centralist, but it will in countless cases leave voters on the

---

[9] Michael Balinski, Ron Johnston, Iain McLean and Peyton Young, *Drawing a New Constituency Map for the United Kingdom: The Parliamentary Voting System and Constituencies Bill* (British Academy Policy Centre, 2010) 29. These paragraphs are based on this valuable monograph.

[10] With the exception of the Orkney and Shetland Islands and Comhairle nan Eilean Siar (the Western Isles), and the Isle of Wight.

[11] *Hansard* HC col 742 (19 June 1969).

wrong side of a river, a mountain, a county or ward boundary, or cultural divide, and, thereby fail the fundamental tests that we should be setting'.[12] A Liberal Democrat MP, Andrew George, representing a Cornish constituency, predicted that '[w]hen people wake up to the full reality of the way the boundaries are to be divided, they will understand that it will result in the effective pasteurization of parliamentary constituencies. They will be homogenized and we will see the denigration of place, the denigration of identity and the promotion of placelessness and bland uniformity.'[13] Frequent boundary reviews could mean that MPs will be less accountable to voters if the boundaries of their constituencies alter every five years. This is in a sense ironic, in that one defence of the first past the post system in single-member constituencies is that it makes possible a close relationship between the MP and his or her constituency. In the past, there was an emphasis on stability and continuity rather than on frequent boundary changes. But in the future, constituencies are likely to become more artificial constructs. This may harm the Liberal Democrats, who have often campaigned on community politics, and other parties, such as the nationalists, which rely on local campaigning, and on local tactical voting and the local standing of their MPs as much as their national appeal to win seats. The effect of the new provisions for boundary reviews may, therefore, counteract some of the social changes of recent years and help to entrench the two major parties against their competitors.[14]

One advantage of systems of proportional representation such as the single transferable vote, or the system recommended by the Jenkins Commission for proportional representation based on county constituencies, is that constituencies, which are multi-member, can be based on real geographical units, namely counties. Then, when there are movements of population, instead of altering the boundaries, one simply alters the number of members representing the constituency. Thus, with a reduction of population, a five-member county constituency would become a four-member constituency; with an increase, it would become a six-member constituency.

The regular and more frequent boundary reviews will only achieve the aim of equalising constituencies if the electoral register is efficient. If the register does not include all those eligible and if the inefficiencies are not random but skewed towards one particular type of constituency, then that type of constituency will find itself under-represented. Although every elector is legally required to ensure that her name is on the register, the Electoral Commission has calculated that the register is only around 90% efficient, and that around three million people who ought to be on it, and indeed are legally required to ensure that they are on it, are in fact excluded. These absent names comprise primarily the young, students, and members of ethnic minorities, who are more likely to live in inner city and Labour voting constituencies than in the countryside. In its inner city case studies, the Commission found that 56% of 17–24 year olds, 49% of private sector tenants

[12] *Hansard* HC col 657 (1 November 2010).
[13] ibid, col 680.
[14] I owe this point to Michael Steed.

and 31% of black and minority ethnic British residents were not registered. On the Commission's figures, the number of missing voters exceeded the majority of the sitting MP in 160 seats. The Commission found that the lowest rates of completeness and accuracy of the register were in two densely populated areas, chosen as case studies, with highly mobile populations – Lambeth and the city of Glasgow – where the report suggested that there were around 100,000 unregistered voters. That would mean that Glasgow would be entitled to six constituencies, rather than the five that they would be given on the numbers in the current register. Indeed, the Commission took the view that there could be widening local and regional variations in registration levels. Until the register becomes more efficient, therefore, there will be fewer inner city constituencies than there ought to be, and the Labour Party will be disadvantaged as a result.[15] The government has announced proposals to speed up individual registration to deal with the problem of under-registration and improve the system, but, at the time of writing, these had not been published.

* * *

We have already seen that it took more votes to elect a Conservative MP than it did to elect a Labour MP. The electorate in seats won by Labour is on average smaller than the electorate in seats won by the Conservatives. The figures for 2010 were:

Labour	69,145
Conservatives	73,031
Liberal Democrats	69,610

The gap had been even larger in 2001 and 2005. What are the reasons for this?

The first reason is that Wales is over-represented and Scotland slightly over-represented at Westminster as compared with England. Since Labour is by far the strongest party in Scotland and Wales, this over-representation benefits Labour. The electoral quotas for Wales and Scotland are determined independently of that for England. Wales has been over-represented in relation to England relative to her share of the United Kingdom electorate since 1945, and this probably yields around four seats to Labour. Scotland was similarly over-represented until it was given legislative devolution in the 1998 Scotland Act, when her representation was reduced to the English level.[16] Even so, as we have seen, Scotland remains slightly over-represented.

The second reason for the gap is that the average size of constituencies in England represented by Conservative MPs is larger than the average size of those represented by Labour MPs, precisely because the regular periodic boundary

---

[15] Electoral Commission, *The Completeness and Accuracy of Electoral Registers in Great Britain*, March 2010.

[16] Northern Ireland was deliberately *under*-represented at Westminster during the first period of devolution from 1920 to 1972, but this precedent was not repeated in the case of Scotland.

reviews have failed to keep up with population movements. Between 2001 and 2005, for example, the electorate grew by around 1,000 votes in the average Conservative constituency but fell by around 500 in the average Labour one. The figures on p 87 show that, in 2010, the average size of constituencies won by the Conservatives had 3,886 more names on the electoral register than the average Labour constituency.

In 2010 this difference in constituency electorates was worth 18 seats to Labour out of the total of the 54 extra seats that Labour would have won if its vote had been equal to that of the Conservatives. This, however, means that variations in electorate size cannot be used to explain the whole of the total bias to the Conservatives. Such variations 'have contributed no more than one-third of the total bias'.[17] What are the other reasons for the bias?

There are three other factors – factors which cannot be remedied by any redistribution of constituencies, however speedy and efficient. The first is that turnout is higher in Conservative than in Labour constituencies – 68.4% as compared to 61.1% in 2010. On average, 4,161 more voters turn out in a Conservative constituency than in a Labour one. If one adds this to the 3,886 more names on the electoral register in Conservative constituencies, differential turnout means that the average Conservative constituency contains 8,047 more voters than the average Labour one. Differential turnout probably accounts for 32 of the 54 seats that Labour would have won if its vote had been equal to that of the Conservatives.

A second factor that has disadvantaged the Conservatives in recent elections, though not in 2010, is that the Labour vote was more concentrated than the Conservative vote and therefore better distributed from the point of view of winning seats. The Liberal Democrat vote is the least concentrated of the three major parties, though its vote was more concentrated in 2010 than it was in 1983 when for 25% – a quarter – of the vote, it won just 23 out of 650 seats. In elections before 2010, Labour won more seats than the Conservatives by narrow majorities and wasted fewer votes building up large majorities in safe seats or coming a good second. Therefore it won a larger number of seats than the Conservatives for any given share of the vote. In 2010, for purely contingent reasons, there seems to have been no geographical effect of this sort between the major parties.

The third factor is the differential effect of tactical voting. In 2010, Labour voters proved more willing to vote Liberal Democrat in Conservative/Liberal Democrat marginals so as to defeat the Conservatives, than Conservative voters were to defeat Labour in Labour/Liberal Democrat marginals. This differential effect probably cost the Conservatives another four seats, bringing the total to 54.

The bias against the Conservatives, therefore, does not arise solely, or even primarily, from constituency malapportionment, but from three other factors – differential turnout, differential concentration of the vote, and the differential effects of tactical voting. These effects cannot be corrected by any boundary review, however efficient.

---

[17] Balinski et al (n 9) 30–31.

Under the first past the post electoral system, the number of seats a party wins will depend not only upon how many votes it receives, but also upon how that vote is distributed geographically. A party whose vote is more concentrated will in general win more seats for a given share of the vote than a party whose vote is more evenly spread. This geographical bias is the Achilles' heel of the first past the post electoral system. It is also the Achilles' heel of any alternative single-member constituency system such as the alternative vote, the system with which the Liberal Democrats hope to replace first past the post, and the fundamental reason why, as we shall see, the alternative vote does not yield proportional representation.

Electoral bias cannot be eliminated by reform of the rules under which the Boundary Commissions operate. Supporters of the reform exaggerate its likely benefits. The bias can be removed only by introducing a proportional electoral system.

III. THE REFERENDUM ON THE ALTERNATIVE VOTE

In 2010, the Conservative election manifesto promised to maintain the first past the post system, while the Liberal Democrat manifesto continued the party's long-time advocacy of proportional representation, and the Labour manifesto promised a referendum on the alternative vote. Indeed, clauses on the holding of a referendum on the alternative vote had been added to the Labour government's Constitutional Reform and Governance Bill early in 2010, but the reform was not enacted due to lack of parliamentary time.

The Coalition Agreement promised a referendum on the alternative vote. The bill providing for this would be made subject to the whip of both parties, but there would be an 'agreement to differ' on the proposal itself during the referendum campaign. The referendum question will be:

> Do you want the United Kingdom to adopt the 'alternative vote' system instead of the current 'first past the post' system for electing Members of Parliament to the House of Commons?

The referendum will be decided by a simple majority.

The referendum will, however, in contrast with the proposal of the Labour Party, both in its Constitutional Reform and Governance Bill and in its manifesto, be a binding referendum. Labour had proposed a consultative pre-legislative referendum. If the referendum yielded a sufficient majority on a reasonable turnout – and what constituted 'sufficient' and 'reasonable' would be for Parliament to decide – then it would legislate for the alternative vote. The coalition, by contrast, decided upon a binding post-legislative referendum. Legislation providing for the alternative vote will be passed before the referendum. The alternative vote will come into force for the next election unless it is defeated in the referendum, so long as an order has been introduced to initiate the new boundary review equalising constituencies, so that the Conservatives will be compensated for any loss of seats they might suffer following introduction of the alternative vote. Parliament will not be able to reconsider following the referendum. This of course makes it possible for the alternative vote to be introduced if the referendum yields a small majority for it on a low turnout. If turnout is 24% with 13.5% voting 'Yes' and 12.5% voting 'No', the alternative vote will be introduced. Problems might also ensue if, in what is now a multinational country, the majority in Scotland were different from that in England. It would be possible, therefore, for a change in the electoral system to be brought about by a small majority on a low turnout in the referendum.[18]

The referendum in May 2011 will be Britain's first binding referendum. All previous referendums have been advisory, except for the devolution referendums of 1979. These had contained a threshold: in addition to a majority of those voting, 40% of the electorate were required to vote 'Yes' for devolution to come into effect. If these two conditions were satisfied, the outcome would bind Parliament. If, however, the 40% threshold was not achieved, as indeed proved to be the case, the legislation would return to the Commons for further consideration. So, with a 'Yes' vote the referendums would have been binding; with a 'No' vote they were consultative.

The 2011 referendum will be Britain's second national referendum. The first, held in 1975, was on whether Britain should remain in the European Community on the terms renegotiated by the Labour government. There have also, of course, been a number of sub-national referendums on devolution as well as various local referendums.[19] The 2011 referendum is due to be held on 5 May, the first Thursday in May, the same day as English local elections and elections for the devolved bodies in Scotland and Wales. It has been argued that this might prejudice voters in favour of change, since voters in Scotland and Wales will be using a system of proportional representation, not first past the post.[20] In its Twelfth Report, *Referendums in the United Kingdom*, the House of Lords Select Committee on the Constitution declared that 'there should be a presumption against holding referendums on the same day as elections but . . . this should be judged on a case-by-case basis by the Electoral Commission'.[21]

In the referendum, the likelihood is that most Liberal Democrats will support the change, while most Conservatives will oppose it. Although Labour proposed the change in its election manifesto, the party could prove less enthusiastic for it when it is being proposed by its political opponents. The new leader of the Labour Party, Ed Miliband, has indicated that he will vote 'Yes' in the referendum, but will not campaign for change. Perhaps the outcome will depend upon the extent to which Labour activists are in fact willing to campaign for change.

---

[18] It is perhaps ironic that the coalition government has also proposed a European Union bill, one of whose sections declares that Parliament is sovereign! It is not clear how this declaration is compatible with a provision for a binding referendum.

[19] For a discussion of the referendum in Britain see Vernon Bogdanor, *The New British Constitution* (Hart Publishing, 2009) ch 7.

[20] See, for example, the view of David Owen in Andrew Duff (ed), *Making the Difference: Essays in Honour of Shirley Williams* (Biteback, 2010) 59.

[21] Referendums in the United Kingdom, 2009–10, HL 99, recommendation 145.

It is sometimes thought that proposals for electoral reform require all-party support. Indeed, in a research paper published in 2007, the House of Commons Library claimed that there is a 'constitutional convention that changes to the electoral system should be agreed as far as possible on an all-party basis'. Somewhat confusingly, it went on to declare in the next sentence, 'This convention is not universally observed.'[22] There is in fact no warrant for assuming that such a convention existed during the twentieth century. In 1931, for example, the second Labour government, a minority government, introduced a bill providing for the alternative vote, which was strongly opposed by the Conservatives and by the House of Lords, which duly wrecked it. But, to prevent a government manipulating the electoral system for partisan reasons, it has come to be accepted that the electoral system should not be changed without a referendum. In 1997, Tony Blair indicated that any proposal for change recommended by the Jenkins Commission on Electoral Reform would have to be endorsed by the electorate in a referendum.

The proposal for a referendum on the alternative vote system was the product of a deal between the Conservatives and the Liberal Democrats, a deal without which the coalition would almost certainly not have been possible. The alternative vote is not the preferred choice of either party. The Liberal Democrats would prefer proportional representation, and indeed, during the election campaign, Nick Clegg denounced the alternative vote as 'a miserable little compromise', though he did admit that the alternative vote would be 'a baby step in the right direction – only because nothing can be worse than the status quo'.[23] The Conservatives, by contrast, believe that first past the post should remain. The only party to have proposed a referendum on the alternative vote in its election manifesto was, ironically, Labour. This was the first occasion since the war that a governing party specifically proposed electoral reform, and it was in fact in the context of Labour's proposal, not a proposal from the Conservatives, that Clegg made his comment concerning the 'miserable little compromise'.

If introduced, the alternative vote will be the sixth electoral system in operation in Britain. The others, in addition to first past the post, are:

- The supplementary vote, by which the voter can indicate two choices rather than one as under first past the post. This system is used for mayoral elections, including the London mayoral election.
- The additional member system of proportional representation. This system is used to elect the Scottish Parliament, the National Assembly of Wales and the London Assembly.
- The regional list system of proportional representation. This system is used to elect members of the European Parliament, except in Northern Ireland.

[22] House of Commons Library, Standard Note: *Speaker's Conference*, SN/PC/4426, 12 September 2007, p 1.

[23] 'I Want to Push This All the Way, Declares Clegg', *The Independent*, 22 April 2010. David Owen has suggested that many Liberal Democrat supporters will support a 'Yes' vote 'holding their noses', since they would much prefer proportional representation (Owen (n 20) 60).

- The single transferable vote system of proportional representation. This system is used for all elections in Northern Ireland, except elections to the House of Commons, and for elections to Scottish local authorities.

The purpose of putting a proposal to the people through referendum is to enable the people to make a choice. But the choice that the people are being given is one already pre-cooked by the two parties to the coalition. It may not be the choice that the people themselves would want to make, given the opportunity. David Owen has argued that the proposal for a referendum on the alternative vote was an 'inter-party fix agreed as part of the coalition agreement', and that Parliament should not 'feel pre-empted' by it.[24] There is a striking contrast between the way in which reform of the electoral system has come onto the political agenda in Britain, and the procedure adopted by New Zealand, another Westminster system without a codified constitution. In New Zealand, reform was preceded by a Royal Commission of Inquiry into the Electoral System, and by a two-stage referendum process in 1992 and 1993, the purpose of which was on account of 'the wide diversity of public opinion on this issue', to give 'as far as possible . . . a range of options for the public to choose from'.[25]

The first stage of the referendum process, held in 1992, asked two questions. The first was:

> Should the current first past the post system be retained?

The second was:

> Regardless of how you voted under Part A, if there was a change to another voting system, which voting system would you choose?
>
> I would choose the **Mixed Member Proportional** system (MPP)
> I would choose the **Preferential Voting** system (PV)
> I would choose the **Single Transferable Vote** system (STV)
> I would choose the **Supplementary Member** system (SM)

The Mixed Member Proportional system is the system known in Britain as the Additional Member system, as used in elections to the devolved bodies in Scotland and Wales and the London Assembly. It had been recommended for adoption in New Zealand by the Royal Commission. The Preferential Voting system is the alternative vote. The supplementary member system is *not* the system known in Britain as the supplementary vote, which is used to elect the mayor of London and for other mayoral elections, but a system which adds to first past the post various supplementary seats so as to provide a greater measure of proportionality.[26]

On a turnout of 53.9%, 84.7% voted for change, and just 15.3% voted to retain first past the post. On the second question, voting was as follows.

---

[24] Owen (n 20) 60.

[25] Ryan Malone, *Rebalancing the Constitution: The Challenge of Government Law-Making under MMP* (Institute of Policy Studies, Wellington, 2008) 40n.

[26] More detailed descriptions of these systems can be found in, for example, Vernon Bogdanor, *Power and the People: A Guide to Constitutional Reform* (Gollancz, 1997).

	% vote
Mixed Member Proportional	70.5
Single Transferable Vote	17.4
Preferential Vote	6.6
Supplementary Member	5.5

It is interesting to note that the preferential vote, which is being offered to British voters in the referendum in May 2011 as the alternative vote, secured the support of just 6.6% of the voters in New Zealand.

This first referendum was advisory. But the government was committed to putting the preferred alternative in this first referendum, ie Mixed Member Proportional, to a binding second referendum against first past the post. The second referendum took place on the day of the 1993 general election. Turnout as a result was higher, 82.6%, and the result of the referendum was a victory for the Mixed Member Proportional system, which received 53.9% of the vote, with 46.1% voting for first past the post. This system was therefore introduced for the general election of 1996.

In 1993, voters were promised a review after two elections. That was delayed until, in 2008, New Zealand's National Party promised another two-stage multi-option referendum. This will in a sense be a mirror image of the referendums held in 1992 and 1993. The only difference is that this time both referendums will be held on the same day as general elections to maximise turnout; and although the New Zealand Prime Minister and leader of the National Party, John Key, favours change, it is not, at the time of writing, wholly clear what change he favours since he does not, apparently, seek a return to first past the post.

The first question in the first referendum will ask voters whether they wish to remain with the Multi-Member Proportional system or whether they wish to alter it. The second question will offer four alternatives to voters, including first past the post. This first referendum is advisory, but, if a majority of voters opt for change, the government has promised to hold a second binding referendum on the same day as the 2014 general election, asking voters to choose between Mixed Member Proportional and the preferred alternative selected in 2011.

The New Zealand procedure has the advantage over that adopted in Britain of being both more measured, due to the lengthy investigation of the issue by a Royal Commission, and also more democratic, thanks to the multi-option referendum. But, in addition, the Citizens Initiated Referenda Act of 1993 enables New Zealanders to *require* the government to hold an advisory referendum if a petition secures the signatures of 10% of all eligible voters. This means that electors could insist that they had the chance of voting on a proportional system even if the government sought to deny them that option. There is no provision for a citizen-initiated referendum in Britain. So, although it is probable that most of those in Britain who favour electoral reform would prefer a system of proportional representation to the alternative vote, by contrast with New Zealanders, they will not be given the choice. The referendum option is to be restricted to that favoured by the politicians.

On 12 October 2010, Caroline Lucas, the Green Party MP, proposed an amendment in the Commons to the Parliamentary Voting Systems and Constituencies Bill, providing that there should be, as there had been in New Zealand, an option in the referendum allowing voters to express a preference for proportional systems. The original question contained in the bill read:

> Do you want the United Kingdom to adopt the 'alternative vote' system instead of the current 'first past the post' system for electing Members of Parliament to the House of Commons?

Ms Lucas proposed to replace this with the following questions:

(1) Do you want to change the current 'first past the post' system for electing Members of Parliament to the House of Commons?
(2) If there were a change, list your order of preference, 1,2,3, for the United Kingdom to adopt:
    (a) The 'alternative vote' system
    (b) The 'additional member' system
    (c) The 'single transferable vote' system with multi-member constituencies

During the debate, Ms Lucas declared that it was 'contradictory for the coalition to be talking about electoral reform while seeking to offer little more than a Hobson's choice, between the alternative vote and first past the post'.[27] A YouGov poll commissioned by the Constitution Society in September 2010 showed that on the whole the public agreed with Caroline Lucas. Only 14% believed that Parliament should set the choice in the referendum. 40% of those surveyed wanted a wider choice, while 32% did not. Of those who favoured the alternative vote, 59% wanted a wider choice; of those opposed to the alternative vote, only 32% wanted a wider choice.[28] The implication is that support for a change from first past the post is not necessarily to be understood as support for the alternative vote.

Caroline Lucas's amendment was defeated by 346 votes to 17. Before the general election, the Liberal Democrats had tabled an amendment to Gordon Brown's Constitutional Reform and Governance Bill, substituting the single transferable vote for the alternative vote; and, in their election manifesto, they had declared that they would introduce 'a fair, more proportional voting system for MPs. Our preferred Single Transferable Vote system gives people the choice between candidates as well as parties.' Despite this manifesto commitment, 54 of the 57 Liberal Democrat MPs voted against Ms Lucas's amendment, and one acted as a teller for the Noes. No Liberal Democrat MP voted for it, although three Conservatives voted against their party and in favour of the amendment. The Liberal Democrats

---

[27] *Hansard* HC col 280 (12 October 2010).
[28] The poll also showed, as one might expect, considerable lack of knowledge of electoral systems. Only 33% claimed to understand how the alternative vote works, while 32% had never heard of it.

felt committed by the Coalition Agreement to vote against the amendment, since, had it been passed, the Conservatives, bitterly opposed to proportional representation, would have withdrawn their support for a referendum. The rejection of proportional representation, therefore, was a consequence of the coalition with the Conservatives. Had there been a rainbow coalition with Labour, by contrast, there is some chance that a multi-option referendum, including proportional representation, would have been possible. As it was, the two parties to the coalition, one of which proclaims its belief in first past the post, the other its belief in proportional representation, propose a referendum on an electoral system in which neither of them believe and which neither of them supported during the election campaign.

IV. THE WORKING OF THE ALTERNATIVE VOTE

The alternative vote is a system of preferential voting in single-member constituencies. Instead of putting an 'X' on the ballot paper, the voter marks the paper with a '1' by the most favoured candidate, a '2' by the next favoured candidate, and so on. If a candidate has an absolute majority of first preference votes, he or she is elected. But, if no candidate has won an absolute majority of first preference votes, then the candidate at the bottom of the poll is eliminated and second preferences are redistributed. The process continues until one candidate has an absolute majority of the votes. This system is used in just three nations for national elections – Australia, Fiji and, since 2007, Papua New Guinea.

The following example of how the system might work is taken from the Oxford West and Abingdon constituency in the 2010 general election, where the result was as follows:

	Votes	% vote
Nicola Blackwood, Conservative	23,906	42.3
Evan Harris, Liberal Democrat	23,730	42.0
Richard Stevens, Labour	5,999	10.6
Paul Williams, UK Independence Party	1,518	2.7
Chris Goodall, Green	1,184	2.1
Keith Mann, Animal Protection Party	176	0.3

The Conservatives won the seat with a majority of 176. But, under the alternative vote, the outcome might have been different. With no candidate achieving 50% of the vote, the candidate with the fewest votes, Keith Mann, would have been eliminated. Let us assume that, of the 176 votes cast for him, 100 of the second preferences had gone to the Green candidate, and that the other 76 would have indicated no second preference. Chris Goodall would then have been eliminated. Let us assume that, of his 1,284 votes, including those transferred from Keith Mann, 500 had gone to the Liberal Democrat, 200 to Labour, with the rest indicating no further preference. The UK Independence Party candidate, Paul

Williams, would have been the next to be eliminated. Let us assume that 1,000 of his votes were transferred to the Conservatives, with the remainder indicating no further preference. The Labour candidate, Richard Stevens, would then have been eliminated. Let us assume that 3,000 of his next preferences would have been given to the Liberal Democrats, with the other 3,199 (5,999 first preferences plus 200 transfers from the Green candidate) indicating no further preference. Then the outcome would have been:

- Nicola Blackwood, Conservative, 24,906 (23,906 first preferences plus 1,000 transfers from the UKIP candidate)
- Evan Harris, Liberal Democrat 27,230 (23,730 first preferences plus 500 transfers from the Green candidate, and 3,000 from the Labour candidate)

Evan Harris would, on these not implausible assumptions, have been elected, thanks largely to transfers from Labour.

The purpose of the alternative vote is to avoid the anomaly by which a candidate can win a constituency on a minority of the vote. The number of MPs elected on a minority vote has increased dramatically since the 1950s when, with the Liberal Party and other small parties being weak and contesting only a minority of constituencies, the majority of constituencies were contested only by Labour and the Conservatives. In 1951, for example, just 39 MPs out of 625 were elected on a minority vote; in 1955 the figure was just 37 out of 630, and in 1959 just 80 out of 630 were elected on such a vote.[29] In recent years, however, when no constituency has been contested by just two candidates – in 2010, there was an average of seven candidates in every constituency – the figures have been much larger. Indeed, in the last three general elections, over 50% of MPs were elected on a minority vote; and in 2005 and 2010 that figure stood at around two-thirds. The figures for the last three general elections are as follows:

2001: 333 out of 659 seats
2005: 429 out of 646 seats
2010: 433 out of 650 seats[30]

The figure of 433 elected on a minority vote is the largest since the war.

It is sometimes said that the alternative vote *ensures* that every MP is elected by a majority of his or her constituents. But that is so only if every voter marks all preferences. If voters choose instead to 'plump' for just one or two candidates, then an MP can still be elected on a minority vote. The greater the degree of plumping, the more an alternative vote election turns into a first past the post election. In the limiting case, where every voter marks just one preference, introduction of the alternative vote makes no difference at all. In Australia, where the alternative vote is in operation for elections to the lower house, and voting is compulsory, a voter is *required* to list all available preferences for his or her vote to

---

[29] Colin Rallings and Michael Thrasher, *British Electoral Facts, 1832–1999* (Ashgate, 2000) 86.
[30] I am grateful to the House of Commons Library for supplying me with these figures.

be valid: plumping is not possible. In Britain, by contrast, the indication of preferences will be optional, and a vote will be valid so long as a '1' for a first choice candidate is clearly indicated. Optional preferential voting can operate very differently from compulsory preferential voting, since it allows for plumping. If, therefore, we wish to analyse how the alternative vote might work in Britain, the proper comparison is not with the Australian House of Representatives, but the states of Queensland and New South Wales, where preferential voting for the state legislatures is optional. The experience of Queensland and New South Wales shows that a number of voters do in fact choose to plump. In Queensland, in 2009, where the Labor Party advised its supporters to 'Just vote 1', to give Labor their first preference and not to give a preference to any other candidate, around 63% of voters plumped.

Even where a party does offer advice, that advice may be ignored. In Queensland, the Greens advised that second preferences be given to Labor, but 46% of Green voters decided to plump. In elections for the Mayor of London, where voters are allowed, but not required, to indicate a second vote, 17.1% chose not to use their second vote in the first mayoral election in 2000, and 14.6% abstained from using it in 2004.[31] In South Australia, in the 2003 mayoral elections, where optional preferential voting was used, around 50% of voters plumped. Experience of the alternative vote in elections for the states of western Canada in the first half of the twentieth century confirms that 'when preferences are optional, voters and parties tend to treat the election like a first past the post election', by plumping. Figures for plumping reached a peak of 68% in Manitoba in 1945, 64% in Alberta in 1944 and 1948, and 33% in British Columbia in 1952.[32] When a significant percentage of voters decide to plump, the winning candidate is chosen, not by a majority of the voters, but by a majority of those whose votes are *effective*, ie a majority of those who choose to use all their preferences.

If the alternative vote comes to be introduced for elections to the House of Commons, the percentage of plumpers will depend in part, no doubt, on signals given by the political parties. It is possible that the Conservatives and Liberal Democrats, if their coalition survives, will ask their supporters not to plump but to use their second preferences for their coalition partners; but it is not clear that the Labour Party would advise its supporters to use their second preferences. It might well follow the lead of its Queensland sister party and advise its supporters to plump for Labour and not give a preference to any other party. Even if a party recommends a second preference, it is not clear whether they will advise on how third or later preferences should be used. There will in any case be some voters who cannot conceive of voting anything other than, for example, Conservative, Labour or Green, and will not wish to give third or later preferences for parties for whom they care little. Supporters of large parties are perhaps less likely to indicate

---

[31] Henk van der Kolk, Colin Rallings and Michael Thrasher, 'The Effective Use of the Supplementary Vote in Mayoral Elections: London 2000 and 2004' (2006) *Representation* 99.

[32] Harold J Hansen, 'The Political Consequences of the Alternative Vote: Lessons from Western Canada' (2004) *Canadian Journal of Political Science* 664.

further preferences than supporters of small parties, who will be aware that their votes are more likely to face a transfer.

The alternative vote is not a proportional system. Indeed it can, under certain circumstances, yield an even less proportional result than first past the post. This can clearly be seen from the following imaginary example. Let us suppose that there are just three constituencies, A, B and C, and just three parties competing in the election – the Conservatives, Labour and the Liberal Democrats. Let us assume that first preferences are cast as follows:

	A	B	C
Labour	520	450	550
Conservatives	480	550	450
Liberal Democrats	250	250	250

Under first past the post, Labour, with 1,520 votes – just over 40% of the vote – would win two seats; the Conservatives, with 1,480 votes – just under 40% of the vote – would win one seat, while the Liberal Democrats, with 750 votes – 20% of the vote – would win no seats.

Let us assume that, of the Liberal Democrat vote, 200 went to its coalition partners, the Conservatives, while just 50 went to Labour. Then the Conservatives, with under 40% of the first preference vote, would win all three seats, and the other parties would be unrepresented.

V. SOME POSSIBLE CONSEQUENCES OF THE ALTERNATIVE VOTE

The alternative vote has been part of the electoral reform debate in Britain for over a century. It was advocated, with just one dissentient, by the only Royal Commission on the electoral system that Britain has ever had, which reported in 1910. It was also advocated, by a majority, for rural constituencies by the first Speaker's Conference, which reported in 1917 – the Conference also unanimously recommended proportional representation for urban constituencies. At that time Labour supported the alternative vote, with its leader, Arthur Henderson, declaring that 'he would depend on the alternative vote and on a friendly understanding between Liberalism and Labour to give each other their second choice'.[33] The alternative vote was proposed by the second minority Labour government in 1931 in order to secure Liberal support. A bill providing for it passed the House of Commons, though it did not arouse much enthusiasm. The bill was wrecked by the House of Lords; and, before it could begin its second passage through the Commons in accordance with the provisions of the Parliament Act, the Labour government was blown out of office by the financial crisis. The National Government, dominated by the Conservatives and with a landslide majority, had no interest in pursuing the subject, even though the Liberals pressed it to do so.

---

[33] Trevor Wilson (ed), *The Diaries of CP Scott* (Collins, 1970) 317.

More recently, as David Owen has pointed out, the alternative vote has been rejected by three bodies set up to consider electoral reform – the Liberal/SDP Commission on the Constitution, which reported in 1982, the Plant Committee on Democracy, Representation and Elections, established by Labour in 1990, and the Independent Commission on the Voting System, chaired by Lord Jenkins, which reported in 1998.[34] The main reason why all three bodies rejected the system was precisely because it could lead to even more disproportional and unfair results than first past the post.

The alternative vote has been used in Australia for elections to the lower house, the House of Representatives, since 1918. It does not, any more than first past the post, deliver seats in proportion to votes cast. In 1990, for example, the Australian Labor Party won 52% of the seats on just 39% of the first preference vote. Its opponents, the Liberal/National coalition, gained more first preference votes than Labor – 43% – but won only 46% of the seats. In 1954 and 1961, by contrast, the system kept Labor out office even though the party secured a higher percentage of the first preference vote than the Liberal-National coalition. Indeed, 1961 'has a particular place in Australian political folklore, for it was won and lost on a small number of preference votes in the Queensland electoral division of Moreton. Amongst these preferences were votes that had originally been cast in support of the Communist Party, and these not only helped the Liberal Party to win the seat, but in doing so secured the return of a conservative government'.[35] In 1998, Labor won 40% of first preference votes and the Liberal/National coalition 39%. But the Liberal/National coalition won 54% of the seats and Labor just 45%. In the 2010 general election in Australia, the outcome was as follows:

	% first preference votes	Seats
Labor	38	72
Liberal/National coalition	44	73
Greens	12	1
Others	6	4

The Australian Greens were discriminated against as badly as the Liberal Democrats have been in Britain, winning just one out of 150 seats for nearly one-eighth of the vote. The Liberal/National coalition can also claim that the system worked to their disadvantage, in that a 6% lead over Labor gave them just one extra seat. However, two political scientists have concluded that the alternative vote was, for many years, systematically biased against the Australian Labor Party. The alternative vote, they conclude, has 'produced some notably anomalous results, such as the systematic bias in favour of the Liberal Party in nine elections, (1949, 1955, 1958, 1963, 1975, 1977, 1980, 1986 and 2001) in which it was awarded more seats than Labor despite having won fewer votes'. The alternative vote,

[34] Owen (n 20) 59–60.
[35] Clive Bean, 'Australia's Experience with the Alternative Vote' (1997) *Representation* 107–08.

therefore, 'produces levels of distortion in the electoral result' similar to those produced by first past the post.[36]

Nevertheless, the system probably works better in Australia than it would in Britain. That is because Australia has more of a two-party system than Britain. The urban-based Liberals and the rural-based National Party are complementary, and form a united bloc of the moderate-Right in the Australian parliament, as the CDU/CSU does in Germany. In Britain, by contrast, there are powerful territorial parties, and a party of the centre, the Liberal Democrats, which has far more electoral support than any of the minor parties in Australia. The British party system is much more like a typical western European party system with 10 parties represented in the House of Commons, six of them purely territorial parties, while in the Australian House of Representatives elected in 2010 there were only four, two of which are in permanent coalition with each other, and one of which, the Greens, is very much a minor party, together with four independents. In fact, the Australian system functions much like a two-party system, and the alternative vote, even more than first past the post, works best when there is a strongly defined two-party or two-bloc system, rather than a multi-party system with a centre party of the strength of the Liberal Democrats.

Under the alternative vote it would be perfectly possible for every constituency to be won on a majority vote and yet for the outcome to fail to reflect the majority view of the voters. That would occur if one party were to pile up large majorities in safe seats while the second party won a larger number of seats by much smaller majorities. That occurred in South Africa in 1948, under first past the post, when no seat was won on a minority vote yet the United Party with 52% of the vote won 71 seats, while the Nationalists, with 42%, won 79 seats. The United Party succeeded in winning large majorities in the urban areas while the Nationalists won a number of rural seats by very narrow majorities. The Nationalists used their victory to claim that it gave them a mandate to introduce apartheid.

The alternative vote has never been used in parliamentary elections in Britain, but one general election in the twentieth century – that of 1931 – produced conditions akin to it. As we have seen, in 1931 there was, in the vast majority of constituencies, just one National Government candidate opposing a Labour candidate. The outcome was that a two-to-one majority in votes for the National Government – 67% to 33% – was transformed into a nine-to-one majority in terms of seats – 554 seats for the National Government, 61 for its opponents.

The reason why the first past the post system fails to secure proportional representation of parties in accordance with votes is that, under it, as we have seen, the number of seats a party wins depends not only upon how many votes it receives, but also upon the geographical distribution of those votes. A party whose vote is geographically concentrated, such as Labour in Britain, will win a larger number of seats for a given vote than a party whose vote is more evenly spread, such as the

---

[36] David M Farrell and Ian McAllister, *The Australian Electoral System: Origins, Variations and Consequences* (University of New South Wales Press, 2006) 81.

Liberal Democrats. Under the alternative vote the same is true. The alternative vote does nothing to take the geography out of elections. Indeed, it is not possible to take the geography out of elections with a single-member constituency system, unless that system is supplemented, as in the versions of proportional representation used in Scotland, Wales and the London Assembly, with party lists.

But, although the alternative vote does not yield proportional representation, perhaps it might provide more representative and therefore fairer results than first past the post. It might prove, in Clegg's words, a 'baby step in the right direction'. To consider whether this might be so, we need to look at the party distribution of MPs elected on a minority vote since the war.

	Conservative	Labour	Lib (Alliance), (Lib Dem)	Others	Total
1945	92	71	2	9	174
1950	106	76	5	0	187
1951	25	14	0	0	39
1955	25	11	1	0	37
1959	47	31	2	0	80
1964	154	71	7	0	232
1966	131	43	11	0	185
1970	68	48	6	2	124
February 1974	234	150	9	15	408
October 1974	224	131	11	14	380
1979	107	83	6	10	206
1983	165	141	15	15	336
1987	142	109	19	13	283
1992	125	103	17	15	260
1997	152	105	38	18	313
2001	134	141	37	21	333
2005	144	216	46	23	429
2010	180	182	45	26	433[37]

It will be seen that, at every general election until 2001, the Conservatives won more seats than Labour on a minority vote. Therefore, elimination of the minority vote through the alternative vote would probably have reduced the total number of Conservative seats and increased the total number of Labour seats. It would have helped Labour. So, in elections that the Conservatives won, such as 1983 and 1987, the outcome would have been more proportional. But, in elections that Labour won, such as 1945, 1966 and 1997, the outcome would have been even less proportional and Labour might well have won even larger majorities than it in fact did. In 2001, 2005 and 2010, by contrast, Labour won more seats on a minority vote than the Conservatives, albeit by a small margin in 2001 and 2010.

---

[37] Figures from Rallings and Thrasher, and by courtesy of House of Commons Library.

In 2010, the alternative vote would probably have made little difference to the two major parties. One simulation suggests that the Conservatives would have lost around 22 seats and Labour around 10, both to the Liberal Democrats, who would have won 89 seats.[38] But this simulation was based on the view held by many Liberal Democrats before the election, that Labour and the Liberal Democrats were natural alternatives and that more Liberals would therefore give their second preferences to Labour than to the Conservatives. But, of course, the coalition could alter such calculations, and it is possible that, at the next election, Liberal Democrat voters will regard the Conservatives rather than Labour as their second choice. If that happens, then Liberal Democrat gains will be more likely to be at the expense of Labour rather than the Conservatives.

It is, however, almost certain that the Liberal Democrats will benefit from the alternative vote, and, to this extent, the outcome is likely to prove more proportionate. For the Liberal Democrats will probably be the second choice of many Conservative voters – and perhaps, despite the coalition, of some Labour voters as well. But the alternative vote will not only yield second preference votes to the Liberal Democrats. It may also increase the number of first preferences that they receive. For the alternative vote does away with fear of the wasted vote, since votes cast for unsuccessful candidates are transferred rather than being wasted, as under first past the post. Even so, it does not seem that the alternative vote would have transformed any of the 12 decisive post-war election results into indecisive ones. It might, however, have altered the result in the six indecisive post-war elections or elections which yielded small majorities. In 1950 and 1964, February and October 1974, Labour might have gained a working majority, while 1951 and 1992 might have resulted in hung parliaments. With the trend towards greater third-party representation since 1997, the alternative vote will increase the likelihood of hung parliaments since, by reducing the number of seats won by Labour and the Conservatives, and increasing the number of seats won by the Liberal Democrats, it will decrease the chance of Labour or the Conservatives winning enough seats to ensure an overall majority.

Critics of the alternative vote sometimes ask why the second preferences of losing candidates, such as – taking the example given on p 95 – Richard Stevens, the Labour candidate for Oxford West and Abingdon, are transferred, while the second preferences of the two leading candidates, Nicola Blackwood and Evan Harris, are not transferred. But this criticism is based on a misunderstanding. Under the alternative vote system, the vote may be considered a direction to the returning officer to use one's vote where it can be of the most use. If it cannot be used effectively for one's first choice candidate, because that candidate has no chance of winning, then it should be transferred to a candidate who does have such a chance. The system seeks to make every possible vote effective. It therefore seems to do away with tactical voting and to allow honest voting. One can vote for

---

[38] David Sanders, Harold D Clarke, Marianne C Stewart and Paul Whiteley, 'Simulating the Effects of the Alternative Vote in the 2010 General Election' (2010) *Parliamentary Affairs* 1–19.

one's first choice, even if one's first choice is a small party that is unlikely to win in the constituency – for example the United Kingdom Independence Party – without fearing that this might help a party to which one is strongly opposed – for example the Europhile Liberal Democrats. But, in fact, this appearance of eliminating tactical voting is misleading. To take a hypothetical example, in a close Conservative/Liberal Democrat contest, a Labour voter, who thinks that the Liberal Democrats have more chance of beating the Conservatives than his own party, might well give his first preference vote tactically to the Liberal Democrats rather than Labour, to ensure that the Liberal Democrats are one of the final two parties left in the count. There was a remarkable example of tactical voting under the alternative vote in the 2010 Australian election in the constituency of Melbourne Inner-City. The three leading candidates on the first preference vote were:

	Votes	% votes
Adam Bandt, Green	25,387	36.1
Cath Bowtell, Australian Labor Party	27,771	39.5
Simon Olsen, Liberal	14,030	19.9

After preferences had been transferred, Adam Bandt won the seat with 55.7% of the vote, as compared with 44.3% for Cath Bowtell, the Labor candidate. When their candidate had been eliminated, Liberal voters transferred their votes tactically to the Green candidate in order to ensure that Labor could not win the seat, despite the fact that the Liberal Party is much closer ideologically to the centre-right Labor Party than to the left-leaning Greens, and despite the fact that Green votes would normally transfer to Labor.

It is likely that, under the alternative vote, the two leading parties – the Conservatives and Labour – will receive fewer first preference votes, while third parties – the Liberal Democrats, but also UKIP, the Greens and perhaps the BNP – stand to receive more first preferences. Indeed, there could be many more small parties and many more candidates. But, of these parties, perhaps only the Liberal Democrats are likely to benefit from transfers. The alternative vote benefits centrist parties, which can attract transfers as compared to parties at the extremes, which cannot attract transfers. An example of the way in which the alternative vote system can undermine extremist candidates can be found from the Blair constituency in Queensland, Australia in the election of 1998, contested by Pauline Hanson, leader of an extreme anti-immigration party called 'One Nation'. The percentage of first preference votes was as follows:

	% of first preference votes
Pauline Hanson, One Nation	35.97
Virginia Clarke, Australian Labor Party	25.29
Cameron Thompson, Liberal Party	21.69

Six other independent candidates and candidates from small parties secured a total of 17.05% of the vote.

Under first past the post, Pauline Hanson would have been elected. But, following transfers, on the eighth count, Cameron Thompson, third on the first count, was elected by later preferences. The result after distribution of preferences was:

	%
Pauline Hanson	46.60
Cameron Thompson	52.40

Although extremist parties may not benefit from the alternative vote in the sense of winning more seats, the fact that they attract more first preference votes may earn them a greater degree of legitimacy. Conversely, the fact that the two leading parties receive fewer first preferences may adversely affect the legitimacy of government, even if these parties win nearly as many seats as they would under first past the post. As we have seen, Labour in 2005 won just 35.2% of votes, and the Conservatives in 2010 just 36.1%. Were their first preferences to be even lower than these votes, it would appear that they would be forming governments with fewer than one-third of the voters supporting them.

The alternative vote would assist coalition politics by making co-operation between the parties to the coalition easier. Indeed, this is a much more important effect than any alterations in party strengths which the system might induce. In Chapter 4 we saw that, under first past the post, coalitions face the problem of reconciling co-operation in government with competition in the constituencies. In the past, as we have noted, there were three ways of trying to secure co-operation in the constituencies. The first was a coupon system, whereby party headquarters selected one of the candidates in a constituency as the official candidate of the coalition, as occurred in 1918. The second was mutual and reciprocal withdrawal, as took place in 1931. The third was merger, as occurred in 1912 with the Liberal Unionists and in 1968 with the National Liberals. All these methods have their difficulties, as experience of the Lloyd George coalition and the National Government showed, and disaffection amongst Conservative constituency associations at being asked to support Coalition Liberals was a major reason for the downfall of the Lloyd George coalition in 1922. Merger is by no means always an attractive option for coalition parties, who may wish to maintain their independence and identity while in alliance with another party. The alternative vote, however, obviates the need for a coupon, for reciprocal withdrawal of candidates, or for merger. Each of the coalition partners – the Conservatives and Liberal Democrats – can put up candidates in every constituency, without any loss of autonomy, and urge their supporters to give second preferences to their coalition partners. There would, however, be pressure on the Liberal Democrats to make a clear commitment at the national level in terms of how they would expect their supporters to distribute their preferences. They would find it difficult to repeat the stance which they adopted in 2010 of not indicating which party they would work with in a hung parliament.

Oscar Wilde said of Whistler that he had no enemies but was cordially disliked by his friends. The same is true of the alternative vote: it is a singularly unloved electoral system, 'an orphan, a motherless child'.[39] It is being presented to the electorate not because it is the first choice of either of the partners to the coalition, but as the outcome of a political deal. On a free vote, few MPs belonging to the coalition parties would choose it. The Conservatives hope that it will be rejected, the Liberal Democrats that it will prove a stepping-stone to proportional representation. So the 2011 referendum is unlikely to end the debate on electoral reform since, if the alternative vote is endorsed, the Liberal Democrats will almost certainly press for a second referendum on proportional representation in a few years' time. As the alternative vote is likely to strengthen their position in the House of Commons, they will be in a good position to press for this further reform.

When the alternative vote was last presented to Parliament in 1931, Winston Churchill dismissed it as 'the child of folly', predicting that it would 'become the parent of fraud'.[40] That, perhaps, is to give the alternative vote too much credit. Its effects, in the form in which it is being offered, will not be very great. It will not remedy the geographical imbalance in representation that is perhaps the greatest weakness of the first past the post system. It will not ensure that the Conservatives are better represented in Scotland and Wales, or that Labour is better represented in the south of England. It might perhaps widen the basis of popular consent for MPs, but its effects will be small compared with the introduction of proportional representation. Yet the alternative vote is not a mere technical change. It will have a twofold consequence. First, by increasing Liberal Democrat representation, it will make hung parliaments more likely. Second, it will make life easier for coalitions by enabling them to replicate co-operation in government with co-operation in the constituencies, and that perhaps will be its main consequence. By transforming the conditions of electoral competition, the alternative vote could therefore facilitate future coalition governments in Britain.

---

[39] Nick Cohen, *Standpoint* blog, www.standpointmag.co.uk/nick-cohen, 5 July 2010.
[40] *Hansard* HC col 107 (2 June 1931).

6

Fixed-Term Parliaments

I. EXPERIENCE OF FIXED-TERM PARLIAMENTS

URING THE 2010 election, both the Labour and Liberal Democrat manifestoes proposed fixed-term parliaments, while the Conservative manifesto proposed 'to make the Royal Prerogative subject to greater democratic control so that Parliament is directly involved'. The coalition's Programme for Government declared:

> We will establish five-year fixed-term Parliaments. We will put a binding motion before the House of Commons stating that the next general election will be held on the first Thursday of May 2015. Following this motion, we will legislate to make provision for fixed-term Parliaments of five years.

For the Liberal Democrats, an essential precondition of coalition was control over the dissolution of Parliament. Otherwise, a Conservative Prime Minister could secure a snap dissolution at a favourable moment for his party, breaking up the coalition – at the expense of his Liberal Democrat partners – in an attempt to secure an overall majority. This threat of dissolution could therefore be used, in the event of any policy disagreement, to bring the Liberal Democrats into line. It was vital that the Liberal Democrats should be able to prevent this. They had in any case long supported fixed-term parliaments, which they tended to regard as a corollary of proportional representation.

Amongst western European parliamentary systems, however, all of which – apart from France – use a system of proportional representation to elect their lower house, Norway is the only country that makes provision for fixed-term parliaments, the parliamentary term being four years.[1] This, however, causes considerable difficulty when a government is defeated on a confidence vote in the middle of a parliamentary term. The opposition party or parties which are in a minority then have to continue in government until the general election. This has happened on three recent occasions in Norwegian politics, as shown in the table below.

---

[1] Switzerland also has a fixed-term parliament, but it is not strictly a parliamentary system since the executive is drawn from all the main parties in the legislature, rather than solely from the majority party or parties.

Prime Minister	Took office	Left office	Party (s)
Kaare Willoch	October 1985	May 1986	Conservative, Christian Democratic, Centre
Gro Harlem Brundtland	May 1986	October 1989	Labour
Jan Syse	October 1989	November 1990	Conservative, Christian Democratic, Centre
Gro Harlem Brundtland	November 1990	October 1993	Labour
Kjell Magne Bondevik	October 1997	March 2000	Christian Democratic, Centre, Liberal
Jens Stoltenberg	March 2000	October 2001	Labour

The first occasion was in May 1986, when a coalition government led by the Conservative leader, Kaare Willoch, was defeated on its taxation proposals. The Willoch government was succeeded by a single-party Labour minority government which had to continue in office without any chance of obtaining a majority until the general election of October 1989. After that election, another Conservative coalition led by Jan Syse took office. But it too was defeated just a year later, in November 1990, and was succeeded once again by a single-party Labour minority government until the general election of 1993. The third occasion on which a government was defeated in the middle of a parliament occurred in March 2000, when a Christian Democratic coalition led by Kjell Magne Bondevik was defeated in parliament, to be succeeded by yet another single-party minority Labour government until the elections of October 2001. On none of these occasions were the politicians able to appeal to the voters to resolve the deadlock.

The purpose of the fixed-term parliament rule in Norway was to encourage, if not almost to force, the parties to work together. In practice, even when there is a majority government in Norway, the government seeks to co-operate with the opposition and not to confront it. Most Norwegian governments therefore take on the character of grand coalitions between the major parties. Norwegian culture, in contrast to the adversarial culture of British politics, puts a great deal of emphasis on creating consensus and not rocking the boat. The Norwegian system of fixed-term parliaments worked well when, for much of the twentieth century, there was a straightforward two-bloc system of political parties. But that two-bloc system began to break down after the referendum on the European Community in 1972 when Norway rejected membership. Since then, there has been the growth of anti-system parties – the Progressive Party, an anti-tax party on the Right, and a Socialist Left Party. Because the major parties were unwilling to form governments with these parties, the consequence was the advent of minority governments which could be defeated in Parliament.

The rationale for the fixed-term provision in Norway is that, under a proportional system, a dissolution in mid-term in 1986, 1990 or 2000 might not have altered the situation very much. Under proportional representation it is rare for a party to secure over 50% of the vote, and while the relative strength of the parties might have been different after a general election, this would probably not have altered the basic dynamics of the situation by which majority government was made difficult through the presence of anti-system parties. A general election, therefore, would probably not have produced an overall majority for a single party. It is in this sense that the Liberal Democrat linking of fixed-term parliaments with proportional representation finds some justification. The role of a general election under proportional representation, as has been shown in Scotland and Wales, is bound to be different from its role under first past the post. But in Britain, under the first past the post system, consensus between government and opposition is rare. Whatever the merits of a fixed-term parliament rule in Norway, it would be unlikely to work in the very different culture of Westminster. What is suitable for a proportional system with an ethos of consensualism is not likely to be suitable for a majoritarian system in which gridlock rather than consensus is a more probable result, and where dissolution does, by contrast with Norway, offer the prospect of an overall majority for a single party. There is therefore not much of a case for the introduction of fixed-term parliaments in Britain unless or until the electoral system is made proportional, and even then, as we shall see, there may be good arguments for preserving the power of dissolution.

II. THRESHOLDS FOR DISSOLUTION

The Fixed-Term Parliaments Act is misnamed. It does not provide for fixed-term parliaments on the Norwegian model. Instead it seeks to make dissolution more difficult and no longer at the discretion of the government of the day. To avoid difficulties of the kind that have been so apparent in Norway, the coalition's Programme for Government provided for the possibility of early dissolution if 55% or more of the House of Commons were to vote in favour of one. This provision would not have allowed the Conservatives, a minority in the Commons, to secure a dissolution without Liberal Democrat support. It would therefore have safeguarded the Liberal Democrats against an attempt by the Conservatives to dissolve against the wishes of their coalition partners. It would also have safeguarded the Conservative position by preventing a dissolution engineered by the combined Liberal Democrat and opposition parties. For a Labour/Liberal Democrat combination would command the support of just 53% of MPs in the Commons rather than the 55% required by this provision. Either of the two possibilities prevented by the 55% provision – a dissolution engineered by the Conservatives alone or a dissolution engineered by Labour and the Liberal Democrats against the Conservatives – would have been against the spirit of the coalition. The coalition, which commands around 58% of the seats in the Commons, could, under the 55% provision, have obtained a dissolution if it so wished, but no single party could have obtained a dissolution. The provision therefore made the Coalition Agreement possible by giving the Liberal Democrats an assurance that they would have a veto over any decision to dissolve. It would have helped to ensure the stability of the coalition.[2]

There can, of course, be no objection to a government, whether a single-party government or a coalition, binding itself by particular ad hoc provisions in relation to dissolution. That may be regarded as a matter for the government concerned, and is not constitutionally problematic. In this particular case, the 55% rule may be seen as a declaration of political intent on the part of the Conservatives that they would not extrude the Liberal Democrats at their convenience. But constitutional issues are raised by putting such provisions into statutory form. Of course, arrangements which might be entirely appropriate for the particular circumstances of 2010 might not necessarily be appropriate for future circumstances which, in the nature of things, cannot be foreseen. The provisions of the Coalition Agreement in 2010 were part of a political deal. There is no reason why they should be regarded as permanent principles of the constitution.

By the time the Fixed-Term Parliaments Bill was presented to Parliament in July 2010, the 55% figure had been changed to two-thirds. Under this amended provision, neither of the two possible coalitions in the current parliament – neither a Conservative/Liberal Democrat coalition nor a Labour/Liberal Democrat coalition – can obtain a dissolution without the support of other parties. The two-thirds provision has enabled the coalition to dispose of the accusation that it was seeking to gerrymander the constitution, since the 55% provision would have allowed a Conservative/Liberal Democrat coalition to obtain a dissolution, but not a Labour/Liberal Democrat coalition. The effect of the two-thirds provision is seemingly to put dissolution outside the range of the coalition majority. The coalition can no longer, by contrast with the 55% provision, secure an early dissolution unless it has the support of the opposition; and dissolution remains of course outside the range of any alternative coalition. As the Deputy Prime Minister, Nick Clegg, announced on introducing the bill into the Commons, 'These changes will make it impossible for any Government to force a Dissolution for their own purposes'.[3] So it would seem that an early dissolution will be possible only when both the Conservatives and Labour favour one. The provision will, however, confer on a government which has won a landslide, with two-thirds of the seats in the House of Commons, the special privilege of securing an early dissolution. There were four such governments in the twentieth century, none of them since the war. Three of these governments were coalitions – the Lloyd George coalition of 1918, which won 478 out of 707 seats, the 1931 National Government, which won 554 seats out of 615, and the National Government of 1935, which won 432 out of 615 seats. The only single-party government to have enjoyed such a large majority of seats was the second Baldwin government of 1924, which won 419 seats out of 615 in the Commons, though on under 50% of

---

[2] David Laws is explicit that the motivation of the 55% provision was political, to safeguard the coalition. David Laws, *22 Days in May: The Birth of the Liberal Democrat-Conservative Coalition* (Biteback, 2010) 184.

[3] *Hansard* HC col 23 (5 July 2010).

the vote. It is not clear why governments with such large majorities in the Commons should enjoy this special privilege of being able to secure a dissolution at a time of their own choosing.

It might be suggested that the two-thirds provision does not do enough to avoid a parliamentary deadlock. It will still be possible to have a situation in which, although there is not a two-thirds majority for a dissolution, no viable government is possible. The two-thirds rule might force Parliament to tolerate a minority government or a coalition, even in a situation where the majority of MPs want an election. Suppose, for example, that the Liberal Democrats were to abandon the Conservatives and that a no confidence vote against the Conservatives, who would now be in a minority, were then carried. Suppose, also, that the Liberal Democrats did not want to form a coalition government with Labour. The Conservatives would not be able to secure a dissolution, nor would Labour or the Liberal Democrats. The Liberal Democrats, as a hinge party, would be strengthened, since they could switch sides without facing an automatic dissolution. The outcome in these hypothetical circumstances would be a minority government, perhaps a weak minority government. Thus the Fixed-Term Parliaments Act would seem to end the hitherto automatic link between a no confidence vote and the calling of an election, when no alternative government is available in the Commons. Perhaps, however, this is a very unlikely scenario. For it presupposes that the Conservatives, the governing party, would seek a dissolution, while the opposition, which has just helped to defeat the government in a confidence vote, would reject it. That would be highly unlikely. The opposition would probably want an election just as much as the government. If that is so, then the two-thirds provision might make less difference than seems to be the case at first glance.

Nevertheless, the Fixed-Term Parliaments Act provides for a second method of securing an early dissolution, in addition to the provision for a two-thirds majority. This second method was not mentioned in the Coalition Agreement. An early dissolution can occur after a vote of no confidence in the government is carried if, following such a vote, no alternative government can be formed within 14 days. In these circumstances, the Speaker must issue a certificate to this effect and an early election takes place. This provision is similar to that regulating the Scottish Parliament in the Scotland Act 1998, with two exceptions. The first is that, in Scotland, the Parliament is given 28 days to nominate a First Minister. The second exception is more important – indeed fundamental. In Scotland, if there is an early dissolution following a two-thirds vote or vote of no confidence, the election that follows is termed an 'extraordinary general election', and the 'ordinary general election' held after four years still takes place. Thus, if the Scottish Parliament, elected in 2007, had been dissolved in 2009, there would still be another election in 2011. (The only exception to this provision occurs if the 'extraordinary general election' is held within six months of the date of the 'ordinary general election'. In these circumstances, the ordinary general election is not held.)[4] The provision

---

[4] Scotland Act 1998. See, in particular, s 3(1)(a) and (b) and s 46.

that any general election held after a vote for dissolution or vote of no confidence is an 'extraordinary general election', which does not affect the normal cycle, has the effect of lessening the potential advantage of an early dissolution for an incumbent government. The two-thirds requirement in Scotland has not yet been tested, however, and there have been no successful no confidence votes.

The coalition has decided not to adopt the Scottish provision. This means that a mid-term dissolution initiates a new five-year term. If the mid-term election is held earlier in the year than May, the next general election is held four years later; if later than May, it is held five years later. Thus, a mid-term dissolution in February 2011 would mean that the next general election would be held in May 2015; but a mid-term dissolution in October 2011 would mean that the next general election would be held in May 2016.

There is of course a crucial difference between the Scottish Parliament and Westminster: the former is elected by proportional representation. Under proportional representation, as we have seen in the case of Norway, an early dissolution is much less valuable than it is under first past the post, since a new election is unlikely to transform the political situation by yielding an overall majority for one party. Were Britain to adopt proportional representation for elections to the House of Commons, therefore, the Fixed-Term Parliaments Act would be more persuasive than it is at present.

It is, however, by no means always clear what is to count as a vote of confidence. Clearly an explicit vote of confidence or a defeat on the budget or the Queen's Speech must involve the government's resignation. But a government may choose to regard a quite ordinary motion as a vote of confidence. In 1895, for example, the Liberal government chose to regard the outcome of a snap vote on an opposition motion to reduce the salary of the Secretary of State for War as a confidence motion, even though, with a majority in the Commons, it could easily have reversed the vote. In October 1924, Ramsay MacDonald chose to treat a Liberal amendment to a Conservative censure motion as a vote of confidence, even though the Liberals did not intend it as such, and indeed sought to compromise with the government. Because of the ambiguity over what constitutes a vote of confidence, a government seeking an early dissolution can easily use the excuse of a defeat on a minor motion to resign; and, if no alternative government is available, it will be able to dissolve.[5]

III. THE CONSTRUCTIVE VOTE OF NO CONFIDENCE

An alternative to the provisions of the Fixed-Term Parliaments Act that is sometimes suggested is that the rules of Parliament should be altered so that only constructive votes of no confidence are allowed. The idea of the constructive vote of no confidence is derived from Article 67 of the German Constitution, which provides

---

[5] See, for some Canadian examples, Andrew Heard, 'Just What is a Vote of Confidence? The Curious Case of May 10, 2005' (2007) *Canadian Journal of Political Science* 395–416.

that the Bundestag can declare a lack of confidence in the Federal Chancellor only if there is a positive majority for a prospective successor. It cannot declare a lack of confidence by means of a purely 'destructive' or negative vote. If a constructive vote of no confidence is successful, the Federal President then dismisses the Chancellor and appoints the person nominated by the majority in the Bundestag.

The purpose of the constructive vote of no confidence is to ensure that a government cannot be overthrown by a purely negative vote of incompatible parties, unwilling to join together to form an alternative government. It was argued that such negative votes had undermined the Weimar Republic when Communists and Nazis had combined to remove governments of the centre committed to the parliamentary system, but were not themselves able to form a government. Since no successor government could obtain a majority in the Reichstag, one Chancellor succeeded another with great rapidity. Towards the end of the Weimar Republic, no government representing the democratic parties could secure a majority in parliament, and Chancellors became dependent upon the confidence of the Reich President, Hindenburg, who, in January 1933, appointed Hitler to the office of Chancellor, paradoxically because it seemed that Hitler alone was capable of securing parliamentary support, the Nazis being by then the largest party in the Reichstag.

The constructive vote of no confidence has been used twice in post-war Germany, once unsuccessfully, and once successfully. On the first occasion, in 1972, a constructive vote of no confidence was moved against the government of Willy Brandt. The Christian Democrat opposition believed that it would win the vote, but in fact it failed by two votes. Brandt, however, appreciated that he was losing his majority. But he was in a position of some difficulty, since the German Constitution does not allow a Chancellor, even a Chancellor of a majority government, to secure a dissolution. Article 68 of the Constitution, however, provides that if a government is defeated on a confidence vote in the Bundestag, and no alternative government is available, the President may, upon the proposal of the Federal Chancellor, dissolve the Bundestag. The Federal Chancellor may not ask the President for a dissolution until he has lost a vote of confidence. Brandt was therefore forced to resort to the expedient of putting forward a vote of confidence under Article 68, and deliberately losing it.

The second occasion on which a constructive vote of no confidence occurred was in 1982, when the Free Democrats decided to switch coalition partners from Helmut Schmidt's Social Democrats to Helmut Kohl's Christian Democrats. On this occasion, by contrast with 1972, the constructive vote succeeded by seven votes, and Kohl began his long reign as Chancellor, which lasted until 1998.

A constructive vote of no confidence would certainly be feasible in a bipolar parliament, whether composed of two parties or two blocs; but in these circumstances it would almost certainly be unnecessary. For a vote of no confidence will only succeed where there is a breakdown of cohesion in the governing party or bloc, because one part of the governing party or bloc has decided to vote with the opposition on a key matter, as occurred in Britain 1846 with the revolt over the

Corn Laws, and in 1886 with the revolt over Irish Home Rule. In such circumstances it will be perfectly obvious that a new majority has been created, and the constructive vote of no confidence will do no more than register that fact.

By contrast, in a multi-party parliament, there may well be no alternative majority. There are then two possibilities. The first is dissolution, and the second is for parliament to continue. It is by no means clear that the second alternative is preferable. By making it more difficult to remove a lame-duck government, the effect of a clause providing for a constructive vote of no confidence would be to allow a lame-duck government to hobble on, even when the majority of MPs may want a dissolution. If so, that would be a retrograde step. For governments need a majority not just to survive but to be able to govern effectively. The more difficult it becomes to overthrow the government or to dissolve parliament, the greater the danger of a weak or lame-duck government.

So, in a bipolar parliament, the constructive vote of no confidence would be unnecessary; in a multipolar parliament, it would be undesirable.

IV. EFFECTS OF THE FIXED-TERM PARLIAMENTS ACT

The fundamental purpose behind the Fixed-Term Parliaments Act is to take away the alleged advantage held by an incumbent Prime Minister, who can choose the date of dissolution. A Liberal Democrat peer compared this arrangement to 'a race in which the Prime Minister is allowed to approach it with his running shoes in one hand and his starting pistol in the other'.[6] Of the 18 general elections in Britain since the war, it can be argued that there are five where Prime Ministers have benefited from being able to choose an early date for dissolution – the general election of 1959, called by Harold Macmillan as Prime Minister, the general elections of 1983 and 1987, called by Margaret Thatcher, and the general elections of 2001 and 2005, called by Tony Blair. On the first of these occasions, it was alleged that the Prime Minister, Harold Macmillan, had taken advantage of a pre-election boom which could not be sustained. In 1970 Harold Wilson sought to do the same, but was unexpectedly defeated. It does not of course follow that, in the other cases, the government of the day would have been defeated if the parliament had been allowed to run its full term. Indeed, it is possible to argue that the Macmillan, Thatcher and Blair governments would have won elections whenever they had been held. Perhaps, therefore, the advantage that a Prime Minister can gain from an early dissolution has been exaggerated. It would in any case be difficult to regard the outcome as in any sense undemocratic simply because the people were asked to pronounce on their government one year earlier than expected. Even so, a coalition government could always guard against a snap election by the sort of measure contained in the Coalition Agreement. It does not need the cumbrous legislation which is the Fixed-Term Parliaments Act.

---

[6] Lord Holme, *Hansard* HL col 245 (22 May 1991).

An early dissolution, so it is argued by supporters of the Act, represents an illegitimate attempt by the Prime Minister to gain an advantage from the temporary popularity of his government. But this is not always the case. There are a number of more respectable reasons for an early dissolution. The first is when a new Prime Minister seeks a personal mandate. That was Sir Anthony Eden's motive in going to the country in 1955 in a Parliament which still had 18 months to run. (Critics alleged that he too was seeking to take advantage of a temporary economic boom.) Admittedly, Eden's precedent has not been followed, even though five of the other 12 changes of Prime Minister since the war have occurred between rather than after general elections. Neither Harold Macmillan in 1957, Sir Alec Douglas Home in 1963, James Callaghan in 1976 nor John Major in 1990 considered going to the country immediately after their appointment, and there was, perhaps, little public demand for them to do so. In 2007, however, there was some public feeling that Gordon Brown should go to the country to seek a personal mandate. An Ipsos-MORI poll on 10 October 2007, after Brown announced that he would not go to the country, found that 47% believed that he was right not to call an election, while 42% felt that he was wrong. Perhaps Brown's position would have been stronger if he had in fact gone to the country in 2007. The opposition certainly took up the cry that a new Prime Minister needed a new mandate, and in April 2010, shortly before the general election, David Cameron proposed that a new Prime Minister should go to the country within six months of being appointed.[7] This was perhaps ironic, since the Fixed-Term Parliaments Bill which he was to propose as Prime Minister would make it impossible for a new Prime Minister to follow this course. But perhaps Cameron's position in April 2010 accorded more closely with public feeling than the legislation that he was, as Prime Minister, to introduce. The average length of a parliament since the Great Reform Act of 1832 has been three years and eight months. Very few parliaments have lasted for five years, the most recent being the 1959–64, 1987–92, 1992–97 and 2005–10 parliaments. In those cases, there was pressure from the voters for an earlier general election, not for parliament to sit out its full term. Perhaps, indeed, there is greater public pressure now than in the past for a general election following a change of Prime Minister because, partly due to the role of the media, general elections seem to have become more presidential than they were. Politics has become more personalised. In May 2009, speaking during the expenses crisis, Cameron, although declaring himself sympathetic to fixed-term parliaments, accepted that there were 'strong political and moral arguments' against them –

> Political – because there's nothing worse than a lame-duck government with a tiny majority limping on for years.

> And moral – because when a Prime Minister has gone into an election, and won it promising to serve a full term, but hands over to an unelected leader half-way through, the people deserve an election as soon as possible.

---

[7]   *The Independent*, 24 April 2010.

There would be an even stronger argument for a government to go to the country early were there to be a second change of prime minister within a single parliament. That occurred only once in the twentieth century, in 1940, in the unusual circumstances of war, when Winston Churchill replaced Neville Chamberlain, who had in turn replaced Stanley Baldwin in 1937. It might possibly have happened after 2007, when there was some pressure to replace Gordon Brown, who appeared so unpopular that some Labour MPs believed that they would have a better chance of winning the election with a different leader. But these critics faced the argument that it would be constitutionally illegitimate for a second unelected Prime Minister to take office within the same parliament, and that the Labour government therefore would be morally obliged to go to the country fairly rapidly at a time when opinion poll evidence indicated that it would suffer a heavy election defeat. It is by no means clear that a constitutional change designed to obviate the need for a government to go to the country if it twice replaces its Prime Minister is in the public interest.

A second reason for an early dissolution might be to seek a mandate for a new policy. That was Asquith's reason for seeking two dissolutions in 1910. The first was to secure a mandate in a general election in January 1910 for Lloyd George's 'People's Budget', which had been rejected by the House of Lords; the second was to secure a mandate in a general election in December 1910 for the Parliament Act, limiting the powers of the Lords. Similarly, in 1923, Stanley Baldwin sought a dissolution in a Parliament that was just one year old. He had reached the view that unemployment could be cured only by a protective tariff, but felt bound by the pledge made by his predecessor, Bonar Law, in 1922, that a Conservative government would not introduce a tariff.

In September 1931, the National Government, although it had a majority in Parliament of 311–250, on what was in effect a vote of confidence, decided to seek a dissolution to secure a 'doctor's mandate' for its policies, as well as, no doubt, approval for the formation of the coalition. In February 1974, Edward Heath sought an early dissolution 16 months before the end of the Parliament to obtain a mandate to deal with the miners' strike and the changed economic conditions resulting from the oil crisis which followed the 1973 Yom Kippur war. Under the Fixed-Term Parliaments Act, the Labour opposition might well have opposed a general election in these circumstances, since Labour feared that an issue fought on the issue of government versus the unions would yield a Conservative landslide.

A third reason for an early dissolution might be that the existing Parliament is unviable. That was the reason why Attlee went to the country in 1951 in a Parliament that was just 18 months old. In the preceding general election of 1950, the Labour government had been returned with a majority of only five, and the government had been further weakened when two Cabinet ministers, Aneurin Bevan and Harold Wilson, resigned in 1951 because they could not support the budget. Attlee no doubt took the view that the country had to make up its mind whether it wanted Labour to continue or to put the Conservatives in power.

Harold Wilson went to the country in 1966 for a similar reason in a Parliament that was just 18 months old. Labour had been returned in the general election of 1964 with a majority of four, reduced to two by a by-election defeat. Similarly, in October 1974, Wilson went to the country in a Parliament that was just seven months old, since he no doubt felt that a minority government could not take the difficult economic decisions necessary to combat inflation. Under the Fixed-Term Parliaments Act, it is possible, but by no means certain, that Attlee and Wilson would have secured opposition support for dissolutions in these circumstances. If so, the Act makes no difference; if not, the Act would prove harmful.

There might also be a fourth motive for an early dissolution, which has not yet occurred in Britain, but could do so were we, in consequence of the development of a multi-party system, to move to a situation of regular coalition or minority governments. This fourth motive would be to validate a change of coalition partners. Suppose that, in the middle of this Parliament, the Liberal Democrats decided to desert the Conservatives, and to form a coalition with Labour. It might be argued that the electorate should be given the chance to pronounce on this change of government, and that it would be deprived of its rights if it had no say on the formation of the second coalition in the 2010 Parliament which had not been endorsed by the voters.

Something of this sort happened in Germany in 1982, following the constructive vote of no confidence. In 1972, when the Christian Democrats had sought to remove the Social Democrat government of Willy Brandt, Walter Scheel, the leader of the Free Democrats, who were in coalition with the Social Democrats, declared: 'Today we are faced with an attempt to alter the political majority without allowing the electorate to participate. Whether or not this is technically legitimate, it is an act which strikes at the nerve of our democracy.'[8] In 1982, when the Free Democrats themselves sought 'to alter the political majority' by switching from Helmut Schmidt's Social Democrats to Helmut Kohl's Christian Democrats, these words were quoted with glee by the Social Democrats. The new Chancellor, Helmut Kohl, accepted that he ought to seek electoral endorsement for the new coalition. But since, as we have seen, the German Constitution makes no provision for a government, even a majority government, to call a dissolution, Kohl, like Brandt in 1972, had to engineer the defeat of his government in a vote of confidence. This manipulation was to occur on a third occasion, in 2005, when Chancellor Gerhard Schroeder also engineered a vote of no confidence in his government in order to go the country at what he believed was a favourable moment. Unlike Brandt and Kohl, however, Schroeder made a miscalculation and lost the ensuing election. In both 1982 and 2005 the issue was taken to the Federal Constitutional Court, but the Court did not declare the procedure of engineering a vote of no confidence to be unconstitutional. On both occasions, it is fair to add, all the major party leaders favoured elections. Survey evidence in 1982 also

---

[8] Quoted in Vernon Bogdanor (ed), *Coalition Government in Western Europe* (Heinemann, 1983) 275.

showed a strong majority in favour of new elections so that the voters could pronounce on the change of coalition partners.[9]

A British government could similarly manipulate the provisions relating to the no confidence vote to secure a dissolution. This would not be prevented by the Fixed-Term Parliaments Act. Perhaps in the current Parliament the Conservatives could achieve this end, without the support of their Liberal Democrat coalition partners, if they were to ask their MPs to support a Labour no confidence motion in sufficient numbers. It might be argued that this course would incur such political odium that no government would seek to manipulate the rules in this way. However, three governments in Germany have taken a different view, and a government might well take the risk if political circumstances were sufficiently favourable. It would be difficult for the opposition to attack such a manipulation, since it would then be implying that it wished the government to continue and was fearful of the outcome of an election. The examples from Germany of 1972 and 1983 show that governments do not necessarily pay an electoral price for manipulating the system in this way, since both Brandt and Kohl increased their majorities.

The four motives for early dissolution outlined above are by no means unworthy. Indeed, some might argue that it is desirable that early dissolution should occur in these circumstances. Few, for example, suggested in 1951, 1966 or October 1974 that it would be better to continue with lame-duck parliaments rather than go to the country. It is possible, then, to argue that the value of an early dissolution in any of these four circumstances outweighs the possible disadvantage of a Prime Minister securing an early dissolution for purposes of party advantage. Voters are perhaps capable of making up their own minds about whether the reasons given by a government for an early dissolution are satisfactory, as perhaps was proved both in 1970 and in February 1974. It may be that the defeat of Wilson in 1970 was the product of a popular feeling that his government was seeking to cash in prematurely on an economic recovery, while in 1974, the unexpected failure of Heath to secure re-election may have reflected a sense that the premise on which he had fought the election – 'Who Governs' – was mistaken. It might then be better for the voters to decide whether an early dissolution is justified or not, rather than constraining the process of dissolution with constitutional rules.

The fundamental problem faced by those framing the Fixed-Term Parliaments Bill was that of avoiding the kind of deadlock that has occurred in Norway. Therefore, provision had to be made for a situation in which, despite the fixed-term provision, there could be a dissolution before the end of the statutory fixed term. It is, however, almost impossible to make provision in the statute for all of the possible circumstances in which an early dissolution should be allowed. This means that when a situation arises which is not covered in the legislation, politicians will

---

[9] REM Irving and WE Paterson, 'The Machtwechsel of 1982–83: A Significant Landmark in the Political and Constitutional History of West Germany' (1983) *Parliamentary Affairs* 434.

manipulate it, as they have done in Germany, so as to secure the dissolution that they seek. Therefore the Fixed-Term Parliaments Act may make much less difference than might seem to be the case at first sight; insofar as it would make a difference, it is not clear that it would be beneficial. In particular, if a government seeks a radical change of policy, as Baldwin did in 1923, or if a Parliament is unviable, or if there is a change of coalition partner, the public might well demand of a government, not that it should continue for five years, but that it should test its support at the polls.

Supporters of the bill claim that it will strengthen Parliament, since, so they say, it gives MPs the power to dissolve Parliament, a power which has become in effect the prerogative of the Prime Minister. As Sir George Young, Leader of the House, told Conservative Home Comment on 14 May 2010, 'the mechanism for a no confidence vote in the government is unchanged but what our proposals would do is give parliament a new power to dissolve itself, a power currently only exercised by the prime minister'. The effect of the two-thirds rule as opposed to the 55% rule is that a dissolution can only take place when MPs from all three major parties favour it. This, some argue, will enable Parliament to control Government on the matter of dissolution, instead of, as today, Government controlling Parliament. But that is probably illusory, since, of course, backbench MPs normally obey a party whip. The supposed power of 'parliament' to dissolve itself is the power of the party leaders to decide to dissolve Parliament and whip their followers accordingly. While the Act might conceivably alter the conditions under which political leaders can seek a dissolution, it is hardly likely to give more power to backbench MPs or to strengthen Parliament.

A further reason why the Fixed-Term Parliaments Act may make less difference than its proponents imagine is that the effect of a no confidence vote will probably be no different in the future from what it was before the Act was passed. The implication of defenders of the Act was that before it was passed, any government could secure a dissolution whenever it wanted, even if it was in a minority in the House of Commons. But that does not seem to be so. In the past, a no confidence vote would lead to a dissolution only if there was no viable alternative government within Parliament. Otherwise, the Prime Minister would resign, and the alternative government would take office. There were three defeats in votes of no confidence in the twentieth century. The first was in January 1924, when, as we have seen, Stanley Baldwin was defeated six weeks after losing his overall majority in the election, on the King's Speech. In that situation, it would clearly have been improper for Baldwin to seek a second dissolution, and he resigned. George V then appointed Ramsay MacDonald as Prime Minister of a minority government. In March 1979, when James Callaghan's minority government was defeated in a vote of confidence, in a parliament four-and-a-half years old, he sought a dissolution, which was granted. It was then obvious that an election was necessary, and in any case the existing parliament would reach its maximum term in another six months. The precedent of October 1924 is of greater interest. After MacDonald's minority government was defeated in the Commons on what he chose to regard as a vote of confidence, George V, before granting what would be the third dissolution in two years, inquired, through his Private Secretary, of the two opposition leaders, Baldwin and Asquith, whether they were prepared to form an alternative government. Only after receiving a negative answer and only when it was clear that no alternative government was available did George V agree to a dissolution. He told MacDonald that 'no other Party could form a Government that could last. He would protect himself by sending me a memorandum saying that he granted the election with great reluctance, and hinted that I might say so.'[10]

The Fixed-Term Parliaments Act does nothing to alter the constitutional position in this regard. When a government is defeated in a vote of confidence, either an alternative government is available, in which case the government resigns and the alternative government takes office; or no alternative government is available, in which case there is a dissolution. That was so before the Act. The only difference the Act makes is to allow a lame-duck government to continue in office if it does not wish to manipulate the constitution by securing a vote of no confidence in itself. Perhaps one newly elected backbench MP was not overstating things when he declared of the Fixed-Term Parliaments bill that '[t]he best reason for voting for it is that it is pointless'.[11]

An alternative and simpler proposal to that provided for in the Fixed-Term Parliaments Act would have been to require that a dissolution necessitates a majority vote in Parliament. The political effect of such a provision would be to give greater power to a hinge party such as the Liberal Democrats, who, if they held the balance of power, could prevent one of the other two major parties from securing a dissolution. Thus, in September 1974, Harold Wilson, as the Prime Minister of a minority government, might not have been able to secure a dissolution at a time of his choosing were the Liberal Democrats and of course the Conservative opposition to be against it. But it is by no means obvious that the continuation of a shaky minority government in such circumstances rather than a general election would have been in the best interests of the country.

The Fixed-Term Parliaments Bill was introduced as a reaction to the expenses scandal. It was one of a wide range of constitutional reforms proposed in 2009, many of which had little obvious relevance to the issues raised by the scandal. It seems a particularly perverse reaction. The main problem that appears to have been raised by the expenses scandal was the need to secure greater control over MPs, who, so it was alleged, had become insensitive to the reactions of their constituents. If the Act has any effect, however, it will be to insulate MPs from popular pressure by ensuring that dissolution becomes more difficult and general elections less frequent.

The debate about the Fixed-Term Parliaments Act indicates a conflict between two fundamental principles: the principle of parliamentary government and the

[10] From MacDonald's diary, quoted in David Marquand, *Ramsay MacDonald* (Jonathan Cape, 1977) 377–78.

[11] *Hansard* HC col 675 (13 September 2010), Jacob Rees-Mogg.

principle of democratic government. The former provides that parliament shall choose the government, which is accountable to it; the latter that the people should choose the government, and that government should be accountable to them. Normally, of course, under single-party majority government – the norm since 1945, though not before 1939 – the two principles coincide. But if we are, as this book suggests, moving into an era of multi-party politics, then the principles will come to diverge. Under multi-party politics, the fact that a government enjoys the support of parliament does not necessarily mean that it is acting in accordance with democratic principles if, for example, it forms a coalition after an election which the voters have no chance to endorse, or if it swaps coalition partners in the middle of a parliament without securing popular endorsement for this change.

If we are entering a world of hung parliaments, it by no means necessarily follows that dissolutions should be made more difficult. Indeed, it can be argued that they should become more frequent, since changes of Prime Minister or changes of coalition partner are more likely to occur in a multi-party system than under a two-party system where coalitions are unnecessary. While a democracy cannot survive on an endless diet of dissolutions, making dissolution too difficult could lead to endless parliamentary manoeuvring of the sort that so discredited the Third and Fourth Republics in France. Dissolution, then, is not necessarily a threat to good parliamentary government; it can be one of its most important safeguards, ensuring that governments are accountable not only to parliament but also to the people. If that is so, then it is difficult to see what useful purpose is served by the Fixed-Term Parliaments Act. Either the Act will have little effect, because it will be manipulated by the politicians, in which case it will prove to have been a waste of parliamentary time; or it will have some effect, but that effect will be deleterious because it makes an appeal to the people more difficult. In the past, a Prime Minister may have gained an unfair advantage from an early dissolution. In the new world of multi-party politics and coalition government which we may be entering, dissolution could be an essential weapon for the voters, enabling them to prevent inter-party manoeuvring and coalition deals organised behind closed doors after the votes have been counted. In Third Republic France, in 1902, Prime Minister Waldeck-Rousseau declared: 'The ability to dissolve . . . is not a menace to universal suffrage, but its safeguard. It is the essential counterbalance to excessive parliamentarism, and for this reason it affirms the democratic character of our institutions.'[12] Britain may come to think the same.

---

[12] Quoted in BS Markesinis, *The Theory and Practice of Dissolution of Parliament* (Cambridge University Press, 1972) 234.

7

A New World? Multi-Party Politics and Coalition Government

I. A SERIES OF HUNG PARLIAMENTS?

BEFORE 2010, THE last hung parliament was in February 1974. That hung parliament proved an aberration. Thirty-six years were to pass before there was another. Is the outcome of the 2010 election likely to prove a similar aberration? Is it likely to be followed by a reversion to single-party majority government; or could it, by contrast, prove the harbinger of a series of hung parliaments?

There are two reasons why the 2010 outcome may not prove to be an aberration. The first is the increase in third-party representation. The second is the fall in the number of marginal seats.

In 1951 there were just six MPs – all Liberals – who did not belong to the Labour or Conservative Parties. By February 1974 there were 37, but by 2010 there were 85 – and in 2005 there were 92.

	Third-party seats	Liberal Democrat (Liberal, Liberal/ SDP Alliance) seats
1945	34	12
1950	11	9
1951	9	6
1955	8	6
1959	7	6
1964	9	9
1966	14	12
1970	12	6
February 1974	37	14
October 1974	39	13
1979	27	11
1983	40	23
1987	45	22
1992	44	20
1997	76	46
2001	81	52
2005	92	62
2010	85	57

Part of the reason for this increase is that the Liberal Democrat vote has become more geographically concentrated since the 1970s. This means that the party wins more seats for a given share of the vote. Thus, in 1983, the Liberal/SDP Alliance secured 23 seats for 25% of the vote, but in 2010, it won 57 seats with 23% of the vote. Because the Liberal Democrat vote has become more geographically concentrated, the party's representation in the Commons is unlikely to fall back to the low levels of the 1970s, although it is of course possible that, as a result of their participation in the coalition, Liberal Democrat support will be squeezed between the Labour and Conservative Parties. If that happens, the 2010 coalition could prove a prelude not to multi-party politics, but to realignment and a new two-party system, as the coalitions of 1895, 1918 and 1931 proved to be. But there are good reasons for thinking that this may not be the case.

The first past the post system is often defended for its ability to produce single-party majority government, sometimes equated with 'strong' government since it discourages people from voting for third parties. There is a mechanical factor undermining the strength of third parties, since they are likely to be under-represented; and also a psychological factor, since voters will be told that a vote for a third party is a wasted vote. But these factors are not present when third-party votes become more concentrated, as has now become the case for the Liberal Democrats. For, although the Liberal Democrats are still under-represented, they are less under-represented than they were in the 1970s and 1980s. In addition, the argument that a Liberal Democrat vote is a wasted vote because the party cannot 'win' an election becomes much less plausible when the party has become part of a government for the first time in peacetime since the 1930s. For many opinion polls have indicated that the vote for the Liberal Democrats would be much higher if voters believed that they could 'win'. Therefore, the Conservative/Liberal Democrat coalition may have removed an important constraint that has hindered Liberal progress for over 80 years.

The level of representation of the minor parties is also unlikely to fall. Today, in contrast with 1951, none of the constituencies of Northern Ireland return Conservative MPs. It is difficult to believe that, in the foreseeable future, Northern Ireland constituencies will return many MPs belonging to parties this side of the Irish Sea. Nationalist representation in Scotland and Wales is also unlikely to be seriously eroded. Indeed, the nationalists could easily benefit from their opposition to a Conservative/Liberal Democrat government that enjoys only minority representation in Scotland and Wales, but which is imposing cuts in public expenditure affecting disproportionately these parts of the United Kingdom.

It is difficult, then, to resist the conclusion that the first past the system is no longer preventing third parties, and in particular the Liberal Democrats, from winning seats. This conclusion will, of course, be strengthened if the alternative vote comes into effect. For, as we have seen, one likely result of the alternative vote is an increase in the number of Liberal Democrat seats, since the Liberal Democrats tend to be the second choice of many Labour and Conservative voters.

If, then, future parliaments are likely to include at least 85 MPs from parties other than Labour or the Conservatives, it follows that, to secure an overall majority, one of the main parties needs to secure at least 86 more seats than its rival. But that has occurred in fewer than half of the 18 general elections since the war – namely those of 1945, 1959, 1966, 1983, 1987, 1997, 2001 and 2005. Interestingly, it has not occurred on any occasion when the Conservatives have defeated a Labour government – it did not occur in 1951 when Churchill was returned to power, in 1970, when Edward Heath entered Downing Street, in 1979, the year of Margaret Thatcher's first election victory, nor, of course, in 2010.

But, even if a party does succeed in winning 86 more seats than its rival, that is hardly sufficient to govern. After 1992, John Major found that even an overall majority of 21 was hardly sufficient, and the years 1992–97 bore many of the characteristics of a hung parliament, especially when it came to parliamentary ratification of the Maastricht Treaty, when Major sometimes had to rely on the votes of Liberal Democrats or Ulster Unionists to secure his majority. In any case, John Major's majority did not last the duration of the parliament. By February 1997, thanks to defections and by-election losses, his majority had disappeared, and for the last two months his government was a minority administration. Admittedly, in 1951, Winston Churchill had been able to govern without difficulty with a majority of 17. But party lines today are far more fluid than they were then, and party discipline is now much weaker than it was. Therefore, the margin needed for an effective working majority is probably much higher than it was 60 years ago. A party would probably need at least 110 more seats than its main rival to be confident that it could govern effectively for the duration of a parliament. Such a majority has been achieved on only six occasions since the war – 1945, 1966, 1983, 1997, 2001 and 2005.

There is a second reason why the hung parliament of 2010 may not be an aberration. In the 1980s, psephologists John Curtice and Michael Steed first noticed that there has been a dramatic fall since the 1950s in the number of marginal seats. Curtice has defined a marginal seat as a seat won by either Conservative or Labour and contested by both parties, where the Conservative share of the two-party vote lies within the range 45–55%. In terms of this definition, there were 166 such seats in 1955 but only 85 in 2010.[1] This means that, for any given swing, fewer than half of the seats will switch from one main party to another than would have been the case in 1955.

---

[1] John Curtice, 'So What Went Wrong with the Electoral System?' in Andrew Geddes and Jonathan Tonge (eds), *Britain Votes 2010* (Oxford University Press, 2010) 48.

Marginal seats[2]

1955	166
1959	157
1964	166
1966	155
1970	149
1974 (February)	119
1974 (October)	98
1979	108
1983	80
1987	87
1992	98
1997	114
2001	114
2005	104
2010	86

In 1950 the psephologist David Butler rediscovered the 'cube law', which relates seats to votes. This 'law' states that, if the votes of the two main parties are divided between them in the proportion A:B, then the seats they will win will be in the proportion $A^3:B^3$.[3] Thus a 1% swing would switch 3% of the seats between the major parties. In 1955 the relationship was only a little less than $A^3:B^3$. By the time of the 2010 election, by contrast, the relationship had been halved – it was now around $A^{1.5}:B^{1.5}$. The reason for this has been well stated by Curtice as a 'long-term change in the geography of Conservative and Labour support'. Beginning with local elections in the late 1950s, Conservative support became increasingly concentrated in areas in which they were already strong – the south and the Midlands, and rural areas, while Labour performed better in areas where it was already strong – Scotland, the north, and inner city constituencies. The consequences in terms of long-term variation in swing are shown below.[4] A plus indicates the swing to the Conservatives in the particular area over and above the national swing; a minus shows that the swing was lower than the national swing.

	South	Midlands	North	Scotland	Wales
1955–87	+8.9	+5.9	−8.6	−19.1	+0.6
1987–97	−2.6	−2.3	+1.9	+7.4	+2.0
1997–2005	+1.1	+1.1	−0.9	−4.7	+1.5
2005–10	+0.6	+2.1	−0.4	−7.6	+0.7

[2] I am grateful to John Curtice for supplying me with these figures.
[3] David Butler, 'An Examination of the Results' in HG Nicholas, *The British General Election of 1950* (Macmillan, 1951) 327ff. The statistical basis for the law was analysed by MG Kendall and A Stuart in 'The Law of Cubic Proportions in Election Results' (1951) *British Journal of Sociology* 183–97. The 'law' was first noticed by James Parker Smith in evidence to the Royal Commission on Electoral Systems in 1909.
[4] I am grateful to John Curtice for supplying me with these figures.

The reason for these shifts in voting behaviour is unclear, and the effect was at first very small. But small and cumulative shifts gradually resulted in a fundamental change: the creation of more safe seats for each of the major parties.[5] There have been striking political consequences, since Labour is now much less well represented in rural areas and the south of England than it was in the 1950s, while the Conservatives are far less well represented in Scotland, the north and the inner cities. In 1955, indeed, the Conservatives enjoyed a dominant position in Scotland, enjoying an overall majority of both seats and votes – the only time that this has been achieved by any political party in the post-war years. So, in contrast with the 1950s, when the working of the first past the post system appeared to reflect a homogeneous country, in the early part of the twenty-first century it has made the country appear divided, more divided in fact than it probably is. Britain now seems to be split into two discrete halves. There is of course a divergence in voting behaviour between, say, Scotland and the south of England, but this is given exaggerated emphasis by the electoral system. It is this that gives prominence to the West Lothian Question, a Question which would hardly arise were the balance of seats in Scotland more evenly distributed between the major parties, as it was in the 1950s.

For these two reasons, then – the rise in the representation of third parties and the decline in the number of marginal seats – the outcome of the 2010 election may not be an aberration or an accident, but a harbinger of things to come. Admittedly, four of the preceding six general elections – those of 1983, 1987, 1997 and 2001 – resulted in landslides rather than hung parliaments. The landslide of 1983, confirmed in 1987, was in part due to a patriotic reaction to success in the Falklands, in part due to a negative reaction against the swing to the Left in the Labour Party under the leadership of Michael Foot, and the split in the Left, following the SDP breakaway of 1981. The landslide of 1997, confirmed in 2001, was based on a swing of 10%, the largest since the war, and it occurred after the longest period of single-party government since the Napoleonic wars. The landslide was no doubt a reaction by one party against a government which had been in power for so long. The rise in third-party representation and the decline in marginal seats means that larger swings are today needed to yield a single-party majority than was the case in the past; but it is of course possible that, with an increasingly volatile electorate, such large swings will occur in the future as they did in 1997. It is also, however, possible that the era of single-party majority government, which characterised the post-war period, has now come to an end, and that the future will see an era of multi-party politics and hung parliaments. We may be about to enter a new world in which past signposts prove to be of little value. This concluding chapter seeks to outline the constitutional contours of this new world.

---

[5] Curtice (n 1) 49. For further discussion of the decline of the cube law see John Curtice and Michael Steed, 'Electoral Choice and the Production of Government: The Changing Operation of the Electoral System in the United Kingdom since 1955' (1982) *British Journal of Political Science* 249–98; and John Curtice and Michael Steed, 'Proportionality and Exaggeration in the British Electoral System' (1986) *Electoral Studies* 209–38.

II. CONSEQUENCES OF HUNG PARLIAMENTS

What are the likely consequences of a series of hung parliaments? The first was predicted by David Cameron in an interview with the *Independent* the day before the 2010 election:

> The point about a hung parliament is that the decisions that really matter to people are taken behind closed doors. Instead of people choosing the government, the politicians do. Instead of policies implemented on the basis of a manifesto, there will be compromises and half-measures.[6]

There is a danger that both the government and its policies come to be decided after the votes are counted.

The election is no longer the sole determinant of who is to form the government. The party composition of the government is decided in post-election negotiations, after the votes have been counted. In every other post-war election, with the exception of that of February 1974, the voters directly decided which party was to form a government and who was to be Prime Minister – in 2005, it was to be Labour under Tony Blair, in 1992, the Conservatives under John Major. That was not the case in 2010. No one voted for the coalition, and its coming into existence, although partly an outcome of the arithmetic of the result, was not determined by it. On the Continent, where, with the exception of France, parliaments are elected by proportional representation, arithmetic is by no means always the determining factor. Indeed, if a party does well in an election, the others, fearing its dominance, may well combine to keep it out. In 1977, the Dutch Labour Party gained 10 seats but moved into opposition. In 1981, it lost nine seats but returned to government. There is apparently a Dutch saying that one can win the election but lose the formation![7] With hung parliaments, the function of general elections alters. Instead of directly choosing a government, they will alter the power relations between the parties, thereby affecting the relative strengths of the parties in post-election negotiations. There come to be, then, two stages – not one – in the formation of a government. The first is the election, the second the post-election negotiations. A series of hung parliaments will introduce a system of indirect election in place of the direct election of governments.

As the 2010 general election shows, if the government that emerges from a hung parliament is a coalition, then the role of the party manifesto will change. It no longer offers a reliable guide to what the governing party will do, since elements of it may have to be jettisoned in a coalition agreement. It is this agreement, not the manifestoes of the parties comprising the coalition, that will bind the government, for the coalition agreement will supersede the party manifesto, and supersede even very specific pledges made in a party manifesto. Thus, when Vince

---

[6] 'Fourth Debate', *The Independent*, 5 May 2010.

[7] Jan Vis, 'Coalition Government in the Netherlands' in Vernon Bogdanor (ed), *Coalition Government in Western Europe* (Heinemann, 1983) 155.

Cable, the Business Secretary in the Conservative/Liberal Democrat coalition, was charged on the BBC's *The Politics Show* on 21 October 2010 with having broken his specific pledge that he would not vote for an increase in tuition fees for higher education, he replied that the pledge and indeed the promise in the Liberal Democrat manifesto had been overtaken by the Coalition Agreement, and he was now bound by that rather than by any pledge or manifesto. In future, therefore, if we are entering a world of hung parliaments, the manifesto will be seen as nothing more than a bargaining chip, parts of which can be done away with once the votes have been counted.

There are, however, three problems inherent in the doctrine of the primacy of the Coalition Agreement. The first is that, unlike the manifestoes, it will not have been put before the voters. Therefore, while a single-party government might insist, with varying degrees of plausibility, that it has a mandate for its policies since they were spelled out in its election manifesto, no such claim can be made with regard to a coalition agreement. Not only, therefore, might the government be decided upon after the votes have been counted; so also might the policies. This, as we have seen, could have consequences for the relationship between the House of Commons and the House of Lords, which has hitherto conducted its affairs in the light of the Salisbury convention, requiring acquiescence to measures foreshadowed in the governing party's manifesto. But the doctrine of the supremacy of the Coalition Agreement could also have important consequences for the quality of democracy if voters are denied the sight of a coalition government's policies until after the votes have been counted. That has proved to be a particular problem for the Liberal Democrats, who have repudiated some of their main policies since the general election.

Coalition government inevitably involves compromise. But the Liberal Democrats laid themselves open to the criticism that, on three issues – rapid elimination of the budget deficit, the tripling of student tuition fees and the exclusion of proportional representation from any referendum on electoral reform – they have gone further than compromising their party's manifesto: they have repudiated it, supporting policies directly contrary to those which they presented to the electorate. Voters who supported the party because they believed that it would vote, as it promised, for the abolition of tuition fees, for a slower reduction of the deficit, or for proportional representation, have good reason to feel aggrieved. Yet disappointed voters have no redress.

The second problem with the doctrine of the primacy of the Coalition Agreement is that, in contrast with an election manifesto, it was drawn up in a hurry – in five days in 2010. This hardly allows for detailed scrutiny of policies. A party manifesto, by contrast, is usually the product of a long period of discussion and debate within the party, together with advice from sympathetic think-tanks and various experts; and in recent years it has been the custom for opposition parties to cost their manifestoes. None of this is possible during an immediate post-election scramble. Policies are drawn up rapidly in order to secure an inter-party deal. These hurriedly drawn-up policies then come to be regarded as immutable and engraved on tablets of stone.

The third problem with the primacy of the Coalition Agreement is that party discipline becomes more important than is the case under a single-party government, since a dissenting vote from a member of the governing coalition threatens the agreement and therefore threatens to destabilise the basis of trust upon which the coalition was formed.

In order to mitigate these weaknesses, two things are needed: first, parties should signal their intentions with regard to coalition partners before rather than after an election; and second, more attention must be given to working out the details of coalition agreements.

Before the general election, Lord Owen, as David Owen had now become, established a website, www.Charter2010.co.uk, which was designed to provide information for voters who wished to learn more about the issues surrounding a hung parliament. The first principle of Charter 2010 was 'straightness with the voters'. 'The electors', it declared, 'are entitled to ask that party leaders and candidates are straight with them about a hung parliament before they cast their votes.' For this to be achieved, the parties need to indicate to the voters before the election which parties they would be willing to enter a coalition with, and on what terms. The larger parties will be unwilling to do this so long as they believe that there is a good chance of winning an overall majority, while the Liberal Democrats will want to keep their options open for as long as possible. It is therefore understandable that Nick Clegg was unwilling to give any definite indication before the 2010 election. In 1992, when Paddy Ashdown had indicated shortly before the election that, were there to be a hung parliament, he would be unwilling to sustain a Conservative government, John Major was able to say that a vote for the Liberal Democrats was in effect a vote for Labour. The result was that right-leaning Liberal Democrats swung from the Liberal Democrats to the Conservatives. Clegg, therefore, was maximising his electoral support by refusing to make a commitment before the election.

Surely, though, democratic propriety requires that a party of the centre set out its terms before the election rather than after it. Preferential systems of election such as the alternative vote or the single transferable vote system of proportional representation make this easier by allowing for transfer deals between parties. In Australia, for example, the alternative vote has facilitated the Liberal/National party coalition, while in Ireland, which uses the single transferable vote to elect its lower house, there have often between transfer deals between the Fine Gael and Labour parties in order to help defeat the dominant Fianna Fail party; and in 1996, Fianna Fail for the first time made a transfer deal of its own with the Progressive Democrats.[8]

When parties make transfer deals of this kind before the election, they might also come to produce joint manifestoes; or at least agree which items in their individual manifestoes are bargainable. The alternative would be to spend more time

---

[8] Michael Laver, 'STV and the Politics of Coalition' in Shaun Bowler and Bernard Grofman (eds), *Elections in Australia, Ireland and Malta under the Single Transferable Vote: Reflections on an Embedded Institution* (University of Michigan Press, 2000) 150.

working out the coalition agreement after the election. But this could increase the time devoted to the forming of a government, and, while this is acceptable on the Continent, and also in New Zealand since the introduction of proportional representation, voters in Britain seem to expect a government to be in place rapidly following a general election. There was indeed some disquiet even at the gap of five days after the general election of 2010 before the coalition was formed. If hung parliaments become a regular occurrence, the public will have to learn to become more patient.

With a series of hung parliaments the role of dissolution also alters, for it becomes less profitable to do what Harold Wilson did in October 1974, that is, escape from a hung parliament by dissolving a parliament in which one's party is in a minority. If hung parliaments become the norm, there is no easy escape from the necessity of having to work with other parties. The position of the minor parties will in this way be strengthened. When single-party majority government was the norm, and hung parliaments an aberration, their position was weak since the Prime Minister could dissolve at any time, when they might be squeezed between the two major parties; and they were in a weaker position financially to fight elections than the main parties. That, perhaps, is why the Liberals were able to make so little of what appeared at first sight to be a strong bargaining position in the hung parliaments of 1924, 1929 and 1974. But, if hung parliaments are to become the norm, and dissolution is unlikely to make much difference, the minor parties will have the option of threatening to switch their support from the government to the opposition if their demands are not met. The government will no longer be able to threaten them with dissolution. Under single-party majority governments, a dissolution looks like a safeguard because it makes possible an appeal to the people; it exemplifies the principle of democratic government. But the Liberal Democrats and other supporters of coalitions regard frequent dissolutions as a menace, because they take away the incentive for inter-party bargaining and so militate against consensus.

Under a regime of hung parliaments, it is possible that governments will be formed and change between general elections, as was the case during the previous period of multi-party politics in Britain in the nineteenth century, between the fall of Sir Robert Peel's government in 1846 and the advent of Gladstone's first majority government in 1868. We may come to see a disconnect between two principles which, when there are single-party majority governments, coincide. The first principle is that of parliamentary government – the idea of a government responsible to parliament, and governing with the consent of parliament. The second is that of democratic government – the idea of a government responsible to the people, and governing with the consent of the people. With regular hung parliaments, the two principles no longer necessarily coincide. If a party changes coalition partners without a general election, it can claim that, if the new government enjoys a majority in parliament, this is in accordance with the principle of parliamentary government. But it may not be in accordance with the principle of democratic government if the voters have had no chance to approve the switch.

Parliamentary government may then be seen, not as a means of securing the government of the people, but of subverting it. Indeed, the greater the power of parliament, the less may be the power of the people. The greater the role played by deals between coalition partners, the less leverage there will be for voters. Therefore, if hung parliaments are to become the norm, there needs to be some counter-balance to increase the power of the voter and to enable coalitions formed after the votes have been counted to secure democratic legitimacy. The conclusion to this book outlines what these counter-balancing powers might be. But first we must consider whether the direct election of the second chamber might serve to increase the power of the voter.

III. A DIRECTLY ELECTED SECOND CHAMBER

The Coalition Agreement proposes to create a wholly or mainly elected second chamber, to be elected by proportional representation. Direct election could be expected to strengthen the upper house, but it would create a problem of competing mandates, with two competing chambers each claiming to enjoy democratic legitimacy. This problem might have to be resolved through the creation of new institutional machinery to resolve disputes between the two chambers.

There are a number of alternative methods of proportional representation which could be used to elect the Lords. One possibility would be election by closed lists, the system used to elect British representatives in the European Parliament.[9] Alternatively, there could be open lists, whereby the ordering of candidates is determined not by the party machine but, to a greater or lesser extent, by the voter. A third method would be the single transferable vote, which has the merit of conceptually linking a primary election to a general election. A closed list would mean that the voter simply voted for a representative chosen by his or her favoured party, while an open list would give the voter an element of choice. Greater choice would be attained by means of the single transferable vote. Even so, it is not clear what such choice can really mean if there are regional constituencies, as there are in the elections for the European Parliament, for these constituencies are too large to make possible a meaningful relationship between the voter and his or her representative. Few voters know the names of their MEPs; even fewer know enough about them to be able to make a meaningful choice between them. Choice might be easier in smaller constituencies of the type used in the single transferable vote – constituencies based, for example, on counties. Even so, most of those elected are likely to be party nominees. Few independents are likely to succeed; and therefore the cross-bench element in the Lords will either be eliminated or, if the Lords come to be only partially elected, their numbers will probably be drastically reduced so that the elected element becomes dominant.

A directly elected second chamber would almost certainly seek, unlike the House of Lords, to use its powers to the full. Being more legitimate than an

---

[9] Excluding those from Northern Ireland, who are elected by the single transferable vote.

appointed chamber, a directly elected second chamber would feel more justified in asserting itself against the elected government. Currently, the House of Lords hardly ever uses its power to delay government legislation for the single session permitted by the 1949 Parliament Act, nor its theoretically unlimited power to reject secondary legislation. The House of Lords follows a policy of self-restraint, symbolised by the Salisbury convention, which requires deference to measures foreshadowed in the manifesto of the governing party on the basis that such measures enjoy a popular mandate. Day-to-day relations between the Lords and Commons are, however, largely determined by a process called ping-pong, in which Lords amendments are considered by the Commons and then returned to the Lords, and so on, until agreement is reached. At the end of this process, the Lords normally defer to the Commons. They would be much less likely to do so were they to be directly elected, because they would enjoy a mandate of their own, and would have a responsibility to their electorate. Indeed, their mandate could, for two reasons, appear superior to that of the House of Commons.

The first reason is that, being elected by proportional representation, the directly elected second chamber would be more representative than the Commons. It would be a mirror-image, reflecting opinion in the country, while the Commons would appear as through a distorting mirror, exaggerating some streams of opinion and under-representing others. A witty supporter of proportional representation might suggest that, if the second chamber were to be elected by proportional representation, the House of Commons could then be abolished since it is the house elected by proportional representation that ought to be the representative chamber! It would certainly seem odd if the chamber to which the government is responsible should be less representative than a chamber whose functions are restricted to scrutiny and review, and whose powers are so severely restricted by the Parliament Acts.

The second reason why the new second chamber might claim that its mandate was superior to that of the Commons relates to the timing of elections to the two chambers. Were the new second chamber to be elected at the same time as the Commons, then, as we have seen, it could claim to be more representative of opinion than the Commons. If it were elected at a different time, it could claim not only to be more representative but to enjoy a fresher mandate. Suppose, for example, that there had been elections for a second chamber in 2007, two years after Labour's election victory in 2005. The Conservatives would almost certainly have been returned as the largest party in a 2007 election. They might even have enjoyed an overall majority in the second chamber; or they might have been able to form a coalition in the second chamber with the Liberal Democrats to give the anti-Labour forces a majority. The Conservatives would then undoubtedly claim that, while Labour might have enjoyed a mandate from the people in 2005, that mandate was now exhausted. The people had changed their minds and wished to see the implementation of Conservative, not Labour, policies. Therefore, the Conservatives, so they would argue, would have every right to harass the government as much as they wished. Indeed, they would not be following the wishes of their voters if they failed to do so.

It is true that the government could overcome the opposition of the Lords through the Parliament Act procedure, but its legislation would be very considerably delayed; and the government would not be able to override the rejection of secondary legislation, without which its primary legislation would not be workable, since the Parliament Acts do not apply to secondary legislation and the second chamber therefore has an absolute veto over it. If the directly elected second chamber used its powers in this way, government would become more difficult, with the very real danger that the battle between two chambers with competing mandates would lead to gridlock.

These difficulties are not merely theoretical. They have actually occurred in Australia, where the lower house, the House of Representatives, has been elected by the alternative vote since 1918 and the Senate has been elected by the single transferable vote method of proportional representation since 1948. When the Constitution was being drawn up in the 1890s, one of Australia's founding fathers, in the debates on federation in 1891, declared that quarrels between the two houses could be resolved by 'the good sense of the English race to carry us through'.[10] That proved to be an over-optimistic forecast. When the Australian Senate is controlled by the opposition, it acts as a forum for the opposition. That was what occurred in 1975, when Gough Whitlam's Labor government introduced two appropriation bills into the Senate, which was controlled by the opposition Liberal party. The Senate voted that the bills should not be further proceeded with until the government agreed 'to submit itself to the judgment of the people' – exactly the claim that the House of Lords had made in 1909 when it refused to pass Lloyd George's 'People's Budget' until that had been submitted to the people.

In Australia, in 1975, a startling new constitutional doctrine was put forward: since both chambers directly represented the voters, the government was responsible to both chambers, and not just to the House of Representatives.[11] This doctrine was espoused by the Governor General, Sir John Kerr, by Malcolm Fraser, leader of the opposition Liberal party, who was to replace Whitlam as Prime Minister, and by the Chief Justice, Sir Garfield Barwick. The implication of this new doctrine was that the Senate could force a dissolution of Parliament. That was the very doctrine espoused by the House of Lords when, in 1909, it rejected Lloyd George's 'People's Budget' 'until it had been submitted to the country'. It was a doctrine bitterly opposed by the Liberals in Britain, and the 1911 Parliament Act, restricting the powers of the House of Lords, was the result. A directly elected second chamber might well resuscitate this doctrine. Indeed, with a directly elected second chamber, it would be possible for the Commons to declare its confidence in the government, and for the second chamber to counter with a declaration of no confidence.

Although the Australian constitutional crisis of 1975 was a unique event, it is by no means the only occasion on which the Australian Senate has frustrated the

---

[10] Brian Galligan, *A Federal Republic: Australia's Constitutional System of Government* (Cambridge University Press, 1995) 85–86.

[11] ibid, 64.

elected government. In recent years it has been controlled by minor parties, who use their leverage in order to secure amendments to the annual budget. In 1993, for example, Paul Keating's Labor government faced a check from the Senate, which required him to make significant changes in his budget and in legislation concerning native title land claims. Fears have been expressed that the Australian budget process is becoming 'Americanised': ironically, Malcolm Fraser, the beneficiary of the events of 1975 and now in retirement, has expressed his concern that the Senate 'is running the risk of making Australia ungovernable . . . [by] turning the annual Budget process into a series of bargains and trade-offs similar to those which occur in the United States'.[12] But some of the most vigorous conflicts between the two houses have occurred over legislation. Under the premiership of Kevin Rudd from 2007 to 2010, the Senate blocked the government's proposal for a private health insurance rebate, and three times blocked the government's carbon pollution reduction scheme. This damaged Rudd's standing with the electorate, since he was criticised for backing away from a key election commitment on climate change.

An Australian government does, however, enjoy a power denied to a British government: it can dissolve the second chamber under section 57 of the Australian Constitution, which makes provision for a double dissolution. But, if that does not resolve a deadlock, then it must be resolved by means of a joint sitting in which the House of Representatives, as the larger of the two houses, can overrule the Senate. Such machinery might be even more necessary in Britain, where the government is unable to dissolve the second chamber. But these joint sittings of the two chambers, or, more likely, of delegations from the two chambers, to achieve a compromise on government legislation might create, in effect, a third chamber of parliament. Decisions would be reached through negotiations between representatives of the two chambers in a forum remote from public scrutiny, rather than through open public debate. The public would be further excluded from the decision-making process. Indeed, in both the United States Congress and in negotiations between the European Parliament and the Council of Ministers in the European Union, there are closed conciliation meetings which in effect write law beyond the public gaze. Therefore, paradoxically, a directly elected second chamber would decrease, not increase, the power of the voter, by insulating parliament even further from the voter than it is already.

IV. A CONSTITUTION FOR A POST-BUREAUCRATIC AGE

The constitutional reforms proposed by the coalition follow the long raft of reforms passed by the Blair government after 1997, reforms so wide-ranging that

---

[12] Quoted in John Uhr, 'Generating Divided Government: The Australian Senate' in Samuel C Patterson and Anthony Mughan (eds), *Senates: Bicameralism in the Contemporary World* (Ohio State University Press, 1999) 100.

it was argued that they created a New British Constitution.[13] These reforms followed a long period of debate and discussion during Labour's 18 years in opposition, fuelled primarily by the political Left and by pressure groups associated with the Left, such as Charter 88. But the reforms were in the main a response to practical concerns – the demand of Scots for some degree of self-government; the demand of Londoners for a city-wide system of government; a belief that it was anomalous that, although Britain had ratified the European Convention on Human Rights, the rights it promised could be secured only through an international court at Strasbourg, and not through the domestic courts; and a belief that it was anomalous that two-thirds of the membership of the House of Lords should consist of hereditary peers.

The reforms of the coalition, by contrast, are the product of no such long period of public discussion and debate; rather they result, first from a reaction, sometimes confused, to the expenses scandal of 2009, and, secondly, from a coalition deal concluded hurriedly and under media pressure. Neither the Blair government nor the coalition were required to follow the procedures of the majority of countries with constitutions where constitutional change requires special procedures, such as a super majority in the legislature, or approval in a referendum or at an intervening general election, before constitutional alterations can be enacted. For as long as Parliament is deemed to be sovereign, the procedures applicable to 'constitutional' legislation have to be the same as those applicable to 'ordinary' legislation.

The hurried nature of the drafting of the coalition document and the inevitable compromises which it involves laid the coalition open to accusations of a conflict of interest, of seeking to alter electoral rules for its own benefit. This accusation was made by a number of Conservative MPs in the debates on the constitutional bills. In the Second Reading debate on the Parliamentary Constituencies and Voting Bill, an MP quoted from the website of a Conservative backbencher, Mark Field, who declared that 'the current proposals for the alternative vote and the reduction in the number of parliamentary constituencies are being promoted by party managers as an expedient way to prevent our principal political opponents from recapturing office'.[14] In the debate on reducing the maximum number of MPs, Sir Peter Tapsell, a Conservative MP and Father of the House, declared that the government 'have no mandate for the bill from the country'. He added, 'the wide range of constitutional and electoral changes proposed by the coalition Government, taken as a whole, and introduced so early in the life of a Parliament full of new Members, constitute an attempt at a peaceful, political coup d'etat, with the sole object of securing the position of Ministers'.[15] In the Second Reading debate on the Fixed-Term Parliaments Bill, a Conservative backbencher, Bernard Jenkin, accused the government of 'constitution making on the hoof . . . What we need is a proper constitutional convention to consider such a major change to our

---

[13] See Vernon Bogdanor, *The New British Constitution* (Hart Publishing, 2009).
[14] *Hansard* HC col 47 (6 September 2010).
[15] *Hansard* HC col 113 (25 October 2010).

constitution.'[16] These critics perhaps overestimated the likely effects of the reforms, but they were right to complain about the speed with which they had been enacted, a speed which precluded serious scrutiny.

The central element of the new constitution put into place after 1997 was, it was argued in *The New British Constitution*,[17] the gradual replacement of a system based on parliamentary sovereignty, the unitary state and a largely uncodified constitution, with one based on the separation of powers, a quasi-federal state and a constitution that is coming to be codified. Britain was moving, so it was argued, from a majoritarian democracy, characterised by the doctrine of the sovereignty of Parliament which legitimised a concentration of power in the executive, towards a system of more limited government and the gradual development of a genuine constitution in the form of a higher law providing a reference point over and above that of the government of the day. Britain, it was argued, was in the process of becoming a constitutional state. But it had not yet begun the process of becoming a popular constitutional state. For the effect of the reforms of the Blair era was, admittedly, to disperse power, but to disperse it 'sideways' amongst members of the political and judicial elite rather than 'downwards' to the people. The reforms began the process of introducing checks and balances into the British constitution, but they did not widen the scope of public participation, nor did they yield a much greater degree of popular control of government.

The ideological origins of the movement for constitutional reform lay with the radical liberalism of the nineteenth century. Their impetus was in part genera-tional. Indeed, it was no accident that many of the members of the Blair govern-ment which implemented the constitutional reforms were ideological children of 1968, antagonistic to elitist ideas of democracy, and sceptical of the supposed vir-tues of Britain's traditional constitutional arrangements. They appreciated that the public were no longer content to exercise a mere modicum of power at infre-quent general elections, but sought also to exert influence between elections. Just as the economic system had been opened up in the 1980s and 1990s by the governments of Margaret Thatcher and John Major, so there was now pressure to open up the political system. But the reforms of the Blair government failed to achieve the aim of opening up the political system, and the government failed to achieve its aim of regenerating British democracy. The reforms of the Blair gov-ernment were an insufficient response to the popular and radical forces that had put constitutional change on the political agenda.

The constitutional reforms proposed by the coalition will do little to remedy the deficiencies of the Blair reforms. Their overall effect, indeed, is likely to be small in comparison with the sound and fury that they have aroused. The Fixed-Term Parliaments Act, as we have seen, might make less difference than either its proponents or its opponents imagine, since, despite its title, it offers two possibilities for an early dissolution of Parliament – a vote of no confidence or a

---

[16] *Hansard* HC col 624 (13 September 2010).
[17] Bogdanor (n 13).

two-thirds majority for dissolution. The alternative vote will make less difference than either its proponents or its opponents imagine if, as is likely, many voters decide to plump and not use their preferences to the full. Certainly the reforms will do little to assist in the opening up of the political system. Insofar as they have any effect, they could even put the process into reverse. They could, as it were, put the clock back. For, not only will the reforms do little to reconnect government with the electorate, they could actually serve further to insulate parliament from the people. The Fixed Term Parliaments Act, if it makes it more difficult for a Prime Minister to use dissolution to break parliamentary deadlocks, or to appeal to the country on a clear-cut issue dividing government from opposition, will serve to entrench a weak government in power, while if a party knows that it can switch coalition partners with impunity, because it will not have to face the voters for five years, there could be changes of government between elections without the voters being consulted.

The proposed reform of the House of Lords, transforming it into a directly elected upper house, would appear at first sight to be a step towards opening up the political system. But, as we have seen, that is a misleading impression; a more likely outcome is conflict between the two houses leading to deadlock. If disputes between the two houses require some new mechanism to resolve them, such as joint sittings along the lines of the Australian model, that will render the political system even more remote from the people. Finally, the effect of the alternative vote, if it is endorsed in the referendum, will make hung parliaments more likely since it is likely to increase support for the Liberal Democrats, the second choice party for many Conservative and Labour voters.

A series of hung parliaments will do little to open up the political system. The danger is that decisions about government formation will be taken after the votes have been counted, and, with dissolution being more difficult, the government so formed will become less accountable to the people. Parliamentary government would come to overwhelm democratic government. Westminster could become even more of a house without windows than the public thought it was in 2009 during the expenses scandal. Parliament would come to be characterised by what the French call *la politique politicienne* – manoeuvering which excites the political class but alienates the voter.

If the constitutional reforms of the coalition government together with regular hung parliaments do have the effect of further insulating the political system from the people, rather than opening it up, that would be an unfortunate paradox in the light of the ideological origins of the movement for constitutional reform and the social and electoral changes which led to the hung parliament of 2010. The aim of the movement was to strengthen accountability and increase participation, not to give political leaders and parliamentarians more autonomy and enable them to become more distant from the people.

It was in part discontent with the political system and the desire for a widening of choice that led to the increase in support for third parties since the 1970s. The Liberal Democrats pressed as one of their main themes the need for constitutional reform, while support for Celtic nationalism is in part a revolt against the remoteness and lack of accountability of central government. As early as 1969, Samuel Beer, an American student of British politics, noticed that the rise of student rebellion and Celtic nationalism threatened the ideological bases of the post-war political settlement:

> At first glance these two movements may seem quite unlike and unconnected. Yet each can be considered as a reaction to the increasing scale and intensity of rationalization in both government and society. Each shares an antagonism, not always reasoning, against bureaucracy and technocratic forces, against the impersonal, distant and faceless organisations of modern times.[18]

The outcome of recent general elections, together with the rise in third-party support, may be seen as the culmination of these trends. Even a cursory glance at recent electoral statistics shows that there has been a decline in support for the major parties and that Britain has been in the process of becoming a multi-party system. But, because the first past the post electoral system refracts rather than reflecting social change, this development was not widely noticed; it was not to be reflected in the political system until the accident of the hung parliament and coalition government in 2010. Gradual but cumulative changes in electoral behaviour are leading to changes in the party system and the political system. But these changes in electoral behaviour are themselves a response to social changes that are making Britain at the beginning of the twenty-first century a very different country from the Britain of the immediate post-war years.

The ideological basis of the party system in the immediate post-war era was a consensus on collectivism – a term that has been used to characterise 'government intervention with the economy and social system as a whole'.[19] The purpose of government was to ensure, by means of careful economic management, full employment and stable prices, and to ensure, by means of careful social management, the development of the welfare state based on the principles established by the wartime coalition and the Attlee government that succeeded it. The post-war consensus did not of course preclude important policy differences between the parties. But these concerned mainly means rather than ends. The two main parties, although sharing the aims of full employment, stable prices and the welfare state, differed as to how they should be achieved, with Labour stressing government intervention and the Conservatives envisaging a more restricted role for the state. But what really divided the parties was the social basis of their support. They were divided largely on class lines. 'Class', it was suggested in 1967, was 'the basis of British party politics; all else is embellishment and detail.'[20] In the immediate post-war years, two-thirds of the working classes would normally vote Labour,

---

[18] Samuel H Beer, *Modern British Politics: A Study of Parties and Pressure Groups,* 2nd edn (Faber and Faber, 1969) epilogue, pp 424, 427. The first edition of this book was published in 1965. In a later book, *Britain Against Itself* (Faber and Faber, 1982), Beer suggested that the student revolt and Celtic nationalism were aspects of 'a romantic revolt'.

[19] Beer, *Modern British Politics,* ibid, 80.

[20] PGJ Pulzer, *Political Representation and Elections in Britain* (George Allen and Unwin, 1967) 98.

while no fewer than 90% of the middle classes would support the Conservatives. The parties – Labour in particular – were also tightly disciplined, taking the view that party discipline was essential to ensure the passage of their programme through Parliament. Indeed, party solidarity on parliamentary votes in the 1950s and 1960s was so close to 100% that there was little point measuring it. For Labour, party discipline was an analogue to the solidarity of the trade unions, a political concomitant to class solidarity. As Aneurin Bevan insisted:

> The texture of our lives shaped the question into a class and not into an individual form ... For us power meant the use of collective action designed to transform society and so lift us all together ... We were the products of an industrial civilization and our psychology corresponded to that fact. Individual initiative was overlaid by the social imperative. The stresses of individual initiative therefore flowed along collective channels already formed for us by our environment. Society presented itself to us as an arena of conflicting social forces and not as a plenum for individual striving.[21]

In the Labour Party, as Beer noticed, the basis of a person's party allegiance was 'not so much that he agrees as that he belongs'.[22] Because class lines were so strongly entrenched, electoral alignments during the immediate post-war years were comparatively stable. The two parties, although divided by comparatively little, were aligned against each other in a sort of trench warfare. Two large armies faced each other, arguing over relatively little, while large organisations – and in particular the trade unions – seemed to enjoy some degree of veto power over governments. Britain was perhaps in danger of becoming a blocked society and suffering from what was called 'pluralistic stagnation'.[23] Politics was 'sticky' and not fluid.

In the 1940s and 1950s, the two major parties were genuinely mass organisations in a sense in which they are not today, in that they had a mass membership; but this did not, for most members, involve active participation. In an age of deference, members were generally content to accept the decisions of their leaders. The mass party, even though its inspiration was democratic, tended to 'separate leadership from the rank and file and to accumulate influence in the hands of an elite'.[24] Participation, therefore, was minimal, but that did not seem to matter too much in an age happy to accept that the leaders led and the followers followed.

The post-war system was legitimised, both by Conservative thinkers and by those on the Left. The Conservatives were, naturally, less addicted to theoretical explanation than their Labour counterparts, but legitimacy was given to a system of government concentrating power at the centre and with a minimal role for the people by Leo Amery, a former Conservative Cabinet minister, in his book *Thoughts on the Constitution*, first published in 1947. For Amery, the essence of the British Constitution lay in 'two elements, each of independent and original authority, the Crown and the Nation. The Crown, as represented by the Government of

---

[21] Aneurin Bevan, *In Place of Fear* (Heinemann, 1952) 1–2.
[22] Beer, *Modern British Politics* (n 17) 85.
[23] The term is used by Beer in *Modern British Politics* and in *Britain Against Itself* (n 17).
[24] Beer, *Modern British Politics* (n 17) 405.

the day, is throughout the active, initiating and governing element.'[25] The power of the Crown was original and not derivative. It was the active, initiating element, to whose policies the Nation was asked to give or withhold its consent. 'A British government', Amery believed, 'is an independent body which on taking office assumes the responsibility of leading and directing Parliament and the nation in accordance with its own judgment and convictions.' The Nation was represented in Parliament, but the function of Parliament was not to govern, but, as its etymology would indicate, to legislate, to parley, to hold government to account and to ventilate grievances. Amery believed that there was a separation of powers in British government – a separation between Crown and Nation, between government and parliament, between the active power in the state and the consenting power. For Amery, parliamentary government was, then, government by consent and not by delegation. It was 'government of the people, for the people, with but not by, the people'.[26] His doctrine helped to legitimise the system of strong, disciplined parties and a political system in which the role of the people was essentially passive and responsive.

Constitutional theorists of the Left, such as Sir Ivor Jennings, held – in contrast with Amery – that original power lay with the people. Jennings believed that '[t]he electorate is the basis of all governmental power . . . The Government exists only because the majority of the voters have approved a certain broad policy.'[27] This doctrine was also held by the socialist, Harold Laski. On this view, sovereignty derived from the people, and government needed a mandate from the people if it was to enjoy democratic authority. But this doctrine did not serve to legitimise popular participation: the power of the people had to be shaped and represented by strong, disciplined political parties. Only such parties could fulfil the mandate that the people gave them. Herbert Morrison told the Labour Party conference in 1945: 'Only by a Labour majority – a coherent Labour majority – can our programme be put through. I make no promise about what will happen to that programme if we do not get a clear and coherent and united majority . . .'[28] In his textbook, *Government and Parliament*, published in 1954, Morrison declared, 'the British people rightly attach importance to a party being sufficiently coherent and united to give the country a Government not only of sound policy but of adequate strength and unity of purpose'.[29] Thus, starting from quite different premises, thinkers from the Left came to similar conclusions to Leo Amery, a thinker from the Right, and put forward doctrines which legitimised strong two-party government, untrammeled by checks and balances, and with a minimal role for public participation.

The immediate post-war years were characterised by stable and successful party government dedicated to collective action, and given stability by social forces. But

---

[25] Leo Amery, *Thoughts on the Constitution*, 2nd edn (Oxford University Press, 1953) 33.
[26] ibid.
[27] Ivor Jennings, *Cabinet Government*, 3rd edn (Cambridge University Press, 1959) 472–73.
[28] Quoted in Beer, *Modern British Politics* (n 17) 82.
[29] Herbert Morrison, *Government and Parliament* (Oxford University Press, 1954) 162.

this type of government depended not only upon a particular social and electoral alignment, but also upon a pervasive optimism about what government could do. There was great confidence that the government could resolve complex social and economic problems. That confidence had been generated by success in war and by the radical reforms of the 1940s – the Education Act of 1944, the establishment of the National Health Service and a system of national insurance, and the maintenance of full employment, achieved, so it was believed, by beneficent government action. These reforms generated positive attitudes towards government, attitudes that were to disappear after the 1960s – an era that seemed characterised by the failure of government, not its success.

Since the 1960s, this model of stable two-party government has been superseded by something quite different. In place of the confident collective purpose of the immediate post-war era, there is scepticism as to what government can achieve – a scepticism exemplified both in Tony Blair's New Labour, and in David Cameron's conception of the Big Society, a substitute for the Big Government of the 1950s and 1960s. It is no longer as easy as it was once thought for governments to achieve full employment, while the mixed economy, with its concomitant of the main utilities being under public ownership, no longer exists in a world of privatisation and market power. The welfare state does of course still exist, but its limitations are recognised more widely than they were 60 years ago, and there is a much greater emphasis on individual incentives than on collective action. Government is becoming primarily an enabler rather than a provider of benefits to passive and grateful clients.

Changing conceptions of the purposes of government have been accompanied by social changes and by changes in electoral behaviour. The processes of party and class dealignment, already perceived by Beer in 1969, have gathered pace, with greater home ownership, affluence, and increasing social and geographical mobility. In the 1960s, around half of the voters identified strongly with a political party. Today the figure is around 10%. The outcome has been greater electoral volatility and a greater willingness to vote for parties other than Labour and the Conservatives – parties no longer sustained by powerful class and occupational blocs. The veto power of large social organisations, and particularly the trade unions, has disappeared. As the class and electoral blocs have broken up, so also have the disciplined parties that they sustained. Contrary to public perceptions, party cohesion is far weaker today than it was in the 1950s and 1960s. MPs, far from being timid sheep, are today more prone to rebellion than at any other time since the mid-nineteenth century. As in other walks of life, the leaders still seek to lead, but the followers are no longer always willing to follow.

We no longer live in a collectivist age, and the model of party government of the collectivist age – the model celebrated by Amery and Morrison, by Jennings and Laski – is now out of date. We live instead in an individualistic age that David Cameron and others have labelled a post-bureaucratic age, and our party and political systems will come to reflect this. The essence of a post-bureaucratic society is fluidity. Whereas the characteristic instrument of the collectivist age was the class-based political party, in the post-bureaucratic age it is the individual; and whereas the characteristic purposes of the politics of the collectivist age were economic management and the maintenance of a welfare state, the characteristic purpose of a post-bureaucratic age is the enhancement of individual choice and individual aspiration. In direct contrast to what Bevan believed, 'the texture of our lives' now shapes issues into an individual and not a class form. Far from 'individual initiative' being 'overlaid by the social imperative', it is now individual initiative which overlays that imperative. And society now presents itself to us not as, in Bevan's words, 'an arena of conflicting social forces', but 'as a plenum for individual striving'. Finally, we no longer offer allegiance to political parties because we belong; we offer it because we agree. Whereas the basic unit of the collective society was social class, in the post-bureaucratic society it is the individual.

The contrast may, at the risk of gross over-simplification, be depicted in the following way.[30]

	Post-war era	21st century
Purpose of government	Collective management	Enabling
Mode of representation	Party government	Popular government
Doctrinal basis	Parliamentary sovereignty	Popular sovereignty
Social basis	Class	Individualistic
Nature of society	Blocked	Fluid

If it is to be congruent with a society which has become fluid, the politics of a post-bureaucratic age must also become fluid, more open to the voters, more open to popular control. But the coalition exemplifies parliamentarism, not popular participation or popular control of parliament. It exemplifies the principle of parliamentary government rather than the principle of democratic government, in that neither the formation of the government nor the Coalition Agreement were endorsed by the people; while the constitutional reforms proposed by the coalition might well insulate parliament still further from the people. All of this stands in contradiction to the ethos of the post-bureaucratic age. Popular pressure to open up the system will therefore continue. As long ago as 1969, Beer presciently predicted that 'identifiable present tendencies . . . lead one to expect that the post-Collectivist phase . . . will involve some kind of break from party government'.[31]

The constitutional reforms of the coalition need, therefore, to be counterbalanced by reforms designed to open up the political system, not further to insulate it. That counter-balance is best secured through the instruments of direct democracy. If a government is no longer able to claim a popular mandate for its policies because they are based upon a coalition agreement drawn up after the election, they must seek to achieve that mandate in a different way. *The New British Constitution*[32] proposed that the reforms of the Blair era be complemented

---

[30] This table is based on Beer, *Modern British Politics* (n 17) 397. But I have amended his schema in a number of respects.

[31] Beer, *Modern British Politics* (n 17) 427.

[32] See n 13.

by four institutional instruments designed to open up the political system and to increase participation. They were primary elections, the single transferable vote system of proportional representation, a greater use of the referendum and initiative, and Citizens' Assemblies, enabling the people themselves to legislate on particular issues. These instruments become of even greater importance if we are moving into a world of hung parliaments and coalition governments.

It is of course impossible to predict either the end-point of the current process of constitutional reform, or the precise contours of the new British constitution. But, because there is so profound a conflict between the politics of parliamentarism and the politics of a democratic age – the politics of a post-bureaucratic age – the constitutional changes proposed by the coalition will not end the era of constitutional reform. That era will come to an end only when our political system has come to be congruent with the public philosophy of the post-bureaucratic age, whose watchword is fluidity and whose leitmotif is the sovereignty of the people, the only sure foundation for a new British constitution.

Index